Peer Power

Transforming Workplace Relationships

"This book should be required reading for all team members, whether it is a project team or a small organizational team. The framework and vocabulary in this book are invaluable for day-to-day team experiences, especially when dealing with 'unique' behaviors.

"If you are the leader, get it for the whole team. If you're a team member get it for yourself."

~ Ben Snyder, Systemation, CEO

"Who hasn't had a communication problem with a peer? The authors have outlined five clear and sensible strategies for a lifetime of continued peer interaction. Not that it won't happen again, but this will help when it does! Cynthia and Ray are brave for sharing their own stories of poor communications. It certainly helps readers feel as if they are not alone in their communication missteps. Their experiences will stay with you!

"Bravo to the authors!"

~ Beverly Kaye, Founder and CEO, Career Systems International
Co-author: Love 'Em or Lose 'Em: Getting Good People to Stay

"Peer Power: Transforming Workplace Relationships is my pocket coach. Useful, insightful, and immediately applicable, the book is a life saver in building business relationships and resolving conflicts. It has revitalized my commitment to make the time to focus on building relationships with my colleagues despite the demands of challenging times and circumstances."

~ Pamela J. Schmidt, Executive Director,
ISA – The Association of Learning Providers

"Whether you've been working fifty days or fifty years, you need this book! Its pages are chock-full of valuable insights into others — and more importantly, into yourself. Cynthia and Ray's amazing tools will help you discard any old habits that have perpetuated difficult relationships. You will easily recognize the 'people' described, and be able to empower yourself in repositioning your own relationships.

"I recommend making this book a personal assignment. You'll see the results the very next day."

~ Maryann Nelson, C-Suite Business Consultant and
Executive Coach

"This book offers tools for improving interpersonal relationships, with the improvement always starting 'at home.' The content is presented for quick comprehension. Cynthia and Ray have gone to extraordinary lengths to deepen the readers' understanding of each concept and strategy with real life examples, along with questionnaires at the end of each case chapter. The book is evidence of the authors' rich experience in working with individuals and groups to improve interpersonal relationships."

~ Nancy Scholl, CFO, Wright Hotels, Inc.

"We all work with difficult individuals -- be they colleagues, bosses, subordinates, vendors or customers. Peer Power tells relevant stories, gives concrete examples of solutions and provides real tools to repair relationships with these individuals. Practicing these tools improves effectiveness, reduces stress levels, helps build our company and makes this a better place to work!"

~ Karen Howlett, Owner/President,
McSweeney Steel Company

"Strangely enough, despite our shared humanity, interacting with other people remains the most challenging aspect of work. We all need a 'How-To' book on building and repairing relationships. Peer Power *is just that book. Cynthia and Ray combine social science with experience and common sense to give us a practical guide to creating happier (and more productive) times in the workplace.*

"Regardless of your role—executive, manager, or coworker—read this book. To quote Chapter Two: 'Take Responsibility.' Your organization will thank you!"

~ Ron Gajewski, President, Beyond ROI, Inc.,
The Measurement Experts

"Cynthia Clay and Ray Olitt propose principles and strategies that can significantly increase your productivity and satisfaction in working relationships, especially tough ones. They describe several familiar and troublesome 'mistakes' workmates often make, then help us avoid them by applying four essential principles and five key strategies. As a long-term executive coach and organization development consultant, I find their counsel invaluable in helping any person earn the trust and respect of their colleagues. Peers can create their own 'power'—by establishing perceptions that they are credible (demonstrating competence, propriety, and positive intent) and that there is high potential for mutual benefit in their working relationships (affirming for each colleague that his/her and their objectives will be met).*

"Peer Power *is a valuable addition to each working library!"*

~ Ron Scott, Principal, Scott Associates

"This book gives you practical insights into how you react to people today and what you can adjust in order to get the results you need. As you explore more deeply into what is happening with others, this book will shed light on what is blocking you from getting the results you want. No matter where you are on the scale as a communicator, you will gain new perspective when you read this book and apply what you learn."

~ Anne Warfield, CSP & Outcome Strategist,
Impression Management Professionals

"Peer Power *teaches readers how to reduce workplace tension and have productive business relationships through the principles of open and honest communication. Whether you're a CEO or a line worker, this book is a must read. It's as practical as it is inspiring."*

~Mark Levy , Author of Accidental Genius:
Using Writing to Generate Your Best Ideas, Insight, and Content

Peer Power

Transforming Workplace Relationships

Cynthia Clay & Ray Olitt

Punchy Publishing
Seattle, Washington

International Standard Book Number: 978-0976458722

First printing March 2011

Cover Design by Mao Studios
http://www.maostudios.com/

Punchy Publishing
Seattle, WA 98115

http://www.netspeedlearning.com/

Dedication

For my husband Leo, and my children, Brandon, Grayce, and Jessica:

You continually remind me of how blessed I am. I love you bunches.

— Cynthia

For my wife Harriet:

You are the best peer a person could ever have. I am so fortunate you are mine.

— Ray

contents

Acknowledgments

The journey of co-authoring a book can be a long one and we would not have made it this far without the dedicated support of some important collaborators.

Thank you to Elaine Smith, Operations Manager at NetSpeed Learning Solutions, who not only formatted the entire book, but also edited and proofed its contents, and mediated our disagreements about punctuation and grammar. "Switzerland!" we called out whenever we needed her.

A big hug to Bev Kaye, a mentor and friend, who generously reviewed our drafts, graciously offered feedback, warmly encouraged our efforts, and kindly introduced us to her network of authors.

Appreciation to Sara Glerum who edited our early attempts at writing this book and gave us pointed feedback that kept us on track.

Special thanks to Paul Petrucci, who added his insights and suggestions in the final months of writing and editing. He helped us bridge our writing styles and find our combined voice.

Thanks to Harriet Olitt, who reviewed early chapter drafts and offered feedback to clarify our original ideas.

Last, but not least, we thank Leo Brodie, who shepherded the book to completion, developing the style guide, provided feedback on the final draft, and helped us navigate the mysteries of electronic publishing.

We appreciate you all so much!

introduction

What's the Problem?

The most challenging aspect of any job is working with other people. Difficult coworkers and bosses can test anyone's ability to get along and get things done.

In a survey about workplace conflict conducted by NetSpeed Learning Solutions, 600 respondents felt that interpersonal difficulties had seriously damaged their productivity and job satisfaction. Sixty-two percent of the respondents said they left a job in part because of a difficult person. Thirty percent reported a challenging coworker was currently frustrating them. When asked to write about the frustrating coworker, some of the responses included:

"I dread going to work to be barraged by this individual's negativity."

"I often need to 'run interference' because other employees also find this individual difficult to work with."

For many of the respondents, the person causing them the most trouble was their boss:

"This person is a childish, overbearing micromanager, leaving me powerless to perform my job and therefore feeling demeaned and demoralized."

"I frequently have to circumvent this manager to get projects from their department completed."

How do these difficult coworkers and bosses make things hard for the people around them? Their dysfunctional behavior gets expressed in different ways: the manipulators deceive people to get what they want; the whiners complain about people who bug them; the attackers verbally assault those who won't budge; the bullies intimidate in order to get their way.

As difficult as these relationship problems have been in the past, they are intensified by the demands of the new workplace. Today the need to collaborate with others to get work done has never been greater. But there are business trends that make dealing with others infinitely more challenging. Employees are burdened with increased responsibility but limited authority. They need to deal with people across the country or across the world, in different time zones, with different cultural expectations, yet they don't see people's facial expressions or body language. In work settings like these, a simple e-mail might be misconstrued and create conflict.

With such escalating challenges, is there a way to change the outcome? Yes—by using the principles of open, honest communication, your workplace relationships can be transformed. Let us tell you the story of how we came up with the principles, practices and strategies you're about to learn.

Our Collaborative Insight

Five years ago, Ray and Cynthia met for a networking lunch in a noisy Italian restaurant (picture a cup of crayons and a basket of crusty bread sitting on top of a butcher paper tablecloth). Ray, an organization development consultant, described the workshop he had been leading to help people with little authority get better results at work. Cynthia, the owner of a successful training and consulting company, shared the approaches her organization used to train people in leadership and influence skills. As we compared notes, we realized that we were dealing with similar themes, dissatisfactions, and challenges.

In our classes, we frequently coached disillusioned and frustrated employees who were unable to collaborate with colleagues they neither understood nor appreciated. We wanted to help them but we were stymied by the lack of a comprehensive resource that nailed the critical techniques needed to resolve work challenges.

Sure, there were plenty of communication books out there. One offered a model for having a tough conversation; another described how to kick butt when you work with a toxic person. Some of these books were pretty good but others were full of nice-sounding theories that collapsed when applied in the real world. We found ourselves recommending this chapter from one book and that model from another source, mixed in with our own experiences and opinions.

Like many trainers, we were always on the lookout for the most practical actions and strategies our learners needed. As we talked we realized that we might be just the right people to synthesize some of the critical communication practices we had absorbed, originated, tried out, kept, or discarded over the years. As we grew more excited, we scribbled all over that paper tablecloth. After one hour we had covered it with diagrams, strategies, ideas, and potential content, in a rainbow of colors. Our project was launched.

During our collaboration, we came to appreciate that we were not just two people who were trainers and coaches, but we were also seasoned managers who had experienced dysfunctions in the workplace firsthand. Ray has managed employees in industries as diverse as banking, aerospace, and insurance. Cynthia spent many years managing individuals and teams in banking and healthcare, and now serves as the President/CEO of NetSpeed Learning Solutions.

Like you, we've worked with coworkers who slack off and don't produce. We've endured people who steal credit. We've worked with colleagues who, frankly, just seemed clueless. We've been steamrolled by managers who have to get their own way. We've coped with misguided leaders who were blinded by their prejudices. We've experienced having to go home at night exhausted, trying to figure out how to get through these challenges. And we've suffered the dread of waking up the next day and going back into work to do it all over again.

It's tempting to blame the slackers, the bullies, the whiners, and others for impeding your ability to get the job done. But blaming and attacking others won't produce the results you want. You can't force your peers (or your boss) to change. In fact, there is only one thing you *can* change about these situations: your own behavior.

In writing this book, we started with the premise that everyone is worthy of respect, and that behind every bad behavior there is some internal need that is not being met. In ways that may be hard to see, your own behavior may be influencing the situation. In fact, changing your behavior is the only way you can influence the outcome.

Based on these assumptions, we wrote the book to share practical steps that will end your sleepless nights and stop the recurrent conversations about how to change others. As the book evolved, we've watched people in our workshops use these ideas in their own lives to transform impossible situations into incredible successes. Our hope is that the book will start you on the path of conscious, well-planned interactions that can make an amazing difference in your daily life at work.

It took us five years to analyze our successes and failures, capture our thinking, review the literature, interview experts, survey clients and colleagues, and try out our recommended techniques. Along the way we discarded the silly stuff that sounds cool but just plain doesn't work. We eliminated the fluff, the hype, and the clever hook to zoom in on the core principles, practices, and strategies that will make you successful. We've done this painstaking analysis because we knew that what we wrote had to be immediately applicable (or we wouldn't sell books or get hired to teach your next workshop).

We are grateful for the wisdom of many writers who've come before us: Geoff Bellman (author of *Getting Things Done When You're Not In Charge*), Al Switzler (co-author of *Crucial Conversations: Tools for Talking When Stakes are High*), Roger Fisher and William Ury (co-authors of *Getting to Yes: Negotiating Agreement Without Giving In*), and Mel Silberman (co-author of *People Smart: Developing Your*

Interpersonal Intelligence). Their ideas have influenced our practices over the years. We've included their books as well as resources by other authors in a list of References in Appendix 3.

How to Use This Book

We've called this book *Peer Power* because we believe that you can develop your ability to bring powerful communication practices to relationships with your workplace peers.

You'll build your foundation of interpersonal success using principles of being real, being responsible, extending respect, and building relationships. And you'll learn to apply five strategies (Collaborating, Going Head-to-Head, Compromising, Coaching, and Caring-for-Self) at the moment of need (a deteriorating relationship with a coworker or boss). You'll discover how to win support from others and manage difficult behavior when conflict arises.

Whether you hold the role of boss or employee, you'll find that these techniques will help you feel in control of yourself and your job. The result? Reduced stress, increased productivity, greater collaboration, fewer mistakes, less rework, more effective workplace conversations, and a heightened sense of self-efficacy and self-mastery. Through peer power, we're confident you can transform workplace relationships.

Our book is organized so you can navigate to get what you need. In Chapter 1 we look at interpersonal behaviors that most of us have tried but don't work. In Chapter 2 we introduce the four key principles that will be your foundation for effective communication, and in Chapter 3 we dive into the five strategies that you will use if interpersonal problems become serious. We recommend that you read Chapters 1 through 3 before exploring the case studies you'll find later in the book. The case studies will have greater impact if you've learned the key principles and strategies beforehand.

In the nine chapters that follow, we tackle a challenging character who may bedevil you at work. To maintain reader interest, we alternate behaviors that are aggressive with those that are passive. The title of each case chapter indicates that any challenging character can begin to function more constructively, depending on how you use your peer power. You'll read about:

- The attacker (the colleague who repeatedly expresses his anger and frustration in the form of inappropriate personal criticism)

- The whiner (that coworker who complains without taking responsibility for improving conditions that surround her)

- The scene stealer (the peer who sets about building her reputation at your expense)

- The drive-by boss (a leader who ignores some of his key management responsibilities and doesn't meet the needs of his employees or the organization)

- The manipulator (the coworker who attempts to influence your attitude or behavior through deception or secrecy)

- The clueless colleague (a coworker who is insensitive to her negative impact on the work environment)

- The faux-smart boss (the boss who has unrealistic confidence in his own ideas and skills, often accompanied by a lack of confidence in his employees)

- The slacker (the coworker whose poor performance damages your performance)

- The bully (a colleague who uses unreasonable demands and inappropriate threats to get her way)

Of course, we are using each of these labels as shorthand. People are much more complex than the labels we ascribe. Each of us exhibits a range of behaviors that could potentially place us into one or more of these negative categories. Throughout the book you'll find reminders that we have all exhibited negative tendencies. We also strongly feel that even the most challenging people have many admirable traits and skills.

If there is someone at work you're having a hard time with, complete the questionnaire, "About Them," you'll find at the end of this chapter. (It will help you identity which category he falls into.)

We start Chapters 4 through 12 with case studies so you can vicariously experience the impact of various frustrating coworkers. These characters have all played parts in our own workplace dramas. At times we recommend practices that we may not have had the skills to apply when we originally encountered that challenging person. Of course, we've changed the names and modified the details, but they all represent very real challenging types that you will recognize instantly.

You may notice that the list you just read does not include behaviors that may bother you but rarely harm you. We don't include coworkers who refuse to socialize, have major mood swings, brag a lot, or are very anxious, for example. While these are often frustrating behaviors, we can learn to live with them. Instead, we focused on giving you tools to deal with behaviors that can have a detrimental impact on your performance.

If you'd like to work with a road map, turn to the cheat sheet at the end of each of these chapters. Each case chapter includes clues to look for, assumptions to remember, and principles and practices to use. If you want to read actual dialogue, we've added scripted responses to various tough cases. We also suggest what to do if your initial strategy does not work (Plan B). Our goal is to make it easy for you to use this book to develop practical strategies to get results.

As to the writing convention that we follow, we decided to forgo the tortuous "he/she," "she/he," or "s/he" when referring to an individual in our case chapters. Instead, where the example features a woman, we've referred to the difficult character throughout that chapter as "she." Where the example features a man, we've opted to use "he" throughout. Obviously all the techniques we introduce may be used with both men and women.

Note to Organizational Leaders

We believe that organizations desperately need employees at all levels who use solid communication practices. Based on many years of organization development experience, we know that many organizations are rife with interpersonal friction, turf wars, and destructive conflict. As a result productivity, customer service, and morale suffer. We've written this book for project managers, sales and customer service staff, production personnel, administrative and human resources staff—anyone who must work with and through others to get the job done.

Communication challenges are exacerbated in a time of globalization (workers are often separated by distance and time), mergers and joint ventures (people in different cultures are required to adapt quickly), economic instability (employees face the threat of layoffs and resource constraints), and generational differences (employees now span four generations).

Interpersonal dynamics in the workplace will undergo a sea change in the next decade as a wave of new, less experienced workers flows in, replacing the ebbing supply of skilled, experienced baby boomers. While well versed in the uses of technology (social networking, text messaging, blogging, etc.), these inexperienced Gen Y workers are unprepared to deal with the complexity of organizational politics. When they encounter challenging people or situations, they lack the models and communication skills to get the results they want, even as demands for increasing productivity are escalating. Since the highest work priority for the Y Generation is a "good relationship with bosses and coworkers,"[1] a solid foundation of interpersonal skills is crucial.

Every generation needs to master the communication practices that lead to satisfying and effective work relationships. According to

---

[1] Pew Research Center, "Millennials: A Portrait of Generation Next," February 2010.

the Conference Board Research Group, Americans' job satisfaction fell to a record low at the end of 2009, with ratings for job interest and satisfaction with coworkers declining as well.[2] It's more important than ever to supply your workers with training to help maintain an engaging work environment that leads to higher productivity.

We encourage you to adopt and share the practices in this book with others inside your organization. Deliver workshops; hand out copies of the book as reference tools; listen to our podcasts; engage employees by using our web-based questionnaires. We want to partner with you to meet these challenges. Together we can transform the workplace.

Your Testimonials

We invite you to share your experiences as you begin to implement these practices. As you try out the techniques we recommend, you may find that you get results that thrill you. If so, please share them with us by sending an e-mail to *peerpower@netspeedlearning.com*. On the other hand, you may find that nothing we suggest gets you where you want to go. Tell us that, too.

With your permission, we may post your examples at our website: *www.netspeedlearning.com/peerpower*. We will also give you the opportunity to read challenging case studies and recommend approaches for dealing with these difficult people. If you need help figuring out what's driving you crazy, you'll find the same questionnaires ("About You" and "About Them)" that appear at the end of this chapter on the website as well.

Let's Go

If you're ready to get started, turn to the next page and answer a few questions about your skills and behaviors first (Questionnaire: "About You"). You'll find our commentary about your answers in Appendix 1.

---

[2] Jeannine Aversa, "Americans' job satisfaction falls to record low," *Seattle Times*, January 5, 2010 (http://tinyurl.com/29mq2ag).

Then take a look at the behaviors of your frustrating colleague (Questionnaire: "About Them").

Questionnaire: "About You"

This questionnaire asks you to think about your interpersonal strengths, weaknesses, and beliefs. Answer honestly—no one will see this but you—and then turn to Appendix 1 and see how your answers compare to ours. As you answer the questions openly and review our responses, you'll begin to understand the communication philosophy that underpins all of our case studies. If you would like to complete this questionnaire online, you can find a copy of it at our website: *www.netspeedlearning.com/peerpower*

1.	I can improve my communication skills.	Yes	No
2.	What happens to me at work is usually not related to my own behavior.	Yes	No
3.	I prefer to take responsibility for my own actions.	Yes	No
4.	Even if I change my behavior, the situation usually doesn't change.	Yes	No
5.	I am willing to make the first move to improve a challenging situation.	Yes	No
6.	When someone is behaving badly, it's hard for me to feel compassionate.	Yes	No
7.	It's easy for me to put myself in the shoes of other people to imagine their point of view.	Yes	No
8.	I try to be open about my thoughts and feelings.	Yes	No
9.	I find gossip to be a great stress reliever.	Yes	No
10.	I discourage complaining.	Yes	No

		Yes	No
11.	I wish that the top leaders in my organization would just fix the messes at work and leave me out of it.	Yes	No
12.	I strive to listen before I speak.	Yes	No
13.	If I have an opinion, I always put it on the table first.	Yes	No
14.	I often feel impatient with others.	Yes	No
15.	I try to leave my emotions at the door when I arrive at work.	Yes	No
16.	I expect others to apologize when they offend me.	Yes	No
17.	I offer an apology even though I may not be 100 percent at fault.	Yes	No
18.	I make sure I know who's at fault when things go wrong.	Yes	No
19.	When it gets confrontational, I shut down.	Yes	No
20.	I reach out to someone I may have offended.	Yes	No
21.	If I'm not sure what someone is thinking or feeling, I ask for his or her thoughts.	Yes	No
22.	I take people at face value.	Yes	No
23.	I'm good at reading others, so I rarely need to ask their opinions.	Yes	No
24.	I thank others often.	Yes	No
25.	My communication skills are as good as my technical skills.	Yes	No

Questionnaire: "About Them"

The "About Them" questionnaire helps you identify which challenging behaviors you are dealing with in your work environment. Before you begin, it might be helpful to list the key people with whom you interact and then rate the quality of your relationship. For each of those with a low rating, complete the questionnaire.

Simply circle "yes" or "no" for each question. Answer honestly—no one will see this but you. If you would like to complete this questionnaire for multiple people, you can find a copy of it at our website: *www.netspeedlearning.com/peerpower.*

Does your boss or coworker...

1.	Use name-calling, sarcasm, or cursing?	Yes	No
2.	Verbally abuse you?	Yes	No
3.	Blame you personally for problems?	Yes	No
4.	Tease you about your mistakes or weaknesses?	Yes	No
5.	Blame problems and conditions on others?	Yes	No
6.	Not appear willing to be personally responsible for negative outcomes?	Yes	No
7.	Talk endlessly about problems instead of taking action?	Yes	No
8.	Constantly criticize others' work behind their backs?	Yes	No
9.	Appear friendly to your face yet criticize you often behind your back?	Yes	No
10.	Take over tasks that don't belong to him/her?	Yes	No
11.	Take credit for accomplishments that are not his/her own?	Yes	No
12.	Inflate his/her own accomplishments?	Yes	No
13.	Hold staff meetings infrequently or without planning?	Yes	No

14.	Fail to provide his/her employees with clear or reasonable expectations or feedback?	Yes	No
15.	Fail to communicate with his/her employees or keep them informed on important developments?	Yes	No
16.	Ignore performance problems?	Yes	No
17.	Flatter you or act unusually sweet?	Yes	No
18.	Deceive you or cause you to feel deceived?	Yes	No
19.	Present only positive reasons for an action with no balancing negatives?	Yes	No
20.	Misrepresent or exclude data to support his/her position?	Yes	No
21.	Fail to clean up his/her messes?	Yes	No
22.	Borrow items without returning them?	Yes	No
23.	Make inappropriate or loud sounds—whistles, burps, slurps, sniffs, music, etc.?	Yes	No
24.	Make long-winded pronouncements on topics or talk excessively?	Yes	No
25.	Discourage or argue with input from his/her employees?	Yes	No
26.	Micromanage his/her employees?	Yes	No
27.	Take back tasks once delegated?	Yes	No
28.	Rate his/her employees too critically?	Yes	No
29.	Break commitments or not fulfill tasks you need?	Yes	No
30.	Deliver tasks to you late or with poor quality?	Yes	No
31.	Fail to communicate with you or provide you with information you need?	Yes	No
32.	Repeatedly ask for your help?	Yes	No
33.	Make demands that you ignore procedures to meet his/her needs?	Yes	No

34. Threaten to take a problem to your boss rather than trying to resolve it with you first?	Yes	No
35. Delay a decision or withhold support until you comply with a demand?	Yes	No
36. Refuse to listen to your objections to complying with his/her wishes?	Yes	No

Here is the key that matches a label for a challenging character to the statements in the questionnaire.

Statement #s	Label	Chapter
1–4	Attacker	4
5–8	Whiner	5
9–12	Scene Stealer	6
13–16	Drive-by Boss	7
17–20	Manipulator	8
21–24	Clueless Colleague	9
25–28	Faux-Smart Boss	10
29–32	Slacker	11
33–36	Bully	12

Decide which label best describes your challenging person. If you answered "yes" to two or more statements within a set, chances are that you are dealing with a behavior that we discuss in one of the case studies in the book. However, even one item might indicate that is your person, depending upon how serious and pervasive the item is. Before you turn to that chapter, we invite you to read Chapters 1 through 3 to learn more about our mistakes (what not to do), as well as what principles, practices, and strategies we suggest you adopt (what to do).

mistakes we have made (and you can avoid): manipulating, whining, attacking, and bullying

In writing this book, we talked through our failures, embarrassing moments, and just downright humiliating attempts to get others to change their behavior or do what we wanted. It was humbling to revisit the dumb mistakes we made with challenging peers. We attempted to get their support or manage their difficult behaviors by manipulating, whining, attacking, and bullying. We still aren't perfect, but we have learned from these common mistakes and we can speak from painful experience: these behaviors may work in the short run but they rarely work in the long run.

We're going to take them one by one and tell you exactly why they don't work. In Chapter 2 we'll introduce some principles that will get better, consistently positive results. Through mastering these principles, you will begin your journey to developing your peer power.

Manipulating

Cynthia has a confession to make. In the past she has resorted to subtle manipulation to try to get her own way. Once she was responsible for recruiting volunteers to work on the board of a non-profit organization. Her approach to volunteers sometimes involved telling them that her highly intuitive nature gave her a strong feeling that they were "perfect" for the role.

In truth, Cynthia was more worried about filling a vacancy on the board than whether a volunteer was well suited for the job. Often her target would feel special and pleased to be seen as someone who was just right for a spot on the board. Cynthia didn't like the way she felt after these encounters and in time she realized that this form of manipulation preyed on people with lower self-esteem. The result was often mistrust, blame, and board members who quit.

We define "manipulating" as attempting to influence someone's attitude or behavior through deception or secrecy. If you tell someone you don't have adequate resources even though you do so he won't ask for your help, you're manipulating the situation. If you pretend you don't want something from somebody when you do him a favor (but you're really expecting that now he'll "owe you one"), you are manipulating him. If you intentionally make ambiguous statements in an e-mail hoping to buy additional time, you are manipulating the situation. If you pretend to agree with someone to get her to like you, then you are engaging in manipulation. If you withhold critical information that might influence a decision, you are manipulating the outcome. If you flatter someone so she will support you or give you what you want, you are manipulating.

> We define "manipulating" as attempting to influence someone's attitude or behavior through deception or secrecy.

Whether your manipulation becomes blatantly obvious or people simply feel uneasy around you, manipulating is usually discovered. Manipulators often find that it is very hard to keep track of all of the little deceptions they engage in. Ultimately, manipulators damage trust, which can be difficult, if not impossible, to regain. In the long run, manipulators find that they are no longer able to influence others because people begin to go out of their way to avoid being manipulated.

Whining

When Ray worked at an aerospace company, he was unhappy with his colleague Bill. He frequently noticed Bill using a computer for personal business, even though Bill insisted he did not have time to share the workload when Ray was stretched thin. Each time Ray saw Bill slacking off, he became more frustrated and whined to Bill and another peer, Mary. Ray attempted to make Bill feel guilty—

Whining is complaining without seeking to improve the situation.

after all, look how overworked Ray was! And look how unfairly Bill was treating him! In private conversations with Mary, Ray whined about how unfair Bill was being. (Ray winces even now remembering this situation.)

As you can imagine, neither Bill nor Mary appreciated Ray's approach. It only made the situation worse. Bill began to defend himself by complaining about Ray to other coworkers. Mary pointed out to Ray how he had sometimes been unreliable and finally told Ray to knock it off. Ray realized that he needed to find more constructive ways of working with people who disappointed him.

Whining is complaining without seeking to improve the situation. We might whine directly to the coworker who is frustrating us (with an "Oh, poor me" tone of voice): "Shannon, I can't get my work done. This job is just impossible. You're making it so hard for me. I can't even sleep at night." Or we might gossip and whine about Shannon to someone else: "Shannon is driving me nuts. She never gives me what I need."

Whether you whine to your coworker directly, whine to others behind her back, or send whiny e-mails to your peers, you are assuming the role of the victim in a workplace drama. Playing the victim can result in satisfying, self-righteous feelings. But people find whiners to be annoying and rarely respect them. Whiners lose credibility because their complaints often seem exaggerated. When your coworkers listen to you whine about your peers, they probably wonder what you're saying about them behind their backs. And when they learn that you have been whining about them, they may attack you with anger. They may even forward your negative e-mails to the person you're complaining about. You may have experienced the escalating cycle of whining, attacking, whining, and attacking that can be set into motion. Sad to say, whiny victims bring out aggressive attacks from others.

Does this mean you should never discuss your frustrations about someone at work with your friends? Of course not! Talking a problem through with someone you trust can be helpful. Listening to advice can help you prepare to handle a situation. But if you find that you are constantly complaining about the same person or situation to many different people, you've fallen into the trap of whining. If you vent your frustrations about someone without seeking a resolution, you're whining. Instead of tackling an issue head on, you're reinforcing your negative view of a person or situation, intensifying your own anger, damaging someone's reputation, losing your own credibility, and probably annoying everyone around you.

Avoiding whining does not mean you remain silent about workplace problems. Organizations need employees who speak up. Share your concerns with the appropriate people. As long as you do your homework, avoid blaming and embarrassing, and focus on solutions, you are not whining.

Attacking

Cynthia has been known to attack when under stress. (Please note that she has always felt bad when she has resorted to this coping technique.) On one occasion, she prepared to lead an important meeting despite feeling under the weather. She wrote the agenda, created materials for the people who would be attending, and organized binders that were carefully placed on the table for the meeting attendees.

Cynthia was expecting to hear appreciative comments for her efforts. Instead, as the meeting began, one of the participants stated that she didn't think the agenda was on target, didn't agree with the decisions made at the last meeting, and wanted to take this meeting in a different direction. Cynthia lost her composure (imagine a volcano erupting), began to rant about what it had taken her to get ready for the meeting, and verbally attacked the woman who dared to oppose her. After quashing all dissenting opinions, Cynthia led a very quiet meeting to a rapid conclusion.

Attacking is the repeated expression of anger and frustration in the form of inappropriate personal criticism. It often may include name-calling and blaming statements. It rarely gets people to cooperate. Most victims of an attack give in, comply, and bow down to end the aggressive attack.

> *Attacking is the repeated expression of anger and frustration in the form of inappropriate personal criticism.*

If you attack as your method of gaining compliance, you may have experienced verbal abuse or flaming e-mail attacks yourself and believe that it toughens people up. You may think that creating fear will motivate them to change. You're right; fear *is* a motivator. People will do what you want as long as they believe you can harm their careers, their reputations, or their work lives. If you attack your colleagues, you may feel better momentarily and even see immediate results.

In the end, however, those who attack others fail to gain loyalty, trust, enduring relationships, or commitment from others. Instead, people go around them, quit their jobs to escape the attacks, and may eventually respond by attacking the attacker.

Bullying

Ray worked with Brit at a data processing company. The two of them were assigned to create a class jointly. Ray worked very hard to prepare his portions of the class. Usually when he met with Brit to review their progress, she indicated she had not been able to complete her segments.

> *Bullying occurs when someone makes unreasonable demands or uses inappropriate threats that exceed natural and appropriate consequences.*

After a while Ray began to bully Brit to deliver on her promises. When these demands were ignored, Ray told Brit that he would just prepare the class by himself, but would let others know of her lack of cooperation. As a result of that threat, Brit contributed a bare minimum of work. In the end, Ray was forced to share credit with Brit for a successful class, which he resented, just as Brit resented Ray's attempts to bully her. Tension between the two of them continued for several months. In looking back, Ray realized that Brit lost all desire to collaborate with him because of his bullying.

Bullying occurs when someone makes unreasonable demands or uses inappropriate threats that exceed natural and appropriate consequences. The bully stamps his feet, raises his voice, and insists that others do what he wants. If they don't, the bully will make sure there are negative consequences. You've probably run across a bully before, whether on the school playground, in your neighborhood, or in the next cubicle at work.

Be honest now: Have you ever prematurely told someone you'll go over her head if she doesn't do what you want? You've engaged in bullying. Have you ever copied someone's boss on every little issue or problem? That's a form of virtual bullying. Have you ever pushed hard to get someone to do something with a tone that implies she has little choice? That's bullying. Have you ever threatened to drag your heels on a decision or undermine someone else's initiative? That's actually a form of bullying as well.

The problem with bullying is that it often produces long-lasting resentment and retaliation. Bullies have few allies at work (except those people who align themselves with the bully as a way to protect themselves or gain power from the association).

Where We're Headed

It was embarrassing to write this chapter because we like to think we were born with superior peer power. You may have winced, chuckled, or cried at our examples. Perhaps you saw yourself or others reflected in the stories. We encourage you to complete the self-assessment at the end of this chapter to see whether you may have unintentionally adopted these four powerless behaviors.

If you are using some of these ineffective practices, you'll find practical suggestions for modifying your behavior in the next chapter and throughout this book. If you need to deal with these behaviors when used by others, explore our case studies. We've developed practical strategies for handling manipulating, whining, attacking, and bullying (in Chapters 8, 5, 4, and 12 respectively), as well as many other unproductive behaviors.

Personal Self-Assessment

We've bared our souls and shared some of the disastrous mistakes we've made in the past. We invite you to follow our example and approach this simple self-assessment with honesty.

We've listed several behaviors that people often use to get what they want. Place a ☑ in the column that indicates how frequently you use that behavior. When you've completed the assessment, we'll provide a simple scoring key that will point you toward the four key principles that support better behavioral choices in the workplace.

Behavior	Never	Rarely	Sometimes	Often
1. I tell "white lies" to get what I want.				
2. I point out problems, but no one solves them.				
3. I pretend to agree with people to make them happy.				
4. If someone makes me angry, I raise my voice to express my concerns.				
5. I speak directly to the person I'm having difficulty with.				
6. I have to mention problems over and over again to get people to change their behavior.				
7. I gain cooperation by forcefully presenting my position.				
8. I consider others' needs when making requests.				
9. I push people to do things my way.				
10. I withhold my support or cooperation to make sure my needs are addressed.				
11. I manage my emotions when upset with someone.				
12. I retaliate if people treat me disrespectfully.				
13. I complain about one or two people at work to my colleagues.				
14. I share both the pros and cons of my recommendations.				
15. People tell me I am intimidating.				
16. I lose my temper when people aren't doing the right thing.				

Personal Self-Assessment Scoring Key

For each statement in the scoring key below, find the score that corresponds to your response and write that score in the empty box on that line. For most of the statements, the higher scores indicate behavior we don't encourage. However, for each category there is one statement (grayed area) for which the point scale is reversed. (These grayed areas contain behaviors we do encourage.)

Total your points for each behavior. The higher your score, the more likely you are using this inappropriate coping strategy. Your score for each behavior will fall somewhere between 0 and 12.

Behavior	Never	Rarely	Sometimes	Often	Manipulating	Whining	Attacking	Bullying
					Enter your score in the empty box			
1. I tell "white lies" to get what I want.	0	1	2	3				
2. I point out problems, but no one solves them.	0	1	2	3				
3. I pretend to agree with people to make them happy.	0	1	2	3				
4. If someone makes me angry, I raise my voice to express my concerns.	0	1	2	3				
5. I speak directly to the person I'm having difficulty with.	3	2	1	0				
6. I have to mention problems over and over again to get people to change their behavior.	0	1	2	3				

	0/3	1/2	2/1	3/0				
7. I gain cooperation by forcefully presenting my position.	0	1	2	3				
8. I consider others' needs when making requests.	3	2	1	0				
9. I push people to do things my way.	0	1	2	3				
10. I withhold my support or cooperation to make sure my needs are addressed.	0	1	2	3				
11. I manage my emotions when upset with someone.	3	2	1	0				
12. I retaliate if people treat me disrespectfully.	0	1	2	3				
13. I complain about one or two people at work to my colleagues.	0	1	2	3				
14. I share both the pros and cons of my recommendations.	3	2	1	0				
15. People tell me I am intimidating.	0	1	2	3				
16. I lose my temper when people aren't doing the right thing.	0	1	2	3				
Total Points for each Behavior:								

No matter what your scores in these areas, there are probably techniques in your repertoire of behaviors that don't really serve you. None of us is perfect! We invite you to explore more constructive principles and practices in Chapter 2 that will improve your relationships by quantum leaps in the weeks ahead. You're on the way to becoming a powerful peer.

what we have learned: four key principles

We hope you felt a little better reading about some of our embarrassingly human moments. We have given up these ineffective coping tactics, practiced healthier techniques, and have developed four key principles that are diametrically opposed to manipulating, whining, attacking, and bullying. In every situation you encounter at work, these principles will give you the springboard for an effective, satisfying interaction. For each of these principles, we also describe some related practices that work best with workplace colleagues.

Of course, we can't give you a cookie cutter approach to working with your coworkers, customers, or bosses. Instead, we will introduce you to critical principles and practices in this chapter. Any time you work with vexing people, these general principles and practices will help increase your peer power and transform your relationships. As you begin to read the situations and case studies in Chapters 4–12, you will see how we apply the relevant approaches for specific workplace challenges you may face.

Four Key Principles

Let's leave behind manipulating, whining, attacking, and bullying and replace them with these four key principles:

Be Real: Be open and authentic rather than manipulative.

Take Responsibility: Choose to be accountable instead of whining.

Extend Respect: Treat people with kindness instead of resorting to personal attacks.

Build Relationships: Partner with others instead of bullying them.

Take a moment to review the self-assessment you completed at the end of Chapter 1. If you scored high on manipulating, then pay

> *When you converse with someone who is authentic, you feel a sense of connection and trust.*

particular attention to the key principle Be Real. If your score was highest in whining, then focus on the key principle Take Responsibility. If you scored highest in attacking, then carefully explore the key principle Extend Respect. If your weakest score was in bullying, then attend to the practices we suggest for the fourth key principle, Build Relationships.

Be Real

When people are real, they are genuine, sincere, and open. How they present themselves outwardly is completely in alignment with what they are thinking and feeling on the inside. When you converse with someone who is authentic, you feel a sense of connection and trust. You may think of him as honest, as real, as credible or trustworthy. There are no hidden agendas, game-playing, manipulating, or dishonesty when someone lives by this principle.

If you want to Be Real, we suggest two important practices:

- Share your thoughts.
- Acknowledge reality.

Share Your Thoughts

Let people know how you feel or what you think about what's happening. This is not an invitation to gossip or to deliver subtle messages by teasing others, but rather an opportunity to disclose your point of view openly. If you see something that concerns you (or pleases you), acknowledge it. Don't assume people can read your mind. (We haven't met any skilled mind readers in our work with thousands of people inside organizations.)

Be careful about performing your own mind-reading tricks. When we assume we can correctly interpret others' emotions or attitudes, we're usually wrong. How often have you been convinced that someone was upset with you, only to find that she was just having a bad day? Or mistakenly concluded that her actions were based on bias or prejudice? Instead of speculating, invite your coworker to share her thoughts with you.

Organizations need people who are willing to speak up when they see problems that need to be addressed. People won't always agree with you, but they will know where you stand and that's an important element in developing trust. Talk directly to people who trouble you, rather than about them to others. If you have a clear intention to be helpful, to be of service, or to contribute to a solution and you demonstrate respect, people will probably appreciate your candor.

Being Real doesn't mean you say everything you feel or think. It means sharing your opinions when they will make a significant difference. It also means being honest even when you may feel uncomfortable.

This principle requires some degree of self-awareness. It's hard to be open about your views and intentions if you don't know what you think, feel, or want. In a tense or confusing work situation, you may

> *Being Real doesn't mean you say everything you feel or think.*

need to take some time by yourself to figure out just what's happening inside instead of indulging in a damaging knee-jerk reaction.

Acknowledge Reality

That may sound like an unusual practice, but the truth is that we often ignore the obvious. No one brings up the layoff that was announced last week, hoping the change won't affect the team. Everyone avoids mentioning the death of an employee's father because it might be too painful. Someone loses a promotion that he really worked for, and you're afraid to discuss it because he might get angry. A coworker breaks down into tears during a meeting while you look away and wait for the discomfort to pass.

The principle Be Real is supported by the practice of acknowledging "what is so" in the moment. When we don't face reality, it's usually because we believe that avoiding the feelings will make them disappear. You may have heard the expression, "What you resist persists." The irony is that talking about uncomfortable feelings, even for a few minutes, often minimizes their influence, while attempting to ignore or avoid those same feelings may actually magnify them.

A short time after Cynthia's mother passed away suddenly, a colleague at work asked her why she looked so sad. Cynthia responded that someone she loved had died the previous week. The colleague hesitated for a second and then changed the subject to her plans to attend a party that night. She was clearly uncomfortable with the difficult subject she had opened up. And her discomfort led her to respond in a completely insensitive way.

Cultivate the practice of saying "what is so" whenever you become aware of underlying emotions or tensions. Speaking the truth gently can help to clear the air and may make it possible for people to move forward.

Take Responsibility

Responsibility is one of those principles that sounds like a burden you want to put down rather than a principle you want to embrace. When you think of Taking Responsibility, imagine yourself making a passionate commitment to yourself and others. There is enormous freedom that comes to those who choose accountability over whining.

What practices support this principle? We suggest four:

- Be responsible for your experience.

- Respect your needs.

- Communicate with others.

- Perform well.

Be Responsible for Your Experience

Being accountable to oneself requires giving up blame and victimization. People who are involved in conflicts tend to demonize their adversaries (making them bad, evil, and unredeemable) so that they can justify their own actions. At the same time, they tend to view themselves with biased self-regard (they are virtuous, in the right, and blameless). Think of someone who has gone through a messy divorce. Recall the angry words, the accusations, and the negative judgments verbalized by one or both partners in the marriage. And yet, there was certainly a time when both people fell in love with all that was attractive in their partner. There was a time when the same person could do no wrong!

Being responsible for your own experience means that you put yourself in the driver's seat of life. No one has the power to make you think, feel, or act in a certain way. You choose the experience you wish to have.

Take a deep breath before you read the remainder of this sentence: most difficulties you experience are caused at least partially by your own actions and reactions. You might unintentionally encourage the

> *Being accountable to oneself requires giving up blame and victimization.*

behaviors that frustrate you. For example, you express sympathy when someone whines to you. Or you jump in to help someone who is not performing his duties. You don't operate in a vacuum and neither do your coworkers. Instead of making excuses or blaming others when things go wrong, focus on what role you might have played in the outcome. Let's say the team missed a critical deadline. Instead of blaming or selling out a peer, acknowledge your contribution to the result. You can make this acknowledgement without beating yourself up. You might say, "I'm disappointed that we didn't make that deadline. I realize that I probably waited too long to give you the report. I'm sorry and I'll make sure that it gets in your hands early next month."

Any time you aren't getting what you need, ask yourself, "What can I do?" instead of waiting to see if others are going to give you what you need. Don't play the Gotcha Game with others. Ray remembers having a new boss who did not give him information he obviously needed for an ongoing project. Ray waited patiently because he realized his boss was very busy learning new responsibilities. Eventually his patience wore thin and he started saying to himself, "What's the matter with this guy? It's obvious I need this information." Finally it dawned on Ray that it would not help to play the Gotcha Game. He got what he needed when he asked for it assertively.

Respect Your Needs

We have some good news: Being responsible for your own experience does not mean that you have to be a doormat! In fact, when you are accountable for your happiness, your success, your relationships, and your life, you also respect your own needs. The magic word is balance. When you respect your needs, you balance your needs and the needs of others. Remember that video on the airplane about oxygen masks? When your mask drops down, put it on first and you'll be able to assist others.

If someone is pushing you to accomplish an impossible task, push back. It won't be the end of the world if you say "no" to a challenging request. You may be able to suggest alternatives that will allow the other person to meet her deadline without you. Any effort to manage your stress level shows respect for your needs.

Another way to respect your needs is to maintain your own self-esteem. When you make mistakes, be gentle with yourself. You're human. You don't need to blame anyone when a mistake occurs, even yourself. You can acknowledge any error openly without judging yourself or others harshly. In fact, by adopting this practice, you may find that your stress levels are significantly reduced.

Once Cynthia was treated at a hospital for a painful spasm in her upper gastro-intestinal tract. The doctor gave her an upper GI cocktail and told her to drink up. She was delighted to experience instant relief! If you need a self-esteem cocktail, review and celebrate your strengths, improvements, and successes. Keep a folder with positive comments, thank you notes, grateful comments, and nice observations from others. When you're feeling a painful self-esteem spasm, drink up those positive feelings.

Communicate with Others

When you're responsible, you also communicate with people. It's a great practice to gain agreement to ground rules and expectations upfront, instead of waiting for conflicts or disagreements to occur. When you begin to work with someone on an assigned task, consciously devote your first few conversations to clarifying your (and his or her) expectations around how you'll get things done together. When you join a new team, encourage the team to have the same kind of conversation before they tackle the goals, tasks, or problems on their

It's never a waste of time to focus on your interpersonal agreements before you knuckle down to getting the job done.

plate. It's never a waste of time to focus on your interpersonal agreements before you knuckle down to getting the job done.

Instead of assuming that everyone knows what you're up to, keep your colleagues, customers, and boss informed of your activities, progress, and results. Make it a practice to respond quickly to e-mail messages from your boss and coworkers, even if it is only to say, "I'll get back to you soon." When we consult with teams inside organizations, we are often amazed at the amount of unnecessary conflict that people are experiencing simply as a result of insufficient communication.

Perform Well

Taking Responsibility means performing well. Another way to say this: Do your best work no matter what the circumstances. Notice we didn't say, "Do perfect work," just "Do your best work."

When you choose to be responsible to others, you do your best possible work given the goals, resources, and time constraints. When you are accountable to others, you clearly tell people what they can expect from you without making promises that you can't keep. You keep your commitments and don't violate confidences. You strive for accuracy, no matter how fast you're moving. If the workday begins at 8:00 a.m., then you arrive on time. You model the behavior you want from others. As others learn that they can rely on you to perform well without excuses, you'll build and sustain trust.

Extend Respect

This third principle is essential to successfully working with people. Have you ever worked with someone who sneered, rolled his eyes, sighed, or tapped impatiently while you were speaking? We're certain you felt disrespected and were probably not highly motivated to collaborate with that guy.

What behaviors allow you to demonstrate respect in your dealings with others? We suggest four practices:

- Honor differences.
- Listen, listen, listen.
- Allow others to solve their own problems.
- Respect the organization.

Honor Differences

When you honor differences, you recognize that your colleagues have different personalities and backgrounds. You choose to be aware of and sensitive to cultural differences. If their behavior mystifies you,

you consider the possibility that it might be the product of their cultural background. Ask yourself, "Is this a difference that makes a difference?" Unless the difference affects productivity or morale, embrace it.

In fact, organizations often benefit from these differences. For example, it helps to have people in the workplace who are thorough and methodical as well as others who are fast paced and spontaneous. The folks who focus on keeping people engaged balance those who focus on getting tasks accomplished. The different styles complement each other. Without this mix of complementary styles, organizations can develop blind spots that hinder their ability to serve customers, develop new products, or, for that matter, avoid legal difficulties.

This book is not about personality types, behavior styles, or generational differences, but we think that deepening your understanding of various styles can

> *Ask yourself, "Is this a difference that makes a difference?"*

help you adopt an effective approach more easily when working with others. (In Appendix 3 we offer some resources that may help you.)

Listen, Listen, Listen

We agree with the expression that we have two ears and one mouth because it is more important to listen than to speak. Not all comments deserve your attention, but the best way to get others to listen to you is to listen well to them.

Encourage others to go first and hear them out without interrupting. It helps to enter the conversation with a spirit of curiosity and a desire first to understand. A Buddhist would call this "beginner's mind." Instead of assuming that you know what they are going to say and jumping to conclusions as they begin to speak, empty your mind of your preconceptions and expect to learn something new.

Make it possible for people to express differing opinions. If you want people to say what they think to your face, you'll need to state your own opinions less adamantly. Ask others to raise their concerns and thank them when they do.

We know from experience that it is particularly difficult to listen when someone is criticizing you. Let's face it. You probably don't roll

> *Have you noticed that it is impossible to control what everyone else is thinking, saying, or doing?*

out of bed in the morning, stretch, take a deep breath, and say, "I hope I get buckets of critical feedback at work today." It is very easy to start defending your actions, arguing your point of view, or attacking the messenger. Instead, when criticism happens, ask questions to understand.

Be willing to acknowledge the mistakes you've made. Stop rebutting or defending yourself, and express your appreciation for the feedback instead.

Allow Others to Solve Their Own Problems

This practice is powerful. If you truly want to extend respect to others, then allow them to live their own lives and resolve their own issues. Have you noticed that it is impossible to control what everyone else is thinking, saying, or doing? You can't force people to do what you want. (You may have had bosses who tried to micromanage your behavior. How many creative ways did you and your coworkers try to get out from under the boss's thumb?)

Once one of Ray's close relatives told him about some frustrations she was having with her boss. Shortly into the conversation, Ray began to suggest some things she might do to improve the situation. For each suggestion, she had objections. Finally she said, "Please let me figure this out myself. I think I know more than you do about this situation. I just need someone to serve as a sounding board." In the end the solution she chose was her idea, not his. And because it was her idea, the solution was more likely to work for her—that's human nature, after all.

When you give up the illusion that you can control the behavior of others, then you're ready to stop offering unsolicited advice. We're suggesting that you respect people enough to allow them to succeed or fail without your intervention. That means you may also have to give up the urge to rescue people (unless it's a matter of life or death, of course).

The next time you have the impulse to control others, to give unsolicited advice, or to rescue people in a difficult situation, take a deep breath, count to 20, and wait to see what suggestions they have. Allowing others to solve their own problems is a powerful demonstration of respect that can transform your work relationships.

Respect the Organization

What we mean by this practice is that any organization has a set of relationships, a hierarchy of roles, written and unwritten rules, values, and history. Organizations are complex organisms. The systems that have developed are probably engrained and intertwined. You can be competent, confident, highly experienced—a top performer in one organization—and still fail if you don't take time to learn about and adapt to a new organization.

In practical terms, when you respect the organization, you choose to respect the roles in the hierarchy. If you get frustrated with your boss, you don't go over her head to her boss and attempt to undermine her position. Instead, you do all in your power to help your boss

> *Organizations are complex organisms.*

succeed. If you are concerned about another team's performance, you express those concerns constructively in the right forum.

Another way to think about this is to choose either to play by the rules or to challenge the rules constructively. Don't circumvent policies and procedures. There is nothing sadder to us than working with organizations full of cynical people. It just drains the energy from the place. Cynicism arises when people feel powerless to change the situation or their circumstances.

Cynthia consulted once with a team that was experiencing chaos and confusion. She'll always remember the defiant words of one team member: "It may be a mess but it's OUR mess. We've made many decisions and taken many actions with good intentions." He's right, of course. We need to understand an organization's history before we attempt to change it.

Build Relationships

We know there are a few jobs out there that don't involve working with people. We're confident that you don't have one of them or you wouldn't be reading this book. The fourth principle we want you to embrace is to Build Relationships.

We suggest five relationship-building practices that will help you be successful:

- Network with others.

- Get input.

- Seek solutions that benefit all.

- Build and protect self-esteem.

- Express compassion or empathy.

Network with Others

Networking is a practice that allows you to develop relationships with people across the organization. The best time to build a network is when you don't need one. If you wait to build your network until you've lost your job or desperately need an ally at work, then you're probably too late.

Think of the many reasons you might want to get to know someone better:

- He is on your team or holds a similar position.

- She attended the same college as you did.

- He was promoted into a job that you aspire to.

- She tells great stories and brings a sense of fun to her work.

- He needs help with a critical project.

- She has mastered the latest software.

- He made a compelling presentation at the last meeting.

- She just received public praise or recognition.

Networking involves a natural give and take of interest, support, joint successes, and mutual celebration. When you take the time to network, you're really acknowledging that you can't be successful without others. Extend a hand, ask for help, thank others, congratulate people, and take time to get to know your colleagues.

Cynthia recalls a deep conversation she had with a trusted mentor a few years into their relationship. He disclosed a personal tragedy that had occurred when he was a young man that shaped the adult he became. From his sense of personal responsibility and sadness over what had occurred, he transformed his life into one of service and integrity. After this disclosure, Cynthia viewed him completely differently and her respect for him as a person grew exponentially. Be willing to disclose those kinds of meaningful events in order to build deeper relationships with others.

There was a time when we thought that organizational politics were inherently destructive—until we realized that whenever you have three or more people in a group, politics inevitably emerge. Rather than resist politics, pay attention to the dynamics that revolve around the use of authority and power at work. Notice that truly influential people often have networks of supporters and allies. They don't resort to bullying because they have earned the ability to influence.

> *Networking involves a natural give and take of interest, support, joint successes, and mutual celebration.*

Get Input

Talk things over with others before taking actions that may affect them. This practice prevents you from surprising or antagonizing people. Choose to consult with others and seek their input instead of quashing dissenting opinions.

Ray once coached a manager who was preparing to launch a new initiative. When Ray probed to find out whom the manager had consulted before deciding on this direction, the manager revealed that he had only consulted a few associates who agreed with his decision. When Ray suggested that it might be useful to get input from other employees as well, the manager brushed aside this suggestion as a waste of time. You can imagine what happened after the manager announced the initiative: open rebellion by disgruntled employees who were not at all pleased with the new direction. Beware the "I know best" trap.

Taking the time to consult others, solicit input, and incorporate their ideas leads to stronger relationships and greater cooperation.

Seek Solutions that Benefit All

You may have heard the phrase "win-win" to describe a negotiated agreement. In an argument or disagreement, take the lead in proposing solutions that work for all parties. To do this, you will have to take time to uncover others' needs, instead of focusing only on your needs.

Let's look at an example: Suppose you work with a controlling coworker. She has a need for lots of information. She gets anxious if she doesn't know exactly what is going to happen when. You find this behavior irritating. You have two choices: give her the information she needs when she needs it (which meets her need for control), or ignore her needs and allow her anxiety to rise. Which should you do? If you're applying this practice, the answer is obvious: meet her need for timely information. If you do so, she'll be more willing to collaborate with you.

Build and Protect Self-esteem

At its simplest, this practice means that you pay attention to the self-esteem of others. We all want to feel good about who we are and what we contribute. Look for opportunities to sincerely thank people for their efforts, to praise them for their contributions, and to acknowledge their work on joint projects. Of course, you probably expect your boss to do this! But even if you're not the boss, expressing sincere appreciation builds self-esteem.

In this same vein, share credit with your colleagues. If you're praised for meeting a goal, acknowledge the peers who gave you information or collaborated on a proposal. Spread those good feelings around the team. Your "we're all in this together" attitude creates strong bonds with your coworkers.

Even if you have to give critical feedback, protect others' self-esteem by allowing them to save face. Focus on the specific behavior that troubles you, rather than generalized judgments about their attitudes or personality.

Express Compassion or Empathy

When you empathize with others, you allow yourself to acknowledge their feelings. You don't have to experience their feelings, join them in a pity party, or get mad on their behalf. You simply express your compassion for their situation.

> *We all want to feel good about who we are and what we contribute.*

We live in the Pacific Northwest and there are occasional floods that occur after heavy rains. After one particularly intense three-day rainstorm, Cynthia's basement flooded, creating an expensive, inconvenient, and stressful situation for her family. When she shared what happened with a friend, the judging response was, "You should feel blessed. Your family is healthy and you only lost a few possessions." Cynthia experienced that response as cold and unsympathetic.

Your compassion or empathy is simply a demonstration of concern for the other person. You don't have to fix it, wallow in it, or dramatize it. There are times when the most helpful action you can take is to allow someone else to vent her feelings, or express her frustration, disappointment, or anger while you listen. There may not be much required of you except a concerned facial expression, an occasional head nod, and an acknowledgement of the feeling. Isn't that a relief? You don't have to give advice, make it all better, or agree with her feelings. You just need to bring compassion to the table. Once the venting has stopped, your frustrated colleague may be able to solve her problem on her own.

Conclusion

In Chapter 1 we explored what doesn't work (manipulating, whining, attacking, or bullying). In this chapter we have described what does work (Be Real, Take Responsibility, Extend Respect, and Build Relationships). We want to emphasize that there are no tricks, deceptions, or play-acting that will help you fake these principles. And despite our best attempt to describe these comprehensive principles, we can't guarantee that they will always work. In every human interaction, you'll have to use your best judgment.

What we do know is that at the root of most conflicts there are relationship issues. Beneath the apparent conflict there are usually feelings about how we are being treated by the other person. That's why these principles are so important, and why applying them skillfully will make people want to work with you. If you're the boss, they're the secret for gaining others' commitment and loyalty.

If you do nothing else but adopt these principles and practices as part of your interpersonal interactions with others, you will prevent 75 percent of the conflict and misunderstandings that occur at work. Okay, we made up that 75 percent statistic, but we challenge you to use these approaches consistently with others and watch what happens when you bring peer power to your relationships.

Now that you understand the principles that we recommend, you're ready to dive into the strategies to use when dealing with the remaining 25 percent of difficult situations. Turn now to Chapter 3 to learn more about the strategies that we'll be using throughout the case studies in this book.

PRINCIPLES & PRACTICES

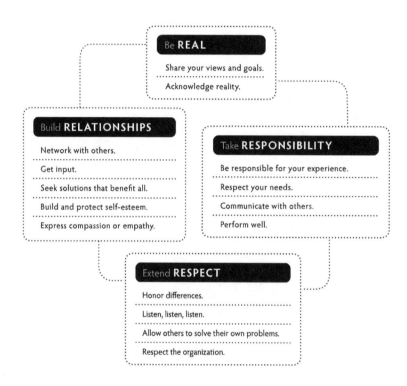

chapter 3

strategies for transforming relationships

Introduction

In Chapter 2 we introduced the principles and practices that will help you work more effectively in challenging situations. You can use the principles as the bedrock that will position you for the most constructive relationships possible. However, they are not sufficient for dealing with a challenging person who is interfering with your significant needs or whose behavior is seriously troubling you. In that situation, you must adopt a specific strategy to turn the situation around. Let's add these strategies to your peer power toolkit.

Most workplace difficulties involve both an immediate issue and a difficult pattern. The story in the first chapter about Ray and Brit involved both the immediate issue of completing the class and the difficult pattern of Ray bullying. Your strategy will focus on resolving the immediate issue; however, dealing with the immediate issue will likely affect the other person's difficult pattern.

In this chapter, we want to share our five practical strategies for any workplace difficulty. We'd like to give credit to Kenneth W. Thomas and Ralph H. Kilmann, whose *Thomas-Kilmann Conflict Mode Inventory*[3] has influenced our thinking.

---

[3] Kenneth W. Thomas and Ralph H. Kilmann, *Thomas-Kilmann conflict mode instrument* (Tuxedo, N.Y.: Xicom, 1974).

The Five Strategies

Let's look at our five strategies that you might adopt to resolve any difficulty when it is too important to ignore:

- Going Head-to-Head (Attempting to meet your needs while preventing others from meeting their needs)

- Compromising (Attempting to meet your needs partially while meeting others' needs partially)

- Caring-for-Self (Attempting unilaterally to meet your needs by limiting the impact of others' behavior without affecting their needs)

- Coaching (With permission, attempting to help another solve a problem or develop skills so the other person gets better results)

- Collaborating (Jointly attempting to meet fully the needs of all parties)

Choosing the right strategy for the right situation is essential. But how can you determine the best strategy? There is no one formula. It depends upon the situation. It depends upon you and your goals. It depends upon your previous history. We will use a simple story to illustrate a few key points about handling difficult situations. (We find this personal example makes it easier to understand and apply these strategies to your work-related situations.)

When Colin and his wife Hannah began to live together, they discovered they had a major difference. Colin likes to sleep with the bedroom window closed, and Hannah likes to sleep with it open. After they would fall asleep, Colin would wake up cold and quietly close the window. After a while he would wake up again, feel cold, and notice that the window was open again. He would quietly close it and go back to sleep, only to find it open again the next time he woke. This pattern continued for several months. As you can imagine, neither Colin nor Hannah was getting enough sleep.

Going Head-to-Head

Colin and Hannah were using the Going Head-to-Head strategy. When you Go Head-to-Head, you seek to meet your needs in a way that blocks the other's needs. It does not mean that you are abusive or hostile, although that sometimes also happens. It happened when Colin and Hannah attempted to have their own way. Colin, sometimes using very critical and harsh language (attacking), insisted that Hannah keep the window shut, and Hannah, now standing her ground, angrily insisted that Colin leave it open. Things did not improve and their close relationship began to suffer.

The Going Head-to-Head strategy has its place, but it was not appropriate in this situation (a loving marriage in which partners want to remain together). When it is critical that you maintain a good relationship with the other person and you need his or her support for actions you take, then you will get better outcomes if you choose one of the other strategies.

The truth is there are times when it's appropriate to use Going Head-to-Head. One night right after a vacation, Colin was sound asleep when Hannah woke him up because she heard strangers in their basement. At first Colin couldn't believe that was possible. But then he realized Hannah was right—there were unusual sounds coming from the basement. As they whispered about what to do, they heard footsteps coming up the stairs toward their bedroom.

> *When you Go Head-to-Head, you seek to meet your needs in a way that blocks the other's needs.*

Colin valiantly adopted the Going Head-to-Head strategy. He told Hannah to stay where she was, leapt from bed, and began shouting at the would-be robbers to leave. He did not consider the feelings or needs of the intruders. Fortunately, they fled, and Colin looked and felt like a hero! (Looking back, Colin thought the intruders had wrongly assumed the house was empty, were equally surprised to hear loud whispering, and probably were starting to retreat by the time Colin started shouting.)

Use the Going Head-to-Head approach when there is very little time, the issue is critical, or when the other person is pursuing unreasonable needs or is making a huge mistake. There are times to politely, but firmly, push for your position or needs while blocking the other's needs. The downside of this strategy is that it can cause considerable long-term resentment. Be sure that meeting your own needs is essential before resorting to it.

> *In Compromising, each party gets some of what he wants and gives up some of what he wants.*

Chapter 6 about the scene stealer will illustrate the effective use of Going Head-to-Head.

Compromising

In dealing with the window problem, Colin or Hannah could have used the Compromising strategy. For example, they might have agreed to keep the window open on alternate nights. Colin could be too cold half the time. Hannah could be too warm half the time. In Compromising, each party gets some of what he wants and gives up some of what he wants. Colin and Hannah considered Compromising but decided to look for a more complete solution.

Compromising is appropriate when time is limited and everyone's needs can't be met. Choose the Compromising strategy when you want to maintain a good relationship and you're willing to give a little to get a little.

To see good uses of Compromising, read Chapter 12 on dealing with the bully.

Caring-for-Self

When Going Head-to-Head did not work, Colin and Hannah sometimes tried the Caring-for-Self strategy (unilaterally meeting their own needs). For example, they would take catnaps during the day when time permitted. They occasionally would sleep in separate rooms just to catch up on their sleep. Caring-for-Self is always useful when other strategies fail or aren't appropriate.

If Colin and Hannah had carried the Caring-for-Self strategy to an extreme, they might have concluded that they should separate. It certainly would have been one way for them to satisfy the need for more sleep. Taking this drastic step would have compromised many other needs, however. (Though Hannah and Colin chose to work out their differences, we know there may be times when it is necessary to leave a difficult situation in your personal life or your work life.)

All of our case chapters illustrate how to use the Caring-for-Self strategy when the initial strategies fail.

Coaching

Coaching is attempting to help another solve a problem or develop skills so the other person gets better results. The Coaching strategy was not an appropriate strategy for Colin and Hannah. (Can you imagine Colin coaching Hannah to leave the window closed if she wanted to get better results? Enough said.) The problem involved both of them and had nothing to do with a skill deficiency.

> *Caring-for-Self is always useful when other strategies fail or aren't appropriate.*

A good workplace coach asks permission to coach before asking questions to help the person get clear on what is happening, determine her goals, and come up with her own solutions. The coach might also provide training, information, and options, depending on the answers to the questions.

Let's look at a work example to illustrate how to use the Coaching strategy. Ray's boss John once proposed a restructuring of his division in order to eliminate some performance problems. Though Ray would not be dramatically affected by this change, he strongly believed it would not work well. With some discomfort, he decided to try to help

John by coaching him. When asked if he would be open to help exploring the situation, John was very receptive. Ray asked John why the performance problems were occurring, how customers and employees would react to the proposed reorganization, and what other reorganizations were possible. Ray indicated his concerns about the proposed reorganization, but allowed John to save face and made it very clear that it was John's decision to make.

> *Coaching is attempting to help another solve a problem or develop skills so the other person gets better results.*

John decided to modify the planned reorganization based on Ray's coaching. To help him announce the new reorganization, Ray also gave John a few useful articles to read. Happily, the performance problems declined significantly in the reorganized division.

Examples of how to apply the Coaching strategy can be found in the case chapters on working with the faux-smart boss (Chapter 10), the drive-by boss (Chapter 7), and the whiner (Chapter 5).

Collaborating

Fortunately, Colin and Hannah both finally realized that Collaborating was the most appropriate strategy for their situation. Together they worked through five steps to overcome their disagreement:

1. Define the problem

2. Generate optional solutions

3. Choose the solution

4. Implement the solution

5. Evaluate the results

These steps worked for Colin and Hannah because they were willing to participate, were skilled at problem solving, and were willing to listen without defending.

Warning: Collaborating can take considerable time. Colin tried to shorten the process by making an assertive request he thought might be acceptable to Hannah that met his needs as well (step 3).

When Colin again got frustrated with Hannah opening the window, he asked her if she would just open it up a little. He hoped that this proposal would provide her with sufficient fresh air while he remained warm. He said to her, "When the window is wide open at night, I become cold and have a hard time sleeping. When the window is closed, you can't sleep. Would you be willing to keep the window open just a crack?" This was a request, not a demand. Colin indicated concisely and non-judgmentally what was troubling him, why it mattered, and what he was hoping would work fully for them both.

Hannah politely, but firmly, turned down this request, saying that this would not give her enough fresh air. While assertive requests are often accepted, it is always appropriate for someone to turn down the request if it does not meet her needs. There is no obligation to give in.

So Colin paraphrased Hannah's response and suggested they define their problem (step 1). Previously they had assumed that the definition of their problem was how to keep the window open and closed simultaneously. This view of their problem prevented progress and was inaccurate.

> *Warning: Collaborating can take considerable time.*

To redefine their problem they had to identify each of their underlying needs. This required some careful thought and a willingness to listen to each other. They concluded that they both needed to get a good night's sleep—Colin needed warmth to accomplish that and Hannah needed fresh air. This led to the following definition of their problem: How can Colin stay warm while at the same time Hannah gets fresh air?

Notice that this definition is free of judgmental terms. It would have been easy for Colin to define the problem as "Hannah wants me to be uncomfortable" or for Hannah to define the same problem as

"Colin always needs to get his own way." These judgments would not have contributed to a solution.

After they defined their problem neutrally, they generated a list of optional solutions (step 2). The list included sleeping in separate bedrooms, separate beds, extra blankets on Colin's side of the bed, heavier pajamas for Colin, a dual control electric blanket, a fan, getting a smaller bed, and moving the bed farther from the window.

A good list of options should also include ideas that are humorous, undesirable, illegal, immoral, and impractical.

Colin and Hannah added to their list getting a divorce, having the dog sleep on top of Colin, letting Colin sleep under the bed, and even shooting each other. A good list of options should also include ideas that are humorous, undesirable, illegal, immoral, and impractical. You probably won't choose these ideas, but they will often foster creativity and help stimulate unexpected ideas you could use. (Difficult problems often cannot be solved without some thinking outside the box.)

Choosing their solution (step 3) was not difficult. After quickly analyzing the advantages and disadvantages of all the options they had generated, they decided on the dual control electric blanket. The window would remain open, but Colin would turn his side of the blanket to very warm and Hannah would keep her side low. With hindsight they realized that calm, clear thinking could have produced this solution much earlier. However, calm, clear thinking is often not present when needs are frustrated.

Hannah and Colin implemented the solution (step 4) by purchasing and installing the dual control electric blanket. (Yes!) A little later in step 5, they concluded their solution just wasn't working. (Oh, no!) The warmth from Colin's side of the blanket would spread to Hannah's side, making her too warm. Sometimes the wires even got crossed, causing Hannah's side to become hot when Colin turned up the knob on his side. They had to return to their list of options. This time they chose separate beds with extra blankets on Colin's bed and the window left open. This solution worked. And Colin and Hannah also realized they needed to change their pattern of focusing only on their own needs.

By moving the beds close together, they were able to maintain closeness. Colin is happy to report that he and Hannah have been married for 35 years.

The same approach adopted by Colin and Hannah may be used when collaborating on a work problem. We recommend the Collaborating strategy whenever finding a solution that meets the needs of all parties is important. This is usually the case at work. Many of our case chapters illustrate how to use this strategy.

Summary of the Strategies

We have identified five strategies for addressing immediate and significant issues with difficult colleagues. Each has its place. (See the following chart.) The key to each strategy is your intention.

Strategy	Use This Strategy When
Going Head-to-Head Attempting to meet your needs while preventing others from meeting their needs	Your needs aren't met. Time is very limited. The issue is critical to you. The other person is pursuing unreasonable needs or is making a big mistake. Maintaining a good relationship is not your top priority.

Strategy	Use This Strategy When
Compromising Attempting to meet your needs partially while meeting others' needs partially	Your needs aren't met. Collaborating fails. Time is limited. Everyone's needs can't be fully met. Maintaining a good relationship is important. You are willing to give a little to gain a little.
Caring-for-Self Attempting unilaterally to meet your needs by limiting the impact of others' behavior without affecting their needs	Your needs aren't met. The other strategies fail.
Coaching With permission, attempting to help another solve a problem or develop skills so the other person gets better results	The other person lacks some key skill and is open to your help. The other person wants your help on a problem.
Collaborating Jointly attempting to meet fully the needs of all parties	Your needs aren't met. The issue is important to all parties. Maintaining a good relationship is important. You need the other party to help carry out an agreement. The needs of each party are not mutually exclusive. There is adequate time.

Using all five strategies requires awareness, skill, and flexibility. As a powerful peer, you must carry each strategy in your hip pocket and be able to pull out the right one. Most people are very good at one or two of these strategies and less comfortable or skilled with the others. They tend to rely on just a couple, regardless of the situation. When you choose the

> *If your initial strategy fails, turn to Plan B to try one of the other four strategies.*

wrong one, you can actually make things worse. As you master the use of these five strategies, you'll find that your work relationships consistently improve.

With the growth of technology, it is tempting to rely on e-mail and other electronic forms of communication when using these strategies. We recommend that as much as possible you rely on face-to-face communication. In Chapter 14 we discuss the advantages of face-to-face interaction and how to use technology when necessary.

Plan B (If Your Initial Strategy Fails)

There is no assurance that the strategy you choose will work. Perhaps your first attempt was not skillful. If so, try again. Or you may have encountered unforeseen obstacles, such as you were unable to reach agreement, your agreed-upon solution didn't work, or the other person failed to follow through. Read Chapter 13 to explore techniques to overcome obstacles like these.

If your initial strategy fails, turn to Plan B to try one of the other four strategies. Colin chose Collaborating when Going Head-to-Head with Hannah failed. He realized he had chosen the wrong strategy. Fortunately Collaborating worked. If it had not, he probably would have attempted Compromising next and finally moved to additional Caring-for-Self. Coaching would be inappropriate in this scenario, but is useful in others.

Your Plan B actions often will consist of two phases. The first is to deal with the immediate issue (the window issue for Colin and Hannah). The second is to deal with a difficult pattern that continues.

Fortunately for Colin and Hannah the pattern of focusing only on their own needs ended (with rare exceptions) as a result of the window incident. In some cases, even when the immediate issue is resolved, the difficult pattern continues. Moving forward, you may need to pick a strategy to address this pattern.

At the end of each of the following case-study chapters, we will suggest which Plan B strategies to turn to when your initial strategy fails.

Let's Get to the Cases

Beginning with Chapter 4, nine chapters discuss how to handle a particular difficulty. These case-study chapters all adhere to the same format:

- First, we define the difficulty and identify some clues to help alert you to it.

- Then we tell you some helpful assumptions to make and which of the principles and practices discussed in Chapter 2 are especially important to remember when facing this difficulty.

- Next, with the aid of some sample dialogues, we recommend which of the five strategies you should initially adopt when an exasperating person interferes with your needs or needs help.

- Finally, we recommend a Plan B—what strategy to turn to and what traps to avoid if your first strategy fails to solve the issue or eliminate your colleague's difficult pattern.

Cheat sheets at the end of each chapter summarize all of these steps. By the time you complete those chapters, you will have all you need to transform workplace relationships through peer power.

THE PEER POWER MODEL

PRINCIPLES & PRACTICES

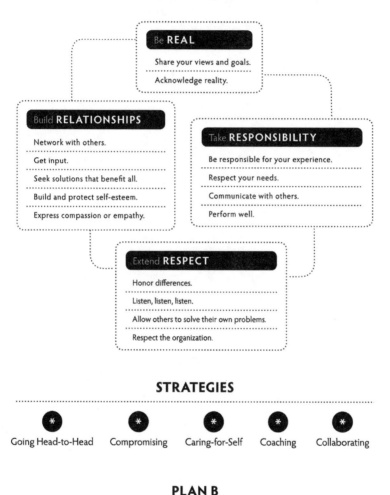

Be **REAL**

Share your views and goals.

Acknowledge reality.

Build **RELATIONSHIPS**

Network with others.

Get input.

Seek solutions that benefit all.

Build and protect self-esteem.

Express compassion or empathy.

Take **RESPONSIBILITY**

Be responsible for your experience.

Respect your needs.

Communicate with others.

Perform well.

Extend **RESPECT**

Honor differences.

Listen, listen, listen.

Allow others to solve their own problems.

Respect the organization.

STRATEGIES

Going Head-to-Head   Compromising   Caring-for-Self   Coaching   Collaborating

PLAN B

When your initial strategy fails.

from the attacker to the constructive critic

When Ray worked as a Manager of Training for a service company, a supervisor in the Marketing Department regularly belittled him. When Josh would pass Ray on the street or in the hallways, he would mock Ray and greet him with apparent sarcasm and derision. This usually occurred in front of others and occasionally in meetings they both attended. Ray suspected the origin of this treatment was Josh's resentment about homework assignments Ray had given in some of the classes he conducted.

Ray did not know how to handle these attacks. Josh was a skilled marketer and popular with some key organizational leaders. Ray was afraid of appearing defensive and alienating Josh further, especially since he was not certain Josh was an attacker. We define the attacker as a colleague who repeatedly expresses anger and frustration in the form of inappropriate personal criticism. His attacks usually include name-calling and blaming, guilt, and sometimes even cursing. Josh's show of derision toward Ray establishes him as an attacker, even though his style was more subtle.

Because of his uncertainty, Ray tried to ignore Josh's comments or laugh at them, pretending they did not bother him. As a result, the comments increased in frequency and Ray's discomfort grew. Ray would avoid Josh whenever possible, but was unhappy when he did that. When he could not avoid Josh, he felt embarrassed, hurt, and angry. He knew something needed to change.

Clues to the Attacker

In Chapter 1 we cautioned against using attacks as a way to affect change. No one wants to work for or with an attacker. Criticism and aggressiveness often show immediate results, but in the long run leaders who attack will find themselves without people to lead, and coworkers who attack will find themselves shunned. And as a customer, a personal attack won't endear you to someone who is there to help you.

Before we discuss how to handle an attacker, let's identify this personality more precisely. You may be dealing with an attacker when a person repeatedly:

- Uses name-calling
- Curses
- Uses sarcasm
- Blames you for problems
- Shouts
- Gives you dirty looks or rolls his eyes
- Teases you or jokes about your mistakes or weaknesses
- Sighs
- Mocks you
- Makes you feel guilty
- Stops interacting with you

Sure, it's possible to experience this unconstructive conduct from anyone who has a bad day. If a valid gripe or need is being expressed (however inappropriately), by all means be attentive to it. But if the behavior is personal, inappropriate, and chronic, then you're dealing with an attacker.

Helpful Assumptions

In other chapters of *Peer Power* you'll find unacceptable coworker behavior that appears to be universally directed, without a specific target. Consider the whiner and the slacker. As much as a whiner's whine may strike a discordant note and a slacker's lack of contribution causes undue burden, you seldom get the feeling that their misfit behavior is directed at you personally. They tend to distribute their offensive behavior without bias.

The attacker is a different animal. If you are his unfortunate target, there's no doubt at whom his anger, name-calling, cursing, and blaming are directed. You are the victim of an attack, pure and simple, and your natural response as a human being is to fight or take flight.

> *Remember that the attacker's acting out is more about him than about you.*

Our advice is to take a deep breath before you respond. Remember that the attacker's acting out is more about him than about you. Think of yourself not as the *victim* of his rant, but as a *recipient* of it. This slight tweak of context will help depersonalize the confrontation.

Staying calm will also buy you time to test some assumptions about the attacker's state of mind and his real motivation. An attacker could be frustrated because he cares a lot about a particular situation or issue. He may be anxious about an upcoming obstacle or challenge. He may be blaming you in order to avoid being blamed or trying to silence you to avoid negative attention from others.

Frustration, anxiety, and fear of blame can cause even upstanding corporate citizens to briefly go into attack mode. In Chapter 1 Cynthia recounted an embarrassing outburst which was chalked up to stress. Most of us can remember a time when we wished we had waited to leave the building before venting.

A genuine attacker, though, displays his aggressive behavior repeatedly. His mishandling of frustration and anxiety is chronic, and its origin more deep-rooted. Attackers are often afraid of being attacked themselves, which is one reason why a knee-jerk counterattack is not a good idea. It's possible they grew up in a home where they were often verbally abused. Even if their childhood environment lacked that kind of drama, it may have spawned a lack of self-esteem or fear of losing control.

Speaking of drama, don't assume that attackers are all loudmouthed and belligerent. As Ray's experience with Josh shows, attackers often utilize more innocuous techniques, like mocking, sarcasm, or humor.

Our peek into an attacker's psyche isn't meant to suggest that you don't have the right to care for yourself against an attacker. But understanding some possible precursors to a person's behavior can help explain his action as an attempt (however inappropriate) to feel better about himself. If you demonize an attacker, you won't be effective in dealing with him.

You'll also be less likely to appreciate the genuine strengths that your coworker contributes to the workplace. His aggression is not necessarily bred from a feeling of incompetence. Due to his passionate nature, he often cares deeply about his performance and the success of his team. Faced with peer power, attackers can even become constructive critics.

Key Principles: Take Responsibility and Build Relationships

A verbal attack in the workplace can be unnerving. It's easy to react in the wrong way without a thoughtful, measured response. And if instead of acting, you choose to ignore the slings and arrows of an attacker, your silence may simply amplify his actions, as Ray experienced.

Incorporating two principles and their practices, Take Responsibility and Build Relationships, can help reduce the consequences of an attack and even keep one from happening in the first place.

Let's examine how Taking Responsibility and Building Relationships can help handle attackers.

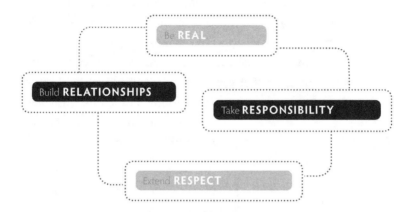

Take Responsibility

If you are the recipient of repeated personal attacks, it may not cross your mind that you share responsibility for the situation. The attacker often has personal issues that are not of your making. His attacks are inappropriate in most settings, especially in a work setting.

That's all likely true, and it may also be true that you are totally blameless in starting or maintaining the conflict. But the practice of being responsible for your experience demands that you assess *your* responsibilities. When dealing with an attacker, this means that you must candidly consider 1) your contribution to the initial confrontation; 2) your contributions to continued confrontations; and 3) how you will take control of your experiences from this moment forward. Your peer power to transform this relationship stems from honestly assessing your role in this situation.

In Ray's case, his initial contact with Josh was in a class that was attended by twenty people. He couldn't recall singling Josh out during the instruction and concluded that he hadn't consciously kindled the flame that sparked Josh's attacks. This is not uncommon with attackers—their anger can be (to all outer appearances) unprovoked, and their targets can be based on a bias or on a whim. But you must still ask the question of yourself and take to heart any insights that result.

Whether or not you had a role in prompting an attack, be honest about how you may be contributing to continued negative attention from an attacker. For example, you may be laughing at his hostile jokes rather than addressing your concern. As tempting as it seems, it does no good to assert that your attacker is evil and obviously in the wrong. Righteous finger-pointing adds to the hostile relationship and solidifies your role as victim who does not control your experience.

> *Your peer power to transform this relationship stems from honestly assessing your role in this situation.*

Taking control removes the attacker's ability to make you think, feel, or act in a certain way. It places that responsibility squarely on your shoulders. Once you accept this responsibility, you can utilize the other Take Responsibility practices.

If you and your attacker have to work together, regular communication and updates may prevent disagreements that might otherwise trip attacking behavior. And if it's possible to become more honest with the attacker and his behavior, your communication could serve to set ground rules and expectations on behavior, instead of waiting for disagreements to occur.

A practice that will help prevent attacks is to perform well. Do the best you can in areas that relate to meeting the attacker's needs. Proactively prevent attacks by anticipating frustrations and model how to handle them if they occur.

While focusing on how you can perform well, don't assume that your own needs are secondary. Aim toward a balance between meeting the needs of attackers and meeting your own needs.

Dealing with an attacker can be a cause for constant worry. It's imperative that you manage your stress before and after attacks, and while you are attempting to communicate with the attacker. Cynthia had a colleague who hated to stand up in front of an audience. Talk about fight or flight—there was no mistaking which choice his body wanted to take! He would stop breathing to the point that his throat constricted and he could only squeak out his prepared remarks. Cynthia coached him in learning how to stay calm, focusing on his objectives and remembering to breathe when his body wanted to turn and run. You can apply similar techniques when experiencing a verbal attack.

Managing stress becomes harder if you don't strike a balance between the Take Responsibility practices. For example, you have a *right* not to be attacked. That might seem contradictory to what we said earlier about honestly assessing any contribution you made to an attacking situation. Be gentle with yourself: don't apply blame, and try to be aware of any feelings of guilt.

Build Relationships

The first Build Relationships practice is to network with others. We tend to network for both personal reasons (like having fun at work) and professional reasons (for help with current and future roles and job positions). The habitual maintenance of a good network of associates will pay dividends if you're attacked. A set of connections provides the strength in numbers that can shield you from a hostile coworker—he is intent on a skirmish, not a battle on multiple fronts. Your associates can also provide one or more sounding boards to help reduce the stress of a protracted confrontation.

Cynthia recently experienced this strength in numbers when a hostile board member attacked her at a board meeting, claiming that Cynthia had just "insulted her by saying that she disempowered others." Cynthia calmly pointed out that she had not made that statement. When the attacker continued to insist that Cynthia had just insulted her, others on the board paraphrased what they heard Cynthia say and agreed that she had not made the statement denounced by the attacker. Failing to get the response she expected, the attacker stopped her attack.

The more expansive your network, the more likely it is to incorporate potential attackers. If Ray had been a known entity, Josh may have been less likely to direct his discontent in the form of an inappropriate personal attack and might have criticized more constructively.

To keep attackers from showing their aggression, there are several good practices that aim to reduce the frustration that may surge into an attack. For example, if you're in a position to take actions or make decisions that affect coworkers or your direct reports, be sensitive to the fact that changes and surprises in the workplace can add to fear and frustration. You can reduce coworker worries by first seeking opinions and input from others. The more control your colleagues or employees have over their fate, the less anxious and frustrated they will feel, reducing their tendencies to attack.

Arguments and disagreements can also breed frustration. When you find yourself in an argument, try to propose a mutually satisfying solution. As is so often the case, good communication is the key to this practice. During discussions, probe your coworker's requirements and wishes, listen well, and seek a remedy that he can feel satisfied with. Frustration (and the likelihood of an attack) is reduced. And because you reached consensus through cooperation, your coworker may act friendlier toward you in the future.

> *You can reduce coworker worries by first seeking opinions and input from others.*

In addition to listening to your coworkers' words, note their feelings. Remember that attackers may have experienced painful abuse themselves. Though it's not an easy undertaking, try to show compassion and empathy when you're in the face of a frustrated coworker, both before and during a harsh personal assault. Simply allowing an individual to express his aggravation may be enough to eliminate an attack scenario. Have you ever dialed a friend on his cell phone and ranted for five minutes after he said "hello"?

More often than not, it's only after you've said, "Thanks, I feel better now," and hung up that you realize that your friend hadn't said a word. Sometimes we just need to vent. Of course, when it's an attacker doing the venting, this doesn't mean that you have an obligation to be a punching bag. It just means you remain calm, open, and honest to the emotional interplay between the two of you.

Consider also the practice of building and protecting the self-esteem of your discontented coworker. Most people want to feel that they are contributing to the success of the team, so look for opportunities to vocally praise and appreciate the positive efforts of others. When people feel good about themselves, they are less likely to attack others.

It may seem as if you can only put this practice into action prior to an encounter, not while the sparks are flying. But as we'll see in the scenarios that follow, fighting the impulse to clash in favor of building self-esteem and partnership is a key to reducing an associate's prickly behavior to that of a constructive critic.

Strategy: Collaborating

The principles and practices that we suggest throughout this book are meant to be incorporated into your everyday behavior. In applying the principles of Take Responsibility and Build Relationships, your chance of being attacked should be reduced.

If you are the recipient of an attack, seek a joint solution through the strategy of Collaborating, especially if your situation includes these elements:

1. The attacks are significant, repeated, or emotionally draining.
2. Your relationship to the attacker is important for you to be effective in your job or goals.
3. It's possible to meet the attacker's needs.
4. You have the time that it takes to implement the strategy.

Going Head-to-Head to confront the attacker might be tempting, but it will only escalate the situation.

The Collaborating strategy can be useful to handle the following scenarios:

- Attacks made in retaliation for a perceived offense
- Unjustified aggressive attacks
- Attacks disguised as humor

Scenario: Someone attacks you because you made a decision that affected him without getting his input

When your attacker appears to retaliate for something you've done to him personally, a Collaborating strategy can defuse the issue. This scenario includes techniques for airing out your differences and jointly finding a solution.

ATTACKER: (Said menacingly, while passing you in the hall)
Hey, if it isn't Mr. High and Mighty. I just want you to remember that pride comes before the fall.

YOU: (Take a deep breath while resolving not to take anything personally. Try to determine the source of the anger.)
Antonio, you've acted upset in the last few weeks. Would you like to talk about it? Does it have to do with something that I've said or done?

ATTACKER: You know what our work schedule in Finance is like. One week out of every month is already taken with month-end accounting. My team has barely enough time to do our current jobs, much less volunteering for a company-wide project. I'd have told you that to your face if you had the courtesy of asking me. If you have any bright ideas on how we can stretch our schedules without doing a half-assed job on both fronts, I'd love to hear it.

YOU: (Allow for venting. Don't rebut the attacker or focus on logic. Instead, paraphrase what he is saying as well as his emotions neutrally. This can help him to hear how extreme his claim is.)
It sounds like you're upset because the decision on this project was made without getting your input first.

ATTACKER: Damn right. Maybe you don't believe in planning, but I for one don't like to shoot from the hip. You have the ear of the boss and think you're a hot shot. That's your problem.

YOU: (Again, paraphrase both the content and the emotion. This should not imply that you agree with him but only shows you are listening.)
So you feel you were blindsided.

ATTACKER: That's right.

YOU: (Apologize for any mistake and thank him for telling you his concern. Compliment him for caring about the issue.)
Well, I appreciate that; I don't like getting blindsided either. You obviously care a lot for your team and want to make sure you do a good job for the good of the company. I'm sorry this decision came out of left field.

ATTACKER: (With scorn)
Well, you can't close the barn door after the horse has bolted. Or don't they have that saying at Yale?

YOU: (The conversation is in danger of getting heated again. If things get derailed, consider taking a break.)
It seems like we are getting into a fight. I really want to resolve our disagreements if we can so we can meet your needs.

ATTACKER: Well, your solutions are already causing my team a lot of unpaid overtime.

YOU: (See how you can help.)
I understand that. What can I do at this point to make it easier?

ATTACKER: That's simple: get us another resource. That way we can get the new project done and make up some of our backlog at the same time.

YOU: (Agree to what the attacker wants unless it doesn't meet your needs. In that case propose some alternatives. This is your chance to collaborate.)
The project doesn't have the budget to do that, unfortunately. But I know that they're going to be using interns in Finance. What if we both make a proposal to the boss to get two of the interns to work on your backlog and help with the month-end close? That

would free up your team a little for the project.

ATTACKER: Well, that might work. I am sorry I unloaded on you. You can tell I was really upset.

YOU: Great. Thanks for taking the time to talk with me. Would you like to set up that meeting with the boss, or should I?

Scenario: Someone attacks you unfairly with cursing or yelling for something you did not do

An aggressive attack is unsettling enough. When it's done for reasons that appear unfair, your knee-jerk reaction is to argue your innocence, which can add fuel to the fire. When it includes foul language, it is hard not to retaliate. Keep your cool and employ some of the Collaborating tips found in the following scenario to meet your need to be addressed courteously and the other person's needs to vent and discover the truth.

ATTACKER: Why don't you get the #@!!% out of my office. I don't want to see your #@!!% face. This is my space; it's for me and my friends.

YOU: (Keep your cool and try to change the tone of the conversation. Ignore the cursing unless it really bothers you.)
Mary, I see you are upset. I want to talk to you about it, but it will be hard to hear your concerns if you continue cursing and yelling at me.

ATTACKER: Sure, let's talk. Why don't you start by telling me why you did it? You know I wanted the Heathridge account. What a coincidence that two days after your meeting with Mr. Mason, the plum marketing assignment went to your best friend. I had no idea you were such a Judas.

YOU: (Take a second to breathe before you respond. Instead of using logic to respond to accusations, paraphrase neutrally both the content and the emotion of your attacker's venting.)
I see. It sounds like you're upset because you think I influenced the boss's decision.

ATTACKER: Don't tell me that you didn't. I'm not as stupid as you seem to think I am.

YOU: (Ask if you can give her your side of things, and then do so only if she allows it.)
May I give you my view of the situation?

ATTACKER: Yeah, go ahead.

YOU: (Don't try to persuade her that she is wrong. Instead, state the facts.)
I did meet with Mr. Mason on Monday about another issue, and I assure you I did not discuss this assignment with him. I know that John also met with Mr. Mason the week before to discuss the assignment. I am not sure how Mr. Mason made his decision.

ATTACKER: So you are saying you had nothing to do with it?

YOU: (Acknowledge that you can see how she might have come to her view.)
Yes, but I can understand how you could conclude that. Anyone would be disappointed not to get this assignment.

ATTACKER: I don't understand why the boss didn't talk to me before announcing the decision. I guess I need to talk to him, don't I?

YOU: I think so.

ATTACKER: Thank you for talking this over with me. I definitely overreacted. I will watch the vulgarity.

YOU: Thanks for toning it down so we could figure this out.

In this scenario, you dealt with a person who appears to fly off the handle at the slightest perceived offense. She may continue to do so, but in dealing with her attack directly, the attacker may think twice before launching curses your way. You are helping her evolve from an attacker to a constructive critic.

Dear Cynthia and Ray,

My boss attacks me frequently, even getting in my face and personal space. I feel physically threatened by him. I have tried many of your ideas, but the pattern continues. Any suggestions?

— At Wit's End

Dear At Wit's,

We often suggest meeting one on one with your attacker. Since you feel the threat of physical violence, it's best to avoid places where you can be cornered. If that is not possible, during your confrontations back away or politely ask him to back up. Maintain a relaxed and non-threatening posture, and talk calmly. Encourage him to keep talking. Focus on listening and letting him vent.

If you've already taken this course of action and the pattern continues, then wait for a time when your boss is not attacking you. Take the opportunity to use an assertive request to collaborate with him. Speak to him frankly, saying something like, "When I am yelled at and criticized harshly, I feel intimidated and am not able to really listen to your concerns. I know the work is very important to you and that intimidation is not your intention. I really want to provide you with what you need from me. I would really appreciate it if when you are bothered by something that I have done that you talk to me calmly about it. Would that work for you?"

Most organizations strive to maintain workplaces that are free of intimidation. If the pattern continues, consider discussing the situation with your Human Resources Department, even though your boss might not be pleased.

— Cynthia and Ray

Scenario: Someone teases you in front of others so the attack is disguised as humor

Remember Ray's experience with an attacker? Josh's mocking and sarcasm were not as dramatic as cursing and yelling. But make no mistake: they were still the weapons of an attacker. The following scenario shows a popular stealth approach, the use of teasing and humor.

ATTACKER: Hey, Borat, how's it going?

YOU: (Some attackers like to play to an audience. Try to get them to meet with you alone now or later.)
John, are you free right now? I'd like to find a conference room and discuss something with you.

ATTACKER: (In a mock East European accent)
Sure. Anything for my friend from Kazakhstan.

YOU: (Once you're alone, don't imply that he must be upset with you; that would be mind reading.)
I doubt it is your intention, but I am uncomfortable with your jokes about me.

ATTACKER: Oh, come on. It's nothing personal. Everyone around here comes from somewhere else; we all have different accents. I like doing accents. It's just a joke.

YOU: I like jokes. But I'm uncomfortable with these jokes.

ATTACKER: Whatever. I'd recommend thicker skin.

YOU: (Try to get him to be direct.)
Am I doing or have I done something that bothers you?

ATTACKER: Not that I can think of. I'm probably not as sensitive as you are.

ATTACKER: (After much more back and forth, denials, and ineffective humor)
It must feel good, having that kind of power in your training class. You give people plenty of opportunities to feel foolish.

YOU: It sounds like you were uncomfortable in our training class last month because of something I did or said.

ATTACKER: Whatever. We can't all be great public speakers.

YOU: I remember that I encouraged you to role-play during our practice exercise. If I did something that made you feel uncomfortable or foolish, I apologize.

ATTACKER: (Remains silent. Bingo.)

YOU: I'd really like to put this behind us. What would you like me to do at this point?

ATTACKER: We can all improve on our presentation skills in front of an audience. I know you're the expert.

YOU: Hardly that. Would you like some help from me to improve your presentation skills in front of an audience? There are some materials I can give you to read, and then you can retake the class. There is another one coming up in two months.

ATTACKER: I'm not comfortable role-playing in front of an audience. Thinking on my feet has never been my strong suit. What would really be nice is to have just the two of us go over the entire class and practice the role-play portion of it.

YOU: (Agree with the suggestion only if it meets your needs.)
I would like nothing better than to give you that kind of one-on-one training. Unfortunately, my schedule doesn't allow that much time. It sounds like you feel your main focus for improvement is in being able to ad-lib in front of an audience. Perhaps we can meet for one or two short sessions on that aspect of the class. Then I could give you specific exercises to follow between our meetings.

ATTACKER: That sounds great. Now that I think about it, that would work well. I happen to have recording equipment. Perhaps we can record the role-playing.

YOU: That's acceptable to me. Of course, I expect the jokes to stop. If I do anything that upsets you, I hope you'll talk to me about it.

ATTACKER: I understand.

YOU: I'm glad we had this talk.

ATTACKER: So am I.

Dear Cynthia and Ray,

A coworker in meetings doesn't attack me verbally, but when I make comments she rolls her eyes, sighs loudly, and looks disgusted. She is also giving me the silent treatment. I definitely feel attacked.

— Sick of Sighing

Dear Sick,

Handle this similarly to a verbal attack. Try to get the person to collaborate by expressing her concerns constructively ("Do you have concerns about me or my point of view?"). The big challenge is that she is likely to deny any concerns. If she does, calmly and non-critically point out the nonverbal signals you have seen and that you thought they might suggest concerns.

Be careful not to embarrass her in front of others, and don't force her to acknowledge her concerns. Chances are good that she will discontinue the eye rolling and sighing because you have brought them out into the open. (Often nonverbal attackers prefer surreptitious attacks.)

— Cynthia and Ray

Plan B (If Your Initial Strategy Fails)

You can't force a person to work toward resolving an issue. If Collaborating fails, turn to the Compromising strategy to try to reach a solution that will work at least partially for both of you. This strategy is also useful when time is limited or when you are willing to make some concessions in order to maintain a good relationship.

Related to attackers, the Compromising strategy may mean that the attacker doesn't necessarily agree to stop the attacking behavior. For example, in the scenario where Mary curses, she may still be upset, but promise not to yell in public. This is not the complete solution, but it's the next best thing.

Negotiating a compromise with a recalcitrant attacker may take tact, courage, and patience. There are a lot of "don'ts" to remember: don't attack back, run away (like Ray did), get defensive, change the subject, or tell the person to get a grip. And when you're away from the attacker, don't vent to others.

You can always employ the Caring-for-Self strategy. Focus on managing your stress. Get coaching from a trusted friend. If the other strategies don't seem to work, caring for yourself may lead to minimizing contact with the attacker. This might take the form of e-mail communication instead of face-to-face. In the extreme case, you may need to find another job.

Moving Forward

If the attacking continues or becomes more and more abusive, so that it becomes clear that the attacker's issue is larger than a single incident, try to Collaborate with the attacker about his general behavior (not the specific issue you are being attacked about). Say, "I would like this behavior to stop. What do you need so that it will?" See if you can agree to a plan. If you are successful and the attacking stops, be sure to acknowledge the improvement. If you are not, you may need to insist that it stop.

The Rest of the Story

After some time, Ray decided to address Josh's behavior. He found the opportunity to confront Josh in private so they could explore each other's needs without involving an audience. Josh continued to insist he was just joking and meant no harm, but he agreed to cut it out and, for the most part, stopped baiting Ray.

Cheat Sheet for the Attacker

Definition: An attacker is a colleague who repeatedly expresses anger and frustration in the form of inappropriate personal criticism.

Clues

The attacker:

- Uses name-calling
- Curses
- Uses sarcasm
- Blames you for problems
- Shouts
- Gives you dirty looks or rolls his eyes
- Teases you or jokes about your mistakes or weaknesses
- Sighs
- Mocks you
- Makes you feel guilty
- Stops interacting with you

Helpful Assumptions

- He is frustrated about a situation or issue he cares about.
- He is facing an obstacle and wants to get his way.
- Sometimes attackers are trying to avoid being blamed.
- You probably have attacked some people, too.
- Attackers are afraid of being attacked themselves.
- Attackers sometimes attack when they are losing control or want to silence you.
- Some attackers lack self-esteem.
- Not all attackers are loudmouthed.
- You have a right to care for yourself.

- Attackers usually have strengths, too.

Key Principles and Practices

Take Responsibility

- Be responsible by looking at your own contributions to the confrontation; take control of your experiences.

- Communicate in order to prevent attacks.

- Perform well: anticipate frustrations; meet the needs of others; model how to handle frustrations.

- Respect your needs through self-knowledge, stress management, and awareness of your rights.

Build Relationships

- Network so people know you and are less likely to attack.

- Get input from others so they feel they have some control and are less likely to get frustrated.

- Seek shared solutions so others are less frustrated.

- Show compassion and empathy.

- Build self-esteem by acknowledging good results.

Strategy: Collaborating

- Take a deep breath and request a break if necessary.

- Allow for some venting. Don't rebut with logic.

- Paraphrase neutrally without the hostile component.

- Acknowledge him for caring about the issue.

- Apologize for mistakes; thank him for sharing his concern.

- If the attack is for something that you did not do, ask to explain your point of view, but don't argue or apologize.

- If the attack involves excessive cursing or yelling, say, "I want to hear what you have to say, but not this way."

- If the attack is public, request to meet privately.

- If someone attacks using humor, say, "I doubt it is your intention, but I am uncomfortable with these jokes about me." Ask if he is upset with you.

- Ask what he would like you to do. Agree to his request or propose some alternatives.

- If the attacks continue during your discussion, say, "I really want to solve this rather than fight."

Plan B (If Your Initial Strategy Fails)

- When Collaborating fails, switch to Compromising.

- Do not attack back or vent to others.

- Do not run away, get defensive, change the subject, or tell him to get a grip.

- Caring-for-Self: Manage your stress; minimize contact with him; look for another job.

Worksheet

1. What clues make you suspect you may be dealing with an attacker?

2. Assuming you've determined the person is an attacker, what might be his legitimate needs?

3. What are this attacker's strengths?

4. What key principles and practices do you want to use with this attacker?

5. Write the opening statement you might use to begin using the Collaborating strategy with this attacker.

6. What response do you anticipate and how will you handle it?

7. What Plan B approach will you use if your discussion is not successful?

from the whiner to the problem solver

There is nothing more taxing than working with someone who feels perpetually victimized by circumstances, people, and outside events. Whiners don't take responsibility for improving the negative conditions that surround them, instead lapsing into blame-filled laments and complaints without offering any solutions. Their complaints, although not harsh personal attacks, might even be about you.

Cynthia once worked closely with a whiner (Lynda) who complained regularly about coworkers who let her down, bad management decisions that affected her, the color of paint on the walls, the sordid state of the refrigerator at work, the company's benefit plans, her inability to get their manager to return her phone calls, the gravel on the walkways outside the building, etc. On and on the complaints went, never with a constructive suggestion.

Like many on the receiving end of Lynda's laments, Cynthia made suggestion after suggestion to empower her to take action. Lynda wanted Cynthia to take action. On occasion, Cynthia would give up and fix whatever was broken to end the whining, resenting every second she spent solving Lynda's problem for her.

Fortunately, like many whiners, attuned to what doesn't work instead of what does work, Lynda would often be the first to spot problems that might threaten to derail important projects. The whiner's early warning system could actually alert the team to issues that needed to be addressed.

Clues to the Whiner

You'll know that you are working with a whiner when you see these clues. Your coworker (or your boss):

- Blames problems and conditions on others
- Talks endlessly about problems with third parties instead of taking action
- Is not willing to be personally responsible for negative outcomes
- Expects the organization's managers to fix mistakes
- Constantly criticizes others' work
- Encourages others to address issues on her behalf
- Avoids direct confrontation or conflict

Because a whiner identifies herself as a victim, her moaning and criticizing are not an occasional reaction to things that go wrong, but an ingrained behavior.

Helpful Assumptions

At the heart of the whiner is fear: fear of assertively requesting a solution, fear of being responsible for the outcome, fear of confrontation, fear of being unseen or unheard, and fear of conflict. Perhaps her attempts to change circumstances or conditions have been met with failure.

If you think about it, there are probably times when you've been fearful yourself and you may have whined to someone about it. Cynthia recalls taking a high ropes course once. She stood at the top of a tree, harnessed up safely, and yet found that she was unable to step off her tree branch to a hanging log. Her conscious mind knew she was safe but her unconscious mind was terrified. She whined to all the instructors who refused to help her step down onto the log. After an hour, she finally succeeded (her colleagues, of course, had long since moved from that hanging log to other treetop exercises). Recalling your own moments of fear may help you feel some compassion for the whiner.

Sadly, perhaps the whiner has drawn attacking and bullying in response to her whining. Some whiners have developed their coping strategy as a way of getting attention or prodding others to take action. Other whiners may have developed a chronic whiny response and, like Lynda, are not even aware of the grating impact of their language and tone of voice on others.

> *Recalling your own moments of fear may help you feel some compassion for the whiner.*

As annoying as a whiner can be, remember there may be a positive aspect to someone who complains. Have you ever wished you had the nerve to speak up about an issue that everyone was ignoring? Cynthia remembers a time when a manager attempted to deceive the team about the company's plans. Though she sounded aggrieved and powerless, Lynda actually voiced what the others were only thinking. Someone had to say it, and Cynthia realized she was thankful that Lynda (and not she) was the one to do so.

In the whiner worldview, however, it may not be safe to step outside the comfortable zone of powerlessness. Cynthia attended a leadership development course once where the focus for several hours was on taking personal responsibility for your life experience. Though the course leader acknowledged that we may not always choose our life circumstances, we can always choose our responses to those circumstances. The leader paired up course participants to talk about who we might become if we released our need to blame others for our life's conditions. Cynthia was paired with a whiner who confessed that she was not the least bit willing to release her identity as a victim of discrimination, a victim of an abusive husband, a victim of a hierarchical company, and a victim of a bad boss.

In a moment of touching self-awareness, Cynthia's partner acknowledged that she had no idea who she would be as a person without these labels. She left at the next break and never returned to the course.

Cynthia realized that, standing at this precipice, the whiner was terrified to take back her power. Without her identity as a Victim (with a capital "V"), the whiner felt stripped of her identity. The bottom line is that whiners have very real needs that may have remained unmet. Unaware that their coping strategy pushes people away, whiners live in a self-reinforcing cycle of perpetual victimhood.

Though you may empathize with the whiner's fears, you don't have to rescue her. In fact, you have other choices that will empower you and the whiner to change some of these chronic whining patterns. With peer power, you can transform this relationship.

Key Principles: Take Responsibility and Extend Respect

The key principles to keep in mind when turning a whiner into a problem solver are the need to Take Responsibility for your own experience and at the same time Extend Respect to someone who feels so disempowered.

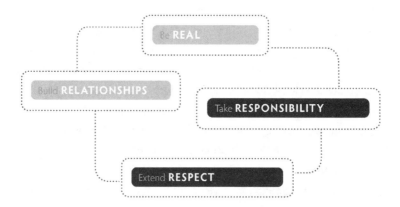

Take Responsibility

When you Take Responsibility, you become responsible for your own experience. You acknowledge your contributions to your difficulties. Ask yourself if you might be encouraging the whiner by responding sympathetically. Do you discourage whining by celebrating positive results when things are going well or praising the whiner's positive statements and productive actions? Do you get others' input before making decisions that affect them?

Perform well by modeling personal accountability. You may have an indirect influence on those who whine. Don't whine about the whiner. Don't whine along with the whiner. Even when the whiner is out of sight and out of mind, monitor your language so as not to lapse into blaming and whining. Make sure your own office is a "No Whining" zone. Eliminate cynical signs masquerading as humor, like "You Want it When?" and "Thank God it's Friday." Don't forward negative e-mails that whine about "dumb" customers. (Refer to Chapter 14 for technology tips.)

Instead, you might follow the example of one of Cynthia's colleagues. His sales team had developed the habit of complaining about management without making any suggestions. He brought in a funny photo of one of his children, face screwed up and crying loudly with arms outstretched towards the camera. The caption under the photo: No Whining!

With a whiner, the practice of respecting your needs may take the form of removing yourself from situations in which the whiner is happily complaining to a group. When the whiner begins her laments, stand up and politely excuse yourself. Avoid hanging out by the water cooler or the lunch room, if these are the whiner's favorite haunts. Ask to be removed from unproductive, whiny e-mail threads.

If the whiner tends to interrupt your work day by dropping into your office and sitting down for a chat, try these techniques: turn your chair away from your office door; find a private place to work; limit your responses; and stand up. If you need to get information from the whiner, go to her space, call her on the phone, or send an e-mail or IM (instant message) with a specific request. With these options, you keep greater control over your time and focus.

Follow the practice of setting ground rules by letting whiners know about your time constraints. A helpful ground rule might be: "I will listen for one minute but then I need to get back to this project." Then do what you say you will do and get back to work at the designated time. Whiners will quickly learn that you are not always available when they start whining.

Extend Respect

There are certainly times when you may choose to practice listening when the whiner complains. If you have time, you may allow her to vent without responding until she's finished. At the end of her venting, the complaint may evaporate or she may be ready to take action. If you want to help someone who is whining shift to problem solving, you have to hear her out before she's ready to do something constructive.

> *Don't fall into the trap of taking action on her complaints to end the whining.*

Don't fall into the trap of taking action on her complaints to end the whining. Part of Extending Respect is to resist the temptation to rescue a coworker. Simply summarize what she has said, restating in neutral language whatever her complaint may be, without expressing concern, empathy, or anger on her behalf. Your job is to keep from being sucked into the whiner's negative vortex.

Because whiners often complain about others in their conversations, it's not unusual to hear complaints about third parties who are not present to explain themselves. This whining tactic is a form of backstabbing best nipped in the bud as soon as it starts. When the whiner begins to tell you about the actions of someone else, expresses outrage over what someone else did or said, or complains about ill treatment at the hands of others, it is important that you step in immediately. You might say, "I'm sorry. I'm just not comfortable

listening to these concerns without the other party at the table."
Whiners will likely begin to avoid complaining to you if they realize
that you are an advocate for openness instead of backstabbing.

If you want to suggest an alternative to the person whining, you
could offer to role-play a difficult conversation to help develop her
confidence in addressing a challenging issue with someone else.

Strategy: Coaching

You may have applied all of these peer power practices, and yet the
whiner persists in complaining to you. It's time to apply the Coaching
strategy (helping her solve her problem or develop her skills) to see if
you can help shift the whiner's behavior to one of greater personal
responsibility and action.

Remember to ask permission to offer coaching or you will be
giving the whiner unsolicited advice, which is often not well received.
If she doesn't agree, turn to Plan B.

Please note that this strategy may not change the whiner's
personality and may not even end her complaining to others,
especially if the motive for whining is to get attention. But it will put
you in a supportive role that may have a positive impact on your
relationship with the whiner and her choice to whine at you. And you
may very well influence her to solve problems rather than complain
about them.

When you choose to coach the whiner, you're firmly leaving the
problems and the potential solutions in her hands. Your goal is to help
the whiner see that the pattern of chronic complaining is not a
successful work strategy.

If you decide to adopt this strategy, tell the whiner that you want
to hear her out but that you also intend to help her focus on potential
solutions. The whiner may vent, complain, lament, and groan about
work conditions, other people, and outrageous events. While you are
listening to her, avoid agreeing or disagreeing. Simply acknowledge
her complaints with neutral responses:

I can tell this has upset you.

You obviously care about this issue.

It sounds like you are angry at this decision.

To help her feel heard and understood, paraphrase her dominant complaint:

So, the bottom line is that you expected to be given that assignment and were angry when it was assigned to Alison. You believe that Alison has less experience than you on projects like this one.

When the whiner exhausts her complaints (and may begin repeating herself), it's time to step in with open-ended questions to figure out what's happening, much as a professional coach might do:

How are other people feeling about the same issues?

What is the impact of your complaints on this situation?

What results are you getting by complaining?

After discussing the current situation, ask questions to help the whiner set goals to resolve the issues she's concerned about:

What is your ideal outcome in this situation?

What is your goal?

Sometimes you'll need to help the whiner figure out what action she's willing to take to resolve a problem and reach her goal:

Where could you get more information?

What small changes can you make in your behavior that might affect this problem?

What are your suggestions for solving this problem?

Would you like to practice having a challenging conversation?

Dear Cynthia and Ray,

Are you kidding me? My whiner constantly texts me with complaints about our coworkers. You sound like I should encourage him to share more. I don't want to paraphrase his concerns and ask him questions that encourage him to process his problems with me. He just tries to get me to agree with him and then fobs his problems off on me to solve. If I respond to his text messages, I'll never get rid of this guy.

— Tired Texter

Dear Tired,

If you're being peppered with whiny text messages, you have a right to set limits. But first, you may want to invite your coworker to talk about his issues. You can make it clear that you see things differently. By allowing him to talk things through constructively, you may eliminate his need to bombard you with negative text messages. Asking thoughtful questions to coach him might help him find his own solution. When he takes positive action, send him a complimentary text message: Way 2 Go.

— Cynthia and Ray

Coaching can be useful in responding to the following scenarios:

- Dealing with backstabbing
- Resolving an organizational issue

Scenario: Dealing with backstabbing

WHINER: I can't believe that Marilyn hasn't answered any of my e-mails! She told us that she wanted this project done by the deadline and we've been jumping through every hoop she has waved at us.

YOU: (Paraphrase her statement, and maintain a neutral tone of voice without agreeing or disagreeing.)
It sounds like you are frustrated by Marilyn's lack of response.

WHINER: She's driving me crazy. She's supposed to be a project manager but she doesn't seem to be managing this project very well.

YOU: (Block backstabbing with a neutral tone of voice.)
I'm sorry, I'm not comfortable talking about Marilyn behind her back. I think you need to take your concerns to her.

WHINER: She doesn't seem to care that we are working hard on these project deliverables but we have no idea whether we are meeting her expectations. I just know she's going to resurface next week like Godzilla and expect us to make changes at the last minute.

YOU: I can't solve this problem for you. I think you need to take your concerns directly to Marilyn. It sounds like you're very upset. I'm sure Marilyn would want to know.

WHINER: Can you just put a bug in her ear that we're all worried about getting this project done on time and we'd really like her feedback?

YOU: (Don't fall into this trap. It's time to ask permission to coach her.)
No, I won't do that, but I am willing to help you come up with some ideas about this. Would you like that?

WHINER: Sure. Anything to get her to respond.

YOU: (Ask open-ended questions.)
What action can you take right now to get Marilyn's feedback? What do you intend to do to resolve this?

WHINER: Me? What can I do? I've already tried to send her e-mails. I mean, I've sent her four or five e-mails in the past week. Each one sounds increasingly concerned. She's not answering any of them.

YOU: (Accept her excuses as valid but continue to ask her to address the problem herself.)
What else could you do to solve this problem?

WHINER: I think your speaking with her might make the difference. Just let her know that the troops are getting angry with her. Tell her that we're all waiting to hear from her and we're stuck until we do hear from her.

YOU: (Time to ask some questions to get the whiner to self-reflect.)
I appreciate that you want me to speak with her. What impact will my sharing your concerns have on her?

WHINER: I don't know. Maybe embarrass her into answering my e-mails. She'll realize that everyone is upset.

YOU: (Continue to ask questions to help the whiner see the impact of her complaining.)
Have your frequent e-mails led to her responding yet?

WHINER: Well, no. Evidently not. She's probably not even opening my e-mails.

YOU: Is it possible that she is ignoring your e-mails because she is too busy with other projects to deal with your complaining?

WHINER: What do you mean?

YOU: You've tried complaining to Marilyn and it doesn't seem to be working. Is there any other way you could approach her that might get a better outcome?

WHINER: Wait a minute. Are you saying that I caused Marilyn not to respond to my e-mails?

YOU: Not exactly. I'm asking you to consider whether you might approach Marilyn a different way to see if you might get a different response. She seems to be ignoring your complaints and focusing on other work.

WHINER: (Sigh)
You mean it's up to me to figure out how to get her to do her job. I hate that.

YOU: It might just be enlightened self-interest. How can you approach her so that she'll give you the feedback you need now?

WHINER: Well, I suppose I could be a little more supportive. I know she's very busy and being pulled in lots of directions. And I think she's got a big conference she's hosting this weekend. I've been pushing her to set up a meeting with me. But what if I send her a handwritten card that acknowledges how busy she is and requests a 15-minute phone meeting after she completes her conference.

That might make it possible for her to give me fast feedback.

YOU: Why don't you try that and see what happens? And be sure to tell me how it goes so we can see if your approach worked.

Scenario: Resolving an organizational issue

WHINER: First they create separate Help Desk groups to support our hardware and software products. Entirely separate. None of their systems talk to each other. Wise move, that. Now because of layoffs and department mergers they put the two Help Desk groups under a single manager. So I'm expected to write a single report that shows metrics for both groups. What a mess!

YOU: (Paraphrase her statement to let her realize that she's been heard. Adopt a neutral tone of voice.)
It sounds like you are frustrated because it will be difficult to do what you've been asked, and you feel the problems are due to poor planning by management.

WHINER: Difficult? Try *impossible*. Management got us into this mess. They should get us out. How am I going to write a single report? It's apples and oranges. It can't be done. These are different systems, the teams use different processes. They even have different databases. How can a single report be written that shows metrics for both groups? What a holy mess.

YOU: (You realize that the whiner isn't whining to get attention, but because she is frustrated and feels powerless to change the situation. Request permission to coach her to help find a solution.)
It sounds like a frustrating situation for you, but I'm not sure I see the problem in the same way. You may have some options. Would you like some help to think it through and find a solution?

WHINER: I've thought it through. The management of this company sucks. But I guess if you could solve their problem, I'd be willing to listen.

YOU: I don't think that I can solve their problem, but you may be able to solve yours. Is there any action you can take to resolve the issue?

WHINER: I already told you. Management just says, "Do it." But they don't realize what's involved.

YOU: What is involved?

WHINER: The two groups collect different information. They call the same things by two different names, and use the same names for two different things. Babel-speak, like I said. It's not my job to fix Babel-speak.

YOU: (Accept her points as valid but continue to ask her to address the problem herself.)
What else could you do to solve this problem?

WHINER: I guess I could suggest that my boss get the managers to talk to each other to see where they differ.

YOU: I hear you saying that by identifying how the two groups differ in how they define their metrics, it might be possible to write a report that adds value.

WHINER: Yes, that's what I'm saying.

YOU: (Since whiners sometimes whine about non-existent issues, encourage them to perform a reality check to make sure there's substance to their complaint.)
Do you think it would be useful to your boss to gather different opinions to check that others see the same problem? Perhaps a different perspective from another team member, or even find best practices from other organizations?

WHINER: Sure, both of those things would help. I admit that the others have more experience with this sort of thing than I do.

YOU: What would be the next steps after you did that?

WHINER: Oh, you're saying that I would be the one to gather the opinions and best practices?

YOU: (Your aim is to help reduce the whiner's feeling of powerlessness.)
Why not? You recognize that there's a problem. You mentioned

that the others have more experience. If they agree with you that there is a problem, you might benefit from their experience. And if you gathered best practices, it would help your boss with the solution.

WHINER: Well, I certainly can't do both. I might make sure there's consensus on the issue, but I certainly don't have time to research other companies' practices.

YOU: And after you reached consensus on the problem? What then?

WHINER: Dunno. That part's not really my job.

YOU: Please explain that. Doesn't somebody have to do an analysis to produce the specs for the report that you would write?

WHINER: Yes, but I've never done that part of it myself. Other report writers also do the analysis, but not me. Someone hands me the specs, and I write the report.

YOU: (Be patient and persistent. Accepting responsibility is new to the whiner. After a few more attempts to have the whiner work through the logical next step [which in this case is having her take responsibility to solve the problem that upsets her by performing the analysis], the coach might need to be more obvious.)
What do you think about creating an action plan that includes researching the problem and performing the report requirements analysis, and bringing it to your manager?

WHINER: (Thinks about it.)
I've never had to do anything like this before.

YOU: You wouldn't have to do it by yourself. There are many resources I can point you to, and perhaps Ted would be willing to mentor you. And I'd be happy to review your work.

WHINER: Well, I would be interested in working with him. I think I might learn something. I guess I could give it a try.

YOU: (Be clear between you on what responsibility the whiner has agreed to take on.)
That's great. Before we break, let's go over how you think you will proceed.

Your objective was to help the whiner gain at least a small degree of personal power in order to take ownership of her problems. Make sure that the action plan allows for many opportunities to praise and acknowledge her success.

Plan B (If Your Initial Strategy Fails)

Unfortunately, Coaching is not likely to work successfully with a whiner who is vying for attention. If you have exhausted all of your Coaching tips and the whiner refuses to take responsibility, you may shift to the Going Head-to-Head strategy to confront the whiner and set boundaries to limit your contact.

For whiners who have developed chronic whiny behavior, you may need to recognize that your Coaching strategy is actually providing the attention they seek without shifting their pattern of complaining. You may realize that, inadvertently, you have created a monster who enjoys these engaging coaching conversations! If that is the case, it may be time to shift to the Going Head-to-Head strategy to put an end to the excessive attention you are giving her. Let's look at how you might do this.

Plan B Scenario: Set boundaries for future contact

WHINER: Well, you're not going to believe what Marilyn has done now.

YOU: (Immediately put a stop to any backstabbing that is about to occur.)
It sounds like you are about to talk about Marilyn again.

WHINER: Yes, I am. She's impossible to work with.

YOU: (Describe in a neutral tone of voice what has happened so far and what you intend to do to meet your own needs.)
I've listened to you process your problems with Marilyn several times lately. I've been willing to coach you in approaching her more constructively. These discussions are not working.
Unfortunately, I'm no longer willing to listen to your complaints about her.

WHINER: I can't talk about Marilyn?

YOU: You have all the skills you need to deal with Marilyn constructively. I'm no longer willing to talk about your frustrations with her.

WHINER: But who will I talk to? You're the only one who understands what it's like to work with her. I can't believe you're not going to let me talk about her!

YOU: (Remain firm despite her response. Clearly describe what action you will take if she complains about others.)
No, I'm not. You'll have to talk with her directly. In the future, if you begin to complain about Marilyn or anyone else, for that matter, I will ask you to leave my office so I can get back to work. I care about teamwork and I'd like to help you, but there's nothing further I can do about these concerns.

WHINER: That's harsh.

YOU: (Offer a constructive option that demonstrates that you're willing to talk about other topics.)
I'm sorry it feels that way. But, you know, I'm happy to talk about anything else but Marilyn. In fact, I want to hear more about that concert you went to last weekend. It sounded like a blast. Can you tell me about it at lunch later?

So, you've asked permission to use the Coaching strategy, asked good questions, made useful suggestions, and supported the whiner to take action. When that didn't work, you shifted to the Going Head-to-Head strategy and confronted the whiner or stopped giving her your attention. Perhaps the whiner continues to bring up her concern.

It's then time to apply the Caring-for-Self strategy. You've used all of the whiner management tools in your arsenal. Now it's time to manage yourself by taking care of your own needs. There's no law that says you have to spend time with whiners.

Cynthia attended a long, personal retreat once to focus on her own life and where she was headed. She arrived at the airport with a woman who began complaining as soon as she stepped off the

Dear Cynthia and Ray,

I love this chapter on whining. In fact, my life is full of customers who whine at me day and night. How can I get them to accept responsibility for the problems they're having with my company?

— Burned Out

Dear Burned,

We hate to say it, but we think that customers have a right to whine. They can complain about things without necessarily having a solution. Certainly ask them for their ideas, but it's not up to them to understand your products, services, and systems. One of the hallmarks of a great customer service provider is the ability to turn a complaint into a solution that satisfies the customer. If you're burned out in your customer service job, you might consider a vacation or a new job.

— Cynthia and Ray

airplane. Cynthia made a couple of attempts to redirect the whiner. However, she quickly decided that she was attending the retreat for personal recharging and chose to spend as little time as possible in the whiner's orbit. When you take care of your own needs, you stop expending energy on whiners.

If nothing else has worked, request to be assigned to other projects, engage in activities that are satisfying and energizing, and don't feel guilty for leaving the whiner out of your life. You may even decide that you'll be happier if you can find a new job working with people who take responsibility for their actions and choices.

Finally, for your own sanity, spend more time with coworkers who have assumed responsibility for their own problems and their own achievements.

Moving Forward

With a chronic whiner whose complaints about everything are interfering with your work, request that this behavior stop. Let her know that you don't want to offend her, but that you don't have time for these conversations. Ask her to agree to raise issues with you only if she has a solution and the issue involves you. Acknowledge improvements when they occur.

The Rest of the Story

Cynthia's relationship with Lynda continued as long as Cynthia jumped when Lynda complained. When Cynthia stopped trying to fix problems that Lynda complained about, Lynda turned to others for support.

Cheat Sheet for the Whiner

Definition: Whiners don't take responsibility for improving the negative conditions that surround them, instead lapsing into blame-filled laments and complaints without offering any solutions.

Clues

The whiner:

- Blames problems and conditions on others
- Talks endlessly about problems with third parties instead of taking action
- Is not willing to be personally responsible for negative outcomes
- Expects the organization's managers to fix mistakes
- Constantly criticizes others' work
- Encourages others to address issues on her behalf
- Avoids direct confrontation or conflict

Helpful Assumptions

- At the heart of a whiner is fear.
- We all have whined at times when we were fearful.
- Some whiners may have experienced abuses.
- Whiners sometimes speak out about something that needs to be heard.
- Whining can be a coping mechanism to gain attention or prod others to take action.
- Whiners may be hesitant to give up their identity as a victim.
- Empathize with the whiner's fears, but don't rescue her.

Key Principles and Practices

Take Responsibility

- Look at your contribution to the problem. Don't reinforce whining.

- Perform well. Don't whine yourself.

- Respect your needs. Don't hang out with whiners.

- Communicate and establish ground rules. Establish time constraints.

Extend Respect

- Listen. Let her vent without responding.

- Resist rescuing. Restate her complaint but don't be sucked into solving her problem.

- Block backstabbing. Become an advocate for openness.

Strategy: Coaching

- Demonstrate that you have heard the complaint.

- Ask permission to offer Coaching.

- Tell the whiner that you want to hear her out, but that you also intend to help her focus on potential solutions.

- Avoid agreeing or disagreeing; acknowledge her complaints with neutral responses. Don't debate or try to control.

- Ask open-ended questions to help her self-reflect.

- After discussing the current situation, ask questions to help the whiner set goals to resolve issues.

- Leave the problems and potential solutions in the whiner's hands.

Plan B (If Your Initial Strategy Fails)

- When Coaching fails, switch to Going Head-to-Head.

- Confront the whiner or stop giving her your attention.

- Caring-for-Self: Stop spending time and energy with the whiner; spend time with coworkers who take responsibility.

Worksheet

1. What clues make you suspect you may be dealing with a whiner?

2. Assuming you've determined the person is a whiner, what might be her legitimate needs?

3. What are this whiner's strengths?

4. What principles and practices might improve the situation?

5. Write the opening statement you might use to begin using the Coaching strategy with the whiner.

6. What response do you anticipate and how will you handle it?

7. What Coaching questions will you ask?

8. What Plan B approach will you use if your discussion is not successful?

from the scene stealer to the ally

Imagine a coworker who constantly undermines you, bad-mouths you to customers, blames you for her mistakes, steals the credit for accomplishments, and tells blatant falsehoods to the boss about your performance. The scene stealer sets about building her reputation at your expense. Friendly to your face, she can appear self-serving in her criticism behind your back.

Cynthia once worked with a scene stealer and experienced the conflict and distrust she created. Rachelle joined the team with smart, fresh ideas and a thirst for recognition. In her first week on the job, she attended one of Cynthia's training programs as an observer and announced to the class that she was there to evaluate Cynthia. Those kinds of inflated statements were a regular occurrence at staff meetings, cross-departmental meetings, and company training sessions. Besides inflating her role, she also lied about Cynthia and others on the team to make herself look good.

Choosing one coworker at a time, Rachelle worked to build relationships with the people who were "for her" and isolate the people who were "against her." When confronted about her lies, misinformation, or blatant falsehoods, she responded with wounded innocence, as if she were the victim of accusations by unreasonable coworkers. In less than two months, she had split a formerly cohesive team into Rachelle's supporters versus her detractors.

Clues to the Scene Stealer

Scene stealers often present themselves extremely well on first impression. After all, they are acutely aware of how you feel about them. What makes it tough to work with them is that most of their energy is directed to maintaining the façade that they are highly capable, perhaps even brilliant. The scene stealer's sense of self is tied to being better than..., smarter than..., more qualified than..., more beautiful than... YOU (or anyone else she works with).

Often the scene stealer attempts to cultivate a relationship with selected people on the team and, at first, may seem friendly and open. But in time, some cracks begin to appear in that carefully crafted façade. Pay attention to these clues as the scene stealer begins to:

- Appear friendly to your face, yet criticize you often behind your back
- Blame you for her mistakes
- Take credit for accomplishments that are not her own
- Tell obvious falsehoods about you that can be countered with fact
- Inflate her own accomplishments
- Build relationships with a chosen few and exclude others
- Take over roles that belong to others
- Criticize you to others or copy others on critical e-mails
- Leave you holding the bag when a project doesn't go as planned

In Cynthia's experience with Rachelle, the scene stealer threatened to turn a highly functional team into a dysfunctional mess.

Helpful Assumptions

The scene stealer wants to be liked, loved, and appreciated, just like the rest of us. Perhaps more than the rest of us. Rather than criticize her or attack her, you'll find it helpful to assume that she has good intentions. She's just developed very poor practices to get the approval, appreciation, and recognition that she seeks.

Like you, she is attempting to get her own needs met (but she's doing it at the expense of everyone else). You can treat her with respect. You can acknowledge her very real talents and abilities. You don't have to like her to work with her effectively. Ask yourself whether you've ever attempted to enhance your reputation, possibly at the expense of someone else's. Most likely you can come up with at least one example. We've all engaged in acts of scene stealing at one time or another.

If you're willing to acknowledge to yourself that you've done the same thing, you may be able to treat the scene stealer with a little less disdain or anger and find some compassion for her poor choices. This does not mean you accept them. It will help you take the focus off her shortcomings and put the focus on how you can build a more open, direct, and constructive working relationship. In time, she may come to value teamwork as a way to satisfy her personal goals.

We have no way of proving that these assumptions about the scene stealer are true. But we do know that you'll get better results and feel more confident that you can handle your scene-stealing coworker if you make these assumptions. It won't help to tell her she's evil (or any other label you may have applied to her). On the other hand, she can become a great resource to you and your team if she can be transformed into an ally. To that end, let's take a look at opportunities to employ the Take Responsibility, Build Relationships, and Be Real principles and practices to enhance your peer power.

> *You can acknowledge her very real talents and abilities.*

Key Principles: Take Responsibility, Build Relationships, and Be Real

When you start to wonder about the scene stealer's motives and behavior, it's time to take action. Rather than wait to see how bad it can get, try these principles and practices to gain commitment, openness, and clarity.

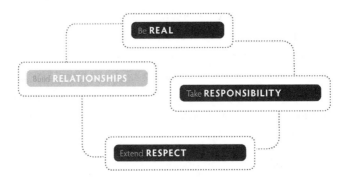

Take Responsibility

In any new relationship, there can be misunderstanding and miscommunication. Rather than allow your frustration to build, choose to be responsible for your own experience. Instead of waiting to see what will happen next in this workplace drama, ask yourself what you can do to ensure that you receive the credit you deserve. Have you neglected to share the details of your contribution with your boss? Have you been too busy to discuss your mutual goals and responsibilities? Are you performing as well as possible?

With scene stealers, communicating with others (one of the key practices within the Take Responsibility principle) takes on critical importance. So take time to clarify your expectations and then ask the scene stealer to clarify hers. In a face-to-face conversation, you can set up a reciprocal give-and-take. If face-to-face is not possible, then talk voice-to-voice to get clear.

You might say, "Rachelle, let's talk about how we communicate for a minute. When you have constructive feedback for me, I'd like you to talk to me first by phone." After you hear her response, summarize and state your willingness to reciprocate: "So you'll call me when you want to give feedback, right? When I have feedback for you, how would you like to receive it?"

You can easily document your agreements and send those to her in a follow-up e-mail. (Refer to Chapter 14 for technology tips.) Once you've established that baseline agreement, it's easier to notice when you are off track.

Another opportunity for communication takes place when documenting meetings. Any time you find yourself on the same project with the scene stealer, make sure that you know who is responsible for which tasks and how you both contribute to the overall project. If no one else is developing a project plan, step into the vacuum, take notes, and send out follow-up e-mails detailing action items, the owner of each task, and anticipated deadlines.

Ray worked with a scene stealer who would appear to be in complete agreement with the team about project goals and team member roles at the end of a meeting, but would later usurp others' responsibilities, to the dismay of her peers. After watching her step on others' toes repeatedly and having to unravel the chaos she caused, Ray realized he needed to document the team's agreements thoroughly and ask everyone to sign off on the plan. It's difficult for the scene stealer to steal the spotlight when there is a clear, specific action plan, particularly if she has approved it or agreed with it, and it's been shared with others.

Let your boss know that you are paving the way for a smooth relationship.

The importance of communication extends to your boss. Here you must remember that you are not tattling on the scene stealer. In the interest of clear communication, you are simply copying your boss on the shared agreements that you are making. Let your boss know that you are paving the way for a smooth relationship. Tell your boss that you want to be sure that everyone is on the same page. If your boss prefers that he not be copied on every passing e-mail, then ask for his guidance. What is the best way to keep him in the loop on a regular basis? Whether that means reporting at a regular meeting or printing out copies for his inbox, follow through to ensure your boss knows about your mutual expectations, ground rules, and project plans with the scene stealer. Keep your boss updated on your accomplishments so that the scene stealer can't claim credit for work that you accomplished.

Watch out for the scene stealer backstabbing you to your boss. In backstabbing, someone goes to a third party to complain or discuss a problem that really should be discussed directly with you. Scene stealers are masters at this tactic. To prevent it, establish a ground rule with your boss: "Boss, I'd like to make a request: if someone comes to you with concerns about me or my performance, please ask them to talk to me directly. In this way, we can resolve issues without wasting your time."

Build Relationships

Recall the importance of the build and protect self-esteem practice of the Build Relationships principle. A little credit, sincere public praise, and recognition can grease the skids for a cooperative relationship with anyone. Take advantage of opportunities to say thank you to the scene stealer in front of others in staff meetings, on conference calls, or in e-mails. Be specific about the actions she took to help you meet a deadline or deal with a difficult customer. Be specific and clear: "Rachelle, I really want to thank you for stepping in when I needed help last week. The time you took to research that problem on the Internet saved me hours of hassle. I really appreciate good teamwork when it happens and I want everyone to know about it."

> *Watch out for the scene stealer backstabbing you to your boss.*

Get input from the scene stealer before you take actions that may affect her. When you propose new ideas, gain her agreement and perhaps include her name as one of the stakeholders on the proposal. Demonstrate the power of building collaborative relationships by considering her needs—in essence sharing the spotlight with her. Cynthia recalls working on a major computer systems transition, helping her team move from one system to a new one. Rather than attempt to influence her peers alone, she engaged the commitment of a scene stealer and allowed her to present aspects of the proposal to the team.

By applying your peer power toward these more proactive approaches, you may very well change your scene stealer's thoughts from stealing credit to becoming your supporter and your team's ally.

Be Real

The Be Real principle encourages you to be genuine, sincere, open, and authentic. This means that you speak up when you hear distorted information, when you're concerned about a problem, or whenever you feel that remaining silent doesn't serve the situation. Rather than allow the scene stealer to run roughshod over your needs, for example, you may choose to step forward, speak directly to her, and ask for what you want clearly.

The practice of sharing your thoughts demands courage. It means that you won't gossip about the scene stealer behind her back. If the scene stealer tells a blatant falsehood, instead of waiting to engage others in a discussion about Rachelle's ethics, ask her a clarifying question: "I'm sorry, Rachelle. Perhaps I misunderstood, but it sounded like you said that you stayed late yesterday to complete my Watson report." The point is not to put the scene stealer on the spot, but to give her an opportunity to correct misinformation or misstatements. These direct conversations (*not* behind her back) may happen face to face, over the phone, or in web meetings.

The Be Real practice of acknowledging reality is important when the scene stealer doesn't get a job or assignment that you got. In such cases, avoid mind reading, but don't be afraid to bring this up. You might say, "Rachelle, I know you applied for this position. If you would like to discuss how you are feeling about my getting it, I would be happy to do that."

Strategy: Collaborating or Going Head-to-Head

Hopefully, the principles and practices suggested in the previous section will be enough to combat scene-stealing behavior. If you're still having significant concerns about the scene stealer, it may be time to adopt the strategy of Collaborating or Going Head-to-Head.

Collaborating may sound synonymous with your communication practices. The difference is that it incorporates your basic principles and practices into a plan of action. When you use the Collaborating strategy, you invite the scene stealer to talk through issues and resolve them together. For example, if you realize that the scene stealer brings issues about you to others, you ask for a meeting (face to face or virtual), rather than using e-mail, to discuss how you plan to communicate with each other more effectively. You document your agreements, share them with others who are affected, and ask her to be accountable. We recommend you use this strategy to enlist her cooperation and turn her into an ally, especially if you believe that no serious damage has been done to your reputation by the scene stealer's actions.

If serious damage *has* been done—as in situations where the scene stealer has clearly acted maliciously or has likely hurt your career—then consider Going Head-to-Head as your initial strategy. As you'll see in our examples, you may need to confront the scene stealer directly. When you Go Head-to-Head, you point out the misstatements and insist that they be corrected and stopped. You may actually escalate the problems to your boss to be handled. You might invite the scene stealer to a meeting with your boss to discuss some of your concerns about the scene stealer. The scene stealer may see that treating you as an ally will be more effective than her current approach.

The Collaborating strategy is illustrated in the first scenario, where no serious damage has been done to your reputation:

- Power grabs

In the second and third scenarios the damage is more critical, so the Going Head-to-Head strategy is appropriate:

- Backstabs
- Credit theft

Scenario: Handling power grabs

When you hear an attempt to grab your responsibilities or roles, a direct and diplomatic response, using the Collaborating strategy, might sound like this:

SCENE STEALER: I was really thrilled that I was able to recruit seven people for that committee. And they've asked me to attend each of their meetings to advise them.

YOU: (Don't accuse her of exaggerating or lying. There's no need to label her statements. Calmly present facts and request information that can be easily confirmed or disputed if that is necessary.)
I'm sorry. I didn't realize that you recruited seven people. On the applications I reviewed, Bob Jones was the only person who mentioned that you recruited him. Who else did you recruit?

SCENE STEALER: I spent a lot of time helping Myra interview a couple of other people.

YOU: (Acknowledge her contribution.)
Yes, Myra told me that she found it helpful to have you sit in on those interviews. Would it be correct to say that you participated in interviewing several people?

SCENE STEALER: Yes, that's right.

YOU: (Openly address an issue that concerns you while allowing the scene stealer to save face.)
There's something else I want to talk about. I'm afraid that there is a miscommunication about who will be advising this committee. Myra told me that I was the assigned advisor. Perhaps I misunderstood. Let's go ask her who is actually assigned so that we can get this cleared up. I'd hate for there to be problems down the road because we have misunderstood our roles.

SCENE STEALER: I don't know what you heard, but Myra assured me that I would be the advisor.

YOU: I'm still confused. Myra didn't tell me that she was making you the advisor to this committee.

SCENE STEALER: Are you telling me that I can't work with this committee? That's not fair.

YOU: (Acknowledge the scene stealer's needs.)
You seem to be saying that it is really important to you to play a significant role on this committee.

SCENE STEALER: Yes, that's true.

YOU: Well, I'm just trying to clarify our roles. I met with Myra yesterday and she told me that she wanted me to be the advisor for the committee. Did she tell you that as well? I think we may need to ask her to clarify our roles.

SCENE STEALER: Well, I'm probably not the formal advisor.

YOU: (Now that the scene stealer has acknowledged her exaggeration, extend a collaborative hand to her.)
But it sounds like you have good ideas for the committee and that you would like a bigger role. Would you like to talk more about that? I'm happy to work with you so that you can play a significant role on this committee. For example, next month's event needs a coordinator. Would you be interested in stepping into that role? Or do you have other ideas about how you could play a significant role?

Scenario: Dealing with backstabbing

If the scene stealer maliciously criticizes or lies about you behind your back to a third party, she's engaging in backstabbing. While her intention is to enhance her reputation, the impact is that it often damages yours. Many scene stealers get a sense of power from reporting to you what someone else thinks about your performance. The scene stealer may try to make it sound like she is doing this for your own good. Don't buy it. She is trying to meet her needs at your expense.

Whenever you face blatantly false statements about you, bring in a third party to verify the facts. In this example, we recommend that you choose Going Head-to-Head as your first strategy. The scene stealer has attempted to undermine you and, even worse, make it appear as if your boss is in agreement with her. Rather than allowing the backstabbing to continue, we suggest you bring the boss in immediately to get issues out in the open. By Going Head-to-Head you block the scene stealer's need to meet her needs at your expense.

Going Head-to-Head in this situation works like this:

SCENE STEALER: I observed your training program and I'm afraid that I had to tell our manager what a poor job you did answering questions from the class.

YOU: What? Can you give me an example of a question that I didn't answer correctly?

SCENE STEALER: There were many examples. That's why our boss is very concerned and has asked me to review the material you're presenting to ensure that it is accurate.

YOU: (You get extra bonus points for paraphrasing and not reacting in anger to this attempt to undermine you.)
I think what you're saying is that you told our manager I didn't answer the group's questions very well, and now our manager wants you to check the material to be sure it's correct. Is that right?

SCENE STEALER: Well, you don't have to get upset. You're really overreacting. I think we should present accurate content in our classes.

YOU: (Again you ignore her attack.)
Of course, we all want the course material to be accurate and we want people to get accurate information. I think we should go to his office now and discuss this issue.

SCENE STEALER: Look, I don't have time for this hostility from you. I'm sure I can help you correct any problems.

YOU: I'm very concerned. I'm going to talk to him right now. Please join us.

YOU: (If Rachelle goes with you, address the boss in front of Rachelle.) I've been talking with Rachelle and I understand that she has raised some concerns about my performance in the classroom. I want to make sure we're all on the same page here and that I'm not missing something.

SCENE STEALER: (Notice that the scene stealer must now attempt to backpedal because your boss is present.)
Nothing major—just some small errors in discussing the attendance and employee relations policies. I told her that I would help her correct them.

YOU: (Continue to speak directly to the boss without looking at the scene stealer.)
Rachelle has not been able to give me any specific examples of questions that I answered in error. Have you received feedback from anyone else about this issue?

SCENE STEALER: What are you trying to say? Are you saying that I'm lying? I'm just trying to help the training team. I care about our reputation.

YOU: (Don't be distracted by the scene stealer's claim of innocence. Continue to speak to the boss.)
We all share the goal of delivering high-quality training programs. Would you like me to compare the attendance and employee relations policies to the training content as it has been designed just to confirm that it is accurate?

By speaking directly to the boss in the presence of the scene stealer you prevent backstabbing. You also expose the scene stealer's use of falsehoods to undermine you. It's up to the boss now to step in and work with Rachelle directly. If Rachelle doesn't want to go with you to this meeting, then take the issue to your boss on your own.

You might want to meet with your boss later and use the Collaborating strategy to gain agreement to the practice of encouraging direct communication between colleagues. It would also be wise to have another conversation with Rachelle to gain her agreement to bring issues to you first before taking them to your boss.

Scenario: Handling credit theft

Scene stealers are adept at making themselves look good and taking credit for actions and results that they may have had little to do with. Though it is important to share credit when you collaborate with others, a scene stealer may actually take credit for your work or your team's work and undermine or damage your reputation. Normally, the scene stealer takes credit behind your back or in a public setting, which makes it difficult to use Collaborating with her because you risk creating an embarrassing scene. When you Go Head-to-Head, you assertively state the facts without allowing the scene stealer to meet her need for an enhanced reputation at your expense.

Here's a scenario in which the scene stealer makes a public pronouncement that is not factually correct, claiming full credit for a successful event your team planned.

SCENE STEALER: I'm glad that you could all be here tonight. It's been my pleasure to organize this leadership event and arrange for the fabulous speakers we've heard.

YOU: (After the applause has died down, you need to speak up diplomatically.)
Thank you, Rachelle, for being a part of the Event Planning team for this event. I'd like to acknowledge Randy and Jane, who researched, interviewed, and contacted the speakers we considered. I'd also like to thank Evelyn and Rachelle, who brought their project management skills to the myriad details that go into organizing a large event like this one. In the many years that I've led the Event Planning team, we've rarely had as talented a team as this year's Event Planning team. Please join me in acknowledging the efforts of each one of my team members.

Dear Cynthia and Ray,

The scene stealer in my life (I'll call her "Alice") helped me get a job in her department. That was seven years ago, but she still takes credit for every promotion I've ever received. Alice tells everyone that she is my "mentor" and expects me to thank her publicly when I receive acknowledgements or rewards for my work. It's really ridiculous, but I can't get her to stop. How would you handle this?

— Annoyed

Dear Annoyed,

It certainly sounds like Alice craves public recognition but she's not really damaging your reputation. So recognize her! Thank her publicly and often for that one action she took seven years ago to launch you on your successful career. It might sound like this: "Thank you, Mr. CEO, for naming me Employee of the Year. I want to thank my boss, Natalie, for her faith in my abilities and her ongoing coaching. And I want to acknowledge Alice for suggesting that I apply for my first job in this department seven years ago."

That may sound like the opposite of what you feel like doing, but recognizing Alice for that one good act will meet her need for recognition while maintaining a collaborative relationship, and it doesn't cost you much in the long run. In time, Alice may even tell you to stop recognizing her publicly for that one action (because it may sound odd, even to her, that you continue to thank her).

— Cynthia and Ray

Plan B (If Your Initial Strategy Fails)

Remember, your primary goal is to turn the scene stealer into an ally and team player. Your initial strategy calls for Collaborating only if serious damage has not yet been inflicted by the scene stealer; otherwise, Going Head-to-Head is the strategy of choice. If your attempt to Collaborate doesn't work, there is little chance that you'll be able to Compromise. You and your organization may have no other recourse than Going Head-to-Head. There is still an opportunity to salvage a good working relationship—in fact, showing "tough love" might be just the wake-up call that the scene stealer needs to realize that cooperation works better than obstruction.

If you run into roadblocks when dealing with a scene stealer, be sure to keep your cool. The worst way to deal with the scene stealer is to engage in scene-stealing behavior yourself. If you do, you'll find that the stakes will escalate rapidly. The scene stealer is very, very good at this game, so you're likely to lose. Avoid sniping and complaining about her to others (while you work up the courage to confront her). With the scene stealer's inflated sense of herself, she's likely to view (and laugh at) your behavior as jealousy or sour grapes.

Don't fall into the trap of sounding like a victim. Your complaining, whining, and begging will turn everyone else off, and the scene stealer will actually look better in comparison.

Don't withdraw totally from working with her because you mistrust her. Tempting though it may be to avoid her, it will decrease your effectiveness. Trust yourself to cope with her behavior effectively.

Don't tell yourself that if you ignore her behavior, it will go away. Remember Rachelle. While everyone ignored what was happening, she was busy building self-serving associations that undermined Cynthia and the team.

Don't try to win her over by telling her confidences or developing a friendship. The sad truth is that scene stealers generally don't have friends and are not very skilled at relationships. They have people around them that they use (and who also may be using them). Your attempts to gain the trust of a Rachelle by sharing confidences will backfire. Either she will share those confidences with others, or she will reveal that you are talking behind someone else's back. Either way, you lose.

If Going Head-to-Head fails, you may have to turn to the Caring-for-Self strategy. Treat your interactions with the scene stealer as an interesting growth opportunity. Discuss her machinations with a coach who can support you as you talk about your relationship. Ultimately, if you continue to be frustrated or harmed by the scene stealer's antics, you may need to look for another job. Some scene stealers have learned to outlast the people they discredit. It's up to you whether you want to suffer a damaged career because of her lies or misstatements.

Moving Forward

While a single case of scene stealing might not do you serious harm, a pattern of scene stealing most certainly will. To block this pattern or behavior, use Going Head-to-Head to insist that the behavior stop or escalate your concern to a discussion with her and her boss. It may require increasingly strong action to break this pattern.

The Rest of the Story

Don't expect the scene stealer to appreciate your forthright approach. Problems may actually escalate before they improve. But that doesn't mean you should give up on the possibility that your scene stealer can get her needs met in a nondestructive way, while allying with the common cause of your team. In Cynthia's experience, Rachelle was eventually forced to modify her behavior when confronted with the impact of her misstatements on others.

Still, not all stories end on a positive note. If the scene stealer is not ready to meet you half way, she may move on or out when she finds that she can't steal credit from you, the boss, or your team.

Cheat Sheet for the Scene Stealer

Definition: The scene stealer sets about building her reputation at your expense.

Clues

The scene stealer:

- Appears friendly to your face, yet criticizes you often behind your back

- Blames you for her mistakes

- Takes credit for accomplishments that are not her own

- Tells obvious falsehoods about you that can be countered with fact

- Inflates her own accomplishments

- Builds relationships with a chosen few and excludes others

- Takes over roles that belong to others

- Criticizes you to others or copies others on critical e-mails

- Leaves you holding the bag when a project doesn't go as planned

Helpful Assumptions

- The scene stealer wants to be liked and appreciated.

- She is attempting to get her own needs met.

- You can treat her with respect.

- You can acknowledge her talents and abilities.

- You don't have to like her to work with her effectively.

- We've all engaged in acts of scene stealing at some time.

Key Principles and Practices

Take Responsibility

- Ensure that you receive the credit you deserve.
- Establish ground rules and document agreements.
- Keep your boss informed about your work and ask him to encourage direct communication between peers.

Build Relationships

- Build and protect the scene stealer's self-esteem.
- Get input from the scene stealer before you take actions that may affect her.

Be Real

- Share your concerns with the scene stealer.
- Offer to discuss her concerns about promotions or assignments.

Strategy: Collaborating or Going Head-to-Head

Collaborating

- Schedule face-to-face discussions to resolve issues.
- Make assertive, clear requests.
- Calmly present facts.
- Avoid labeling or judging the behavior (no name-calling).
- Allow for face saving.
- Paraphrase frequently to demonstrate you are listening.
- Ignore the scene stealer's attacks or excuses.
- Acknowledge her needs.
- Work hard to create joint solutions.
- Acknowledge any improvements afterwards.

Going Head-to-Head (when there is clear malicious intent or your career could be damaged)

- Confront scene-stealing behavior immediately.

- Paraphrase her response and ignore attacks.

- If needed, take concerns to your boss with the scene stealer. If she won't join you, go without her.

Plan B (If Your Initial Strategy Fails)

- When Collaborating fails, Go Head-to-Head.

- Avoid engaging in scene-stealing behavior yourself.

- Avoid sniping and complaining about her.

- Do not withdraw from working with her or ignore her behavior.

- Do not try to win her over by telling her confidences or developing a friendship.

- Caring-for-Self: Treat your interaction as a growth opportunity; find a coach; look for another job.

Worksheet

1. What clues make you suspect that you are dealing with a scene stealer?

2. Assuming you've determined the person is a scene stealer, what might be her legitimate needs?

3. What are this scene stealer's strengths?

4. What principles and practices seem relevant?

5. Which strategy will you use and why will you use it?

6. Write the opening statement you might use to begin Collaborating or Going Head-to-Head.

7. What response do you anticipate and how will you handle it?

8. What Plan B approach will you use if your discussion is not successful?

from the drive-by boss to the engaged leader

Do you have a boss who is often absent or unwilling to support and nurture his staff? Perhaps you need more face time for feedback on your workload or performance. He may not be responding quickly enough to requests for resources, training, or information. Or he might not be addressing team performance issues and conflict.

If any of these situations rings true, you have what we call a drive-by boss. We use this term because your supervisor doesn't appear to be a full-time boss. He seems to be ignoring some of his key management responsibilities and doesn't meet the needs of his employees or the organization.

Ray once had the misfortune of working for a drive-by boss. After a merger, Sam became the Director of Human Resources for the merged organization. Sam had a great deal of expertise on Human Resources issues and policies and gave some excellent presentations to the workforce about the merger.

During the next few months, Ray made numerous unsuccessful efforts to meet with his boss. Sam also seemed to ignore conflicts and tensions within his department, which made it seem as if he wasn't even there. Ray was unable to make any progress on key projects, resulting in customer dissatisfaction and a decline in staff morale.

Finally, he arranged to drive Sam to the airport for one of his business trips. He hoped this would provide an opportunity to address his concerns.

Clues to the Drive-by Boss

Your new boss might be capable and even brilliant in formal presentations to your department or in "managing up" to the higher levels of the company hierarchy. But if the harmonious period of settling in and setting strategy is over, you may come to realize that you are working with a drive-by boss from some common clues. He might:

- Miss meetings or hold them infrequently or without planning
- Fail to provide you with clear expectations or assignments
- Pay very little attention to or have unrealistic expectations about your work or workload
- Give limited praise
- Fail to respond to messages
- Avoid conducting performance appraisals or providing regular feedback
- Ignore critical paperwork
- Fail to keep you informed on important developments
- Provide insufficient resources
- Procrastinate in making decisions
- Limit your training and development opportunities
- Ignore performance problems and team conflicts
- Seem stressed and harried
- Achieve poor results
- Have a demoralized team
- Ignore management functions of planning and monitoring tasks and processes
- Lack the respect of his colleagues

As the clues mount up and the frustration level rises, it may seem like there is little you can do. After all, you report to your boss; he doesn't report to you. Nevertheless, there is much that you not only can do, but *must* do to help your boss become an engaged leader.

Helpful Assumptions

Your ability to work with your drive-by boss will depend upon the assumptions you hold about his behavior. If you assume that his motives are negative, your anger, stress, and sense of hopelessness will increase. At first Ray assumed that Sam let his promotion go to his head or didn't care about Ray or his function. Until Ray reconsidered these assumptions, his resentment festered and he lacked peer power.

> *If you assume that his motives are negative, your anger, stress, and sense of hopelessness will increase.*

Try to imagine that your drive-by boss's actions are the result of his legitimate needs, even if they conflict with your or your organization's needs. For example, if the drive-by boss is stingy with information or feedback, choose to assume that he is extremely busy. If he doesn't offer praise, assume that it's either not his style or will come in time. If your work load is too heavy, make some positive assumptions: he either doesn't realize how busy you are or needs to get a lot done and trusts that you can deliver. If your boss does not appear to be addressing team performance problems, it could be that he is addressing them without your knowledge.

Or consider that a boss's actions may be based on fear and uncertainty. The seeming disinterest of a manager to his direct reports may be due to worry about his job security or a feeling that he is in over his head, and is not the snub that you take it to be. Perhaps his inability to resolve tensions within the team is because he wants to please everyone, is uncomfortable with conflict, or is afraid to offend anyone. If your boss doesn't run an effective meeting, you might simply assume he has not yet learned how.

Another perspective is to assume that your boss's behavior has been at least partially influenced by your own behavior. Ray waited a while before he asked for some time with Sam, who was, by then, overwhelmed by other priorities. And when Ray finally requested meetings, he did not emphasize his urgent need for guidance on some key projects.

If you keep in mind that everyone has both shortcomings and strengths, you can deal with the shortcomings more effectively. Certainly Sam dropped the ball, but he communicated well with employees, oversaw much of the merger effectively, and cared deeply about the organization's survival.

How about you? Have you ever, like Sam, avoided meeting some of your responsibilities? Acknowledging your own shortcomings may help you feel more patient with your drive-by boss.

However, having patience does not mean being passive. The drive-by boss needs to change; you can help him by using the practices in *Peer Power* to influence his growth to an engaged leader.

Key Principles: Take Responsibility, Extend Respect, and Be Real

Even if you rework your assumptions and understand that there are reasons for his behavior, concerns about a drive-by boss often seem clear-cut: they belong to him; they are his to fix. But that assessment does nothing to change his methods or reduce your frustration. Refer to the principles Take Responsibility, Extend Respect, and Be Real and their related practices for an attitude and approach that will benefit you, your boss, and your organization.

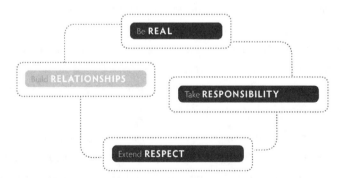

Take Responsibility

An important practice of the Take Responsibility principle is be responsible for your experience. In the drive-by boss scenario, that means refraining from placing the blame and instead focusing on what *you* did to create the situation. Consider your own contributions to your boss's shortcomings. Have you been defensive when given critical feedback and are you receptive to positive feedback? Are you being reasonable in what you expect from the boss? Are your requests clear? Own up to your actions and partner with your boss to achieve team success and promote his development as an engaged leader.

To be responsible also means focusing on what you can do to improve your boss's performance. It does no good to think, "Well, this is not my problem. It is up to my boss or his boss to correct this situation." Nothing will be accomplished by waiting for someone else to take the initiative.

When the clues that you have a drive-by boss accumulate, attempt to identify and eliminate the possible causes of his lack of responsiveness. We have suggested some: your boss is too busy, doesn't know your needs, lacks some skills, or is uncomfortable with conflict. Zero in on the most likely basis for his behavior and work to address it.

Try to help your boss. Every employee's responsibilities include providing support to his boss. Doing so is not inappropriate rescuing and is often essential with a drive-by boss.

For example, there are many ways you can help a boss who is too busy. With his permission, you can perform a supportive task, provide information to help with a decision, or prevent a problem. Save your boss time by limiting your requests, streamlining your communication, and shortening your meetings with him. If you are unsure how to reduce his workload, be willing to ask.

The frustrating behavior exhibited by your supervisor may be due less to his focus outside the team than to his lack of experience or skills as a manager. Jump in quickly to help your drive-by boss fill any skill gaps that are getting in his way. You might drop off a useful article with a short note saying that you thought he might find it to be interesting. If you attend a course that you find helpful, you can leave him the course materials and say, "I found these to be useful and thought you might want to know what was covered in the course." Give your boss practical suggestions, introduce him to good contacts, and serve as a model yourself.

Helping the boss is usually appreciated the most when it is unexpected and gets the boss out of a bind. Ray remembers an incident over 30 years ago. He had agreed to write a corny poem to honor a peer at her retirement party. As the date grew closer, he found he was so busy he couldn't find the time to do it. On the day of the party he was delighted to find a poem, written by his assistant, on his office chair. She had saved the day. When Ray recited the poem at the party, he let everyone know that she had written it. (They probably guessed that, since it was actually pretty good.) Doing something unexpected works wonderfully as long as you know it will be appreciated.

> *Save your boss time by limiting your requests, streamlining your communication, and shortening your meetings with him.*

Another practice within the Take Responsibility principle is communication. Though it may seem that he is not paying attention to your work, it's important to keep your boss informed of your progress and needs. If he doesn't know what you're doing, he can't provide you with the resources and training you need or the recognition you deserve. And if your workload becomes excessive, you can't expect him to assist you if he's not aware that there's a problem.

There are several possible approaches to keeping your boss informed. You can e-mail status reports and project updates, hold one-on-one meetings, share copies of project documents and correspondence, invite your boss to your meetings and events, conduct team briefings, and distribute productivity and project reports. If your team uses an online document sharing site, make it easy for your boss to access your files.

A drive-by boss may declare that he doesn't want to be notified of his team's activities because he trusts them or doesn't have time to review work. Don't let your boss deter you from keeping him informed. If you find getting access to him is difficult, use creativity in communicating your status and issues. While Ray resorted to offering to drive his boss to the airport, another peer posted results and pictures of her team's activities on her cubicle walls.

While communication is key, don't overdo it. Be considerate of his time constraints and pressures. Don't overwhelm your boss with too much information or ask for too much support or assistance. Concisely summarize what you are doing and any relevant needs that you have. Let your boss know how you plan to proceed if he doesn't have time to respond.

Cynthia once worked for a manager who rarely answered her questions or gave her feedback. When she realized that she was peppering him with requests which he rarely responded to, she developed a new approach that respected his work style and time. She set up a 30-minute meeting once a week to discuss various projects. In preparation each week, she concisely summarized the status of projects and any outstanding questions. During the meeting she worked through each project efficiently, with no extraneous chit-chat, and got out of her boss's office quickly. That approach worked well and resolved frustration on both sides.

A difficult question to ask is whether you yourself are performing well. Be honest about your accomplishments and be ready to admit if your results are less than stellar. It's not uncommon for a manager to naturally gravitate toward giving attention to the best producers. Perform well, and your boss will be motivated to help you.

Extend Respect

It might seem challenging to Extend Respect to a drive-by boss, but doing so is a key to improvement. As some of the scenarios later in this chapter show, there are several practices related to Extending Respect that address not only your boss, but your organization.

The practice of listen, listen, listen applies to a boss who seems reluctant to perform a task or make a decision. By giving him your attention, you can understand his reasoning and then address his reservations. Extending Respect by listening is a great way to counteract negative assumptions.

Pay attention to differences in style or work method. You may be fast paced and action oriented, while your boss's analytical or methodical approach takes more time. Honoring these differences, without expecting your boss to bend to your will, is an important indication of respect.

In addition to Extending Respect to your boss, extend respect to your organization—its rules, hierarchy, and culture. Realize that while he is responsible for helping his team attain individual objectives, your boss may be attending to strategic and organizational goals that are not obvious to you. Become aware of these goals and support him in reaching them. By becoming a cooperative partner in his success, you may find that your boss is more willing to share information and give you feedback.

Don't expect that these steps will turn him into a model of confidence. If nothing else, they will demonstrate your kindness and respect.

Be Real

We talked about the Taking Responsibility practice of communicating your needs and the Extend Respect practice of listening. It's essential to supplement these approaches through the Be Real practice of sharing your thoughts about issues and concerns.

A drive-by boss's style may be a conscious approach that has worked in the past or a natural tendency towards less attention to detail. Regardless of its genesis, the behavior is often ingrained. This means that a direct conversation may be the only way that your boss will become aware that there are problems with his team. Though the discussion has the potential of being a difficult one, it may be necessary if you want the situation to improve.

As always, make sure you check your assumptions: just as your drive-by boss won't uncover your apprehension through mind reading, make sure that you have properly pegged the reasons for his lack of engagement with the team. Talk to your boss with honesty and integrity, with an aim toward a solution that benefits everyone.

Remember Ray's assistant who saved the day by writing a poem that he didn't have time to complete? In the first months of her employment, she had approached Ray with some uneasiness about the fact that many of the team seemed to be working more than 40 hours a week. She worried that she might not be meeting expectations and yet felt strongly that her current schedule was as much as she could give. Because she was candid about her concerns, Ray was able to put her at ease, letting her know that the current high workloads were temporary and that longer weeks were not expected.

Strategy: Collaborating or Coaching

If these principles and practices don't work sufficiently, move to either the Collaborating or Coaching strategy. The approach you choose depends on whether your drive-by boss's behavior is primarily affecting you or is primarily affecting the organization. When his behavior affects you personally, choose the Collaborating strategy. When his behavior affects the organization more than it affects you— such as when your boss is ignoring team conflicts and performance problems—choose the Coaching strategy.

Let's look at the Collaborating strategy for dealing with your drive-by boss. Start with an assertive request best made face to face (or voice to voice) and not by e-mail. (Refer to Chapter 14 for technology

Dear Cynthia and Ray,

When my new boss started doling out more duties to me, I took it as a compliment. But after I started working late hours to get all my work done (and noticed that everyone else was, too), I didn't feel as flattered.

Two weeks ago, my husband Rock insisted that I work only 40 hours. Now on top of not getting my work done on time, I'm making more mistakes. I don't see what I can do to make both my boss and my husband happy.

— Between a Rock and a Hard Workplace

Dear Between,

Though it may seem like you don't have good choices, there is a way to satisfy your work requirements without sacrificing your free time. It will require setting up a meeting to talk to your drive-by boss.

At the meeting, remember the importance of both communicating and respecting your needs. Let your boss know how much you appreciate his trust in you and your understanding of the importance of the work he's given you. At the same time, firmly express your concerns: because you don't know how to prioritize your assignments, you're working long hours with more mistakes, resulting in more stress and an unacceptable work/life balance.

Be prepared. Show him how you believe your tasks should be prioritized, and suggest a process that you can follow to make sure you understand the priorities in the future. If your boss responds that all of the tasks are equally important, keep collaborating. Suggest other ways to cope with the work load, such as delegating tasks, getting more resources, or changing task due dates.

— Cynthia and Ray

tips.) Meet privately with your boss. Discuss with him the changes that you'd like to propose, but at the same time give him a way to save face. The solutions that result should meet both of your needs.

It takes some courage to do this with your boss, but the rewards are great.

Let's look at how this might go in two sample cases where your drive-by boss is not meeting your needs:

- Dealing with insufficient information (the situation with Ray and Sam)

- Dealing with lack of feedback

We recommend choosing the Coaching strategy in the third scenario because your boss is not meeting the needs of his team:

- Dealing with a boss who is ignoring team conflict

Scenario: Dealing with insufficient information

YOU: (Begin your discussion with an assertive request while allowing for face saving.)

Sam, I wanted to use this opportunity as we go to the airport to bring up some help I need. I have been hoping to get some input from you on my projects. I realize how busy you are and that it can be difficult to find time to respond to me, but without this information I might not know whether I am working against your priorities and direction. Would it be possible for us to schedule brief weekly meetings to discuss these issues?

DRIVE-BY BOSS: I have just been incredibly busy with the merger. I also did not understand that you needed this information soon. I understood you were doing a good job, so I saw no need to micromanage you.

YOU: (Just accept any excuses you get whether they seem valid or not. Indicate that you have understood his response.)

I hear you, Sam. I understand. You seem to be saying that it has been difficult for you to communicate with me and that you did not understand that it was necessary.

DRIVE-BY BOSS: Correct.

YOU: (Focus on the future and finding out if your boss will agree to your request.)

What do you think about my proposal? Would that work for you?

DRIVE-BY BOSS: (In this case the drive-by boss agrees with your request.)
I think we could do that. Things are starting to ease up for me.

YOU: (Once you get agreement on your solution, pursue how you will implement it.)
Great. I appreciate this. What do I need to do to arrange the meetings?

DRIVE-BY BOSS: Why don't you ask my assistant to put you on my calendar once a week for two weeks? After that, we can assess how it's going and proceed from there.

YOU: Sounds good. I will contact her. As long as we have some more time before we reach the airport, could I check with you now on a few of the most pressing items?

DRIVE-BY BOSS: Let's do it.

Scenario: Dealing with lack of feedback

YOU: (As in the previous scenario, you start with a tactful assertive request. Allow for face saving; stress what's in it for your boss.)
Sam, I would like to make a request. Sometimes I am not clear on how you are feeling about my work. I am the kind of employee who likes somewhat regular feedback, both positive and critical. I know we might not have discussed this before. When I get that feedback I tend to produce my best work, and I really want to help you achieve your goals. Would you be willing in each of our meetings to let me know what you like or dislike about my work?

DRIVE-BY BOSS: (In this case the drive-by boss disagrees with your request.)
I think that is excessive. To do a good job does not require constant praise or criticism. I never have needed that myself. I just don't think we have time for that.

YOU: (When your request is rejected, don't get into a debate. Demonstrate empathy and ignore his personal criticisms.)
It sounds like you are concerned about our not wasting time. I'm also concerned about that.

DRIVE-BY BOSS: Great.

YOU: (Pursue other alternatives that might meet both of your needs.)
Well, let me suggest some options. One would be to just have you
write some brief feedback on each of my status reports. Another
would be for us to meet quarterly to review my work. Either of
those ideas would satisfy me completely. What do you think?

DRIVE-BY BOSS: I think the idea of a quarterly meeting is a good one.
That's not too often. You can schedule them with my assistant
each quarter.

Let's now look at a situation that requires the Coaching strategy
because it affects the organization more than it affects you personally.
Use this strategy only if you have a good relationship with your boss
and you anticipate he will be open to your help and available for a
discussion. Remember that when you Coach, you help your boss solve
his problem or develop his skills. You do this mostly by asking
questions that help him assess his situation, determine his goals, and
come up with solutions. This strategy can be used when the boss is
ignoring his responsibilities or performing them poorly.

Scenario: Dealing with a boss who ignores team conflict

YOU: (Bring up the difficulty using lots of sincere tact, and ask for
permission to provide coaching without using the word
"coaching.")
Sam, as you probably know, there is considerable conflict within
our division between the Recruiting Department and the
Compensation Department. This conflict goes back many years,
long before you were here. I am concerned that things could get
worse unless they are dealt with pretty soon. Would you like me
to give you the history or to explore this situation with you?

DRIVE-BY BOSS: I suppose. I think I know the history.

YOU: You sound concerned. We don't need to have this conversation
unless you think it might help.

DRIVE-BY BOSS: I'm willing to give it a shot.

YOU: I think it's probably tough to deal with a long-standing conflict.

DRIVE-BY BOSS: Well, I have been thinking about this, but I just have been too busy to deal with it.

YOU: (Allow for face saving.)
I realize how busy you have been. That must be very frustrating. What's the best outcome you can envision in this situation?

DRIVE-BY BOSS: I just want these two departments to get along so there is no miscommunication with our new hires. How would you handle it?

YOU: (Avoid the temptation to dominate the conversation. Get his ideas about the causes of the situation or solutions before sharing your ideas.)
I, too, want the new hires to be clear, but I'm not sure what would work. Let's start with what you've been thinking. That might trigger some ideas for me. What do you believe is causing the friction?

DRIVE-BY BOSS: It seems to me that the Recruiting Department resents the Compensation Department's control over the salaries that are offered to new hires. I think the Recruiting Department wants most of the power. Do you agree?

YOU: (Don't backstab your colleagues with their boss.)
I don't think it would be helpful for me to take sides, and I am really not sure where the blame lies. I do agree that there is considerable conflict between those two departments. I think coming up with some steps to understand and address it would be helpful. Had you given any thought to how that could be done?

DRIVE-BY BOSS: I was just thinking of bringing the two supervisors together and just asking them to work out their differences.

YOU: (Don't argue. Ask about possible consequences.)
That is an option. How do you think that would go?

DRIVE-BY BOSS: I don't know. There seems to be so much tension between them, they might not be willing to listen to each other.

YOU: Would you like me to suggest a few other options?

DRIVE-BY BOSS: Sure.

YOU: (Try to give options rather than a single solution.) One possibility would be to hire a consultant to attempt to mediate between them. Another would be to survey both departments to try to determine exactly what the issues are. A third one would be to combine the two departments so that they handle both the hiring and salary functions.

DRIVE-BY BOSS: I really like the second idea. Besides being too busy, I think I have been procrastinating on this because I just have not been clear on what the conflict is about. Would you be willing to help me put together a survey that could be used? After you have done that, I will discuss it with the two supervisors and ask for their support on this.

YOU: Sure. I would be happy to do that. By the way, speaking of being too busy, recently I read a great book about time management. It gave me several new ideas about how to get more done in less time. Would you be interested in looking at it? I've already highlighted some of the main points, so you could skim right through it.

DRIVE-BY BOSS: I'd really appreciate that. Just leave it on my desk, and I'll get it back to you in a few days.

Be sure to follow up on any of these discussions. Summarize your understanding and thank the drive-by boss for changes he makes (otherwise he's likely to regress to his previous pattern). If he does not follow through on his commitments but the issue is still important to you, bring it up again. Explore what is getting in the way and discuss other options so that your agreement sticks. Using peer power to influence your boss to become an engaged leader will benefit you, your boss, and the organization.

Plan B (If Your Initial Strategy Fails)

If Collaborating or Coaching is not successful, avoid the temptation to gain sympathy by venting to others. Your boss will almost certainly hear about your unprofessional conduct. Any allies you gain—and they

---

Dear Cynthia and Ray,

My drive-by boss runs terrible staff meetings. It seems clear that she spends little time preparing for them. There is no agenda, people talk on and on, and nothing is ever decided. I am so frustrated with how much of my time is being wasted, but I am afraid if I skip these meetings that my boss will be angry with me. It seems like there is nothing I can do about this. What do you think?

— Meetinged Out

Dear Meetinged,

Your boss is not ignoring her responsibilities—just doing them poorly. Use Coaching to build her skills.

We often mistakenly think that participants have no control over a meeting run by a higher-up. First, try to educate your boss about good meetings. Offer to do an Internet search and provide her with some articles about running meetings. Do what you can to reduce your boss's workload. It is possible that she is just too busy to plan good meetings. You can even offer to help her put together an agenda.

Turn to Caring-for-Self if Coaching doesn't work. During the meeting, be a proactive participant. If people talk for too long or get off the subject, gently redirect the discussion in a constructive direction. You can participate constructively without attempting to replace your boss as the meeting leader.

— Cynthia and Ray

---

will be few—will be offset by his resentment of being humiliated publicly.

Avoid Going Head-to-Head. Arguing with your boss is never a good idea. If Ray had chosen this route instead of a pleasant conversation outside of the work environment, the situation would only have worsened. Arguing with your boss in front of others is not only disrespectful, it will almost always backfire. Arguing with him privately is usually counterproductive.

Making an end-run around your boss to discuss difficulties with his boss or Human Resources won't get you what you want (unless you want to be fired or demoted). One big caveat to this recommendation: in cases of sexual harassment, unethical behavior, violations of company policy, threats of physical violence, or situations that can do serious damage to the organization, bypassing your supervisor might be entirely appropriate. However, in general it is most helpful to discuss your concerns directly with your supervisor.

If the Collaborating strategy fails, you can try the Compromising strategy. If your boss won't agree to give you frequent feedback, for example, you might offer to write up your own progress report for him to rubber stamp. Or if your boss continues to be so busy that he can't get you important information, you might offer to get it from his assistant.

As a last resort, turn to the Caring-for-Self strategy. Try to meet your own needs. There are a lot of "Sams" in management who provide sparse information. If you can't get information from your boss, seek it elsewhere. If you want more praise, find ways to pat yourself on the back or get praise from someone else. If you are overworked, attempt to be more efficient and manage your time carefully. Determine on your own what priorities to focus on. Seek to gain as much autonomy as you can and continue to do your job as well as possible. You might just be giving your boss too much power by assuming that he is the only one who can meet your needs.

Caring-for-Self might lead you to "fire the boss" by finding another job (or boss) within or outside your organization. You are the best judge of how unpleasant your current situation is and whether it is necessary to head out in a new direction.

Moving Forward

If your boss ignores a whole number of his responsibilities, don't try to Collaborate or Coach him on all of them. That is his boss's responsibility. Just focus on a few that are most critical to you, and you may find that your boss exhibits more of the behaviors of an engaged leader.

The Rest of the Story

Fortunately Sam and Ray were able to work out their difficulty. Using the Collaborating strategy, Ray requested more frequent interaction. Sam agreed, and they became a close, effective team. Ray stayed at that organization for several more years, working productively and happily with Sam.

Cheat Sheet for the Drive-by Boss

Definition: A drive-by boss seems to be ignoring some of his key management responsibilities and doesn't meet the needs of his employees or the organization.

Clues

The drive-by boss:

- Misses meetings or holds them infrequently or without planning
- Fails to provide you with clear expectations or assignments
- Pays very little attention to or has unrealistic expectations about your work or workload
- Gives limited praise
- Fails to respond to messages
- Avoids conducting performance appraisals or providing regular feedback
- Ignores critical paperwork
- Fails to keep you informed on important developments
- Provides insufficient resources
- Procrastinates in making decisions
- Limits your training opportunities
- Ignores performance problems and team conflicts
- Seems stressed and harried
- Achieves poor results
- Has a demoralized team
- Ignores management functions of planning and monitoring tasks and processes
- Lacks the respect of his colleagues

Helpful Assumptions

- Your drive-by boss's actions may be due to real needs and not negative motives.

- Your boss may be failing to give information or feedback because he is extremely busy.

- It may not be his style to give out praise.

- Though overloading you with work, he may not realize that you're busy or trusts that you can deliver.

- You might be unaware of the tasks your boss is actually performing.

- His actions may be based on fear and uncertainty.

- His behavior might be influenced by your own.

- Your boss has strengths; respect them.

- You may have shown some of the same weaknesses.

Key Principles and Practices

Take Responsibility

- Look at your contribution to the situation.

- Focus on what *you* can do about the drive-by boss. Help him and educate him.

- Communicate. Keep your boss informed.

- Perform well (so your boss will want to help you).

Extend Respect

- Listen carefully to his reasons for delaying actions.

- Respect the organization's structure and culture.

- Honor differences in style or work method.

Be Real

- Bring up issues that are on your mind.

Strategy: Collaborating or Coaching

Collaborating (when the issue mostly affects you personally)

- Schedule face-to-face discussions to resolve issues.
- Make assertive requests that meet your boss's needs. Acknowledge his good intentions.
- Don't get defensive or try to convince him he's wrong.
- Paraphrase frequently to demonstrate you are listening.
- Explore alternatives and seek joint solutions.
- When you reach agreement, discuss implementation.
- Acknowledge any improvements afterwards.

Coaching (when the issue mostly affects the organization, not you)

- Approach the issue using sincerity and tact.
- Ask for permission to provide coaching.
- Allow face saving.
- Ask questions that help your boss assess the situation, determine goals, and come up with solutions.
- Listen well to his ideas and paraphrase without arguing.
- Don't dominate the conversation. Get his ideas first.
- Give options rather than a single solution.
- Let your boss come to his own conclusions and decisions.

Plan B (If Your Initial Strategy Fails)

- Avoid venting to others.
- Avoid arguing with your boss.
- Avoid making end-runs around your boss.
- When Collaborating fails, move to Compromising.
- Caring-for-Self: Get information or praise elsewhere; manage your time well; gain as much autonomy as possible; look for another job.

Worksheet

1. What clues make you suspect that you are dealing with a drive-by boss?

2. Assuming you've determined the person is a drive-by boss, what are his legitimate needs?

3. What are this drive-by boss's strengths?

4. What principles and practices are relevant to the situation?

5. Which strategy will you use and why will you use it?

6. Write the opening statement you might use to begin Collaborating or Coaching with the drive-by boss.

7. What response do you anticipate and how will you handle it?

8. What Plan B approach will you use if your discussion is not successful?

from the manipulator to the open communicator

Cynthia once worked in a department that was undergoing a change from one manager (Lucy) to another (Randall). Lucy was usually warm, personable, and focused on developing her people. Randall was quieter, asked lots of logical questions, and analyzed recommendations in great detail. When Cynthia's team shared some concerns about Randall's management style with Lucy, she commiserated with them, fanned the flames of suspicion, and made statements like, "My money is on you. I'm sure you can handle him. It's ten against one."

In truth, she saw this transition as an opportunity to even a political score with Randall, a colleague whose analytical style often conflicted with her people-oriented style. Instead of working to ensure a smooth transfer, Lucy manipulated her team to view Randall's management style with suspicion and mistrust. The manipulator is a coworker who attempts to influence your attitude or behavior through deception or secrecy.

Randall arrived to face a team that was hostile and uncooperative. His early attempts to get to know the team members were met with resistance. Cynthia felt torn between her loyalty to Lucy, who often asked her for confidential updates about how the team was doing, and her desire to work well with Randall, her new manager. The ongoing gossip and tension on the team affected everyone's productivity.

Clues to the Manipulator

Manipulators are often friendly and likeable, and seemingly open communicators. That qualifier "seemingly" is a hint at how manipulators work. Their camaraderie and charm can mask motivations that cause them to exploit your trust in order to fulfill their goals.

You may not initially notice you're dealing with a manipulator, since her behavior doesn't immediately raise red flags. That changes when she needs something from you, and she goes about getting it in a sly, deceptive way. Over time it becomes clear that an ordinary workplace friendship is a charade. Since the manipulator's behavior is subtle, be alert to these clues as your false friend:

- Offers unusual favors or gives you gifts
- Flatters you or is unusually sweet
- Appeals to your sense of guilt
- Deceives you, or you begin to feel deceived
- Presents only positive reasons for an action with no balancing negatives
- Misrepresents or excludes data to support her position
- Whispers in your ear, sharing confidential information with you alone so that you feel privileged or flattered to be selected
- Asks a leading question that she already knows the answer to
- Asks for input when she's already made the decision
- Tells stories that are inconsistent

As we mentioned, the awareness that you're dealing with a manipulator may build gradually. Don't jump to conclusions. But as more odd exchanges occur and a sense of contradiction or falseness builds, your alertness to telltale signs should build, too. Cynthia gradually came to feel like Lucy's accomplice in crime. Once that feeling surfaced, she more readily saw Lucy's comments as innuendos and her friendship as fraudulent.

Nobody wants to be manipulated. Being alert to the signs of deception can keep you from being exploited and embarrassed. And the strategies in *Peer Power* to combat manipulation might also help the manipulator to operate in a more positive fashion as an open communicator.

Helpful Assumptions

If you look closely at the clues of a manipulator's behavior in the previous section, it's easy to track a typical scenario. It starts with signs of friendliness (she flatters you with praise or intimacy). Behavior that is not seen as out of the ordinary eventually exhibits contradictions and untruthfulness (the tale told a second time is different; the reasoned proposal doesn't document the risks).

> *It's natural to feel disappointment and anger at being used and deceived.*

Perhaps her behavior becomes more overt and unusual (appealing to a sense of guilt or asking a leading question that she already knows the answer to). It eventually dawns on you that all those overtures of friendship were for an ulterior purpose.

When the reality does dawn, it can be quite a shock. The manipulator has used a very personal tool—the appearance of warmth and fondness—for seemingly selfish purposes. It's natural to feel disappointment and anger at being used and deceived.

But consider that though a manipulator misleads and deceives, she is not unfeeling. As a matter of fact, her methods are often born of a sense of powerlessness and fear. For reasons unknown or deeply hidden, she fears the consequences of truthful and open communication and may even feel victimized by the circumstances in which she finds herself. She may honestly value you as a friend and may welcome ways you can help her out of her predicament.

When you consider the more overtly self-serving personalities like the scene stealer (Chapter 6) or bully (Chapter 12), notice some contrasts. Those personalities often abuse others to move toward a dishonorable end goal: adulation, enrichment, power. A manipulator may not be characterized by these Machiavellian traits. Though it is possible for her to be motivated by greed or malice, it's just as likely that the manipulator has noble intentions and is afraid you won't share her vision or goals without some maneuvering on her part. She may fear she'll lose your approval if she shares her motives.

Try to resist the tendency to lose respect for the manipulator; instead, seek to understand her motives. Think of the times you manipulated someone to get your way. And if you truly don't have that vice in your toolbox of tricks for goal achievement (good for you), reflect on the times that honesty proved a painful choice. We all have coping mechanisms to ward off pain; the manipulator has chosen hers. This doesn't mean that you don't take care of yourself. Even if you choose to show understanding and empathy, you still have a right to block the manipulation.

Key Principles: Take Responsibility and Extend Respect

As we mentioned, subtlety is a hallmark of manipulators. It takes time to realize that flattery and friendly overtures aren't what they seem. This section presents the principles and practices that can help you avoid manipulation or, if it's too late, deal with the fractured friendship with integrity.

Let's look more closely at how incorporating the principles Take Responsibility and Extend Respect and their related practices into the workplace can prevent manipulation or reduce its fallout.

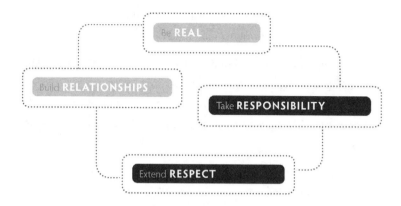

Take Responsibility

In the Helpful Assumptions section, we traced the process of manipulation from the position of the manipulator. Let's switch perspectives and view the scenario from a different vantage point—imagine that *you* are the person being manipulated.

An acquaintance begins to flatter you, suggests spending time, shares intimate information, or otherwise signals her interest in you as a friend in either typical or unusual ways. It feels good, doesn't it? After becoming buddies, you notice contradictions, untruths, or other red flags that signal something unusual in her behavior. You discount it because of your bond. You may even defend your friend from others' suspicions, since you're a very trusting and loyal person. Since you now have an even greater stake in proving everyone else wrong, less subtle behavior—like your friend's appeal to your sense of guilt or an attempt to bolster your ego—is overlooked. You realize you've been manipulated only when your ersatz friend does something truly blatant.

Reflect on how your hypothetical behavior contributed to this harmful ending. What attributes do you possess that are "hooks" to a manipulator? (For example, does your need for approval or camaraderie lead you to respond positively to flattery or overtures of friendship?) You don't need to be distrustful, but it's not unreasonable to demand integrity. This is the best way to employ the practice of being responsible for your own experience.

Honoring an emotional bond isn't synonymous with overlooking unusual behavior. Nor is it the same as ignoring warnings given to you by others. If someone is acting overly nice, ask yourself why. If she misrepresents facts, do your own research to validate or invalidate her conclusions.

Ray remembers a time when a colleague buttered him up via e-mail, complimenting him on his intelligence. Ray was hooked (because who wouldn't want to be thought of as a smart guy?). He agreed to let his colleague include his name in an important recommendation. However, he had some misgivings about his colleague's intentions. To protect himself, he asked to review the recommendation before it was e-mailed to the colleague's boss. By paying attention to his internal warning system, Ray caught several misstatements and exaggerations that would have been embarrassing to him if his name had been included on the recommendation.

> *Once you've become adept at identifying manipulators, go the next step and become someone who can't be manipulated.*

Once you've become adept at identifying manipulators, go the next step and become someone who can't be manipulated. Set ground rules with people you suspect of manipulation. This might take the form of agreeing that your communications will be open and honest, even if it means asking hard questions, pushing back, or challenging a request. By refusing to be shy about blocking manipulation, you are respecting your own needs.

Extend Respect

Extending respect to individuals is largely about honoring others' capabilities to solve their problems, and listening well to others and to yourself (what's that nagging feeling really telling you?).

We often think of manipulators as strong, coercive types. But manipulators can just as easily be timid individuals who realize that emphasizing their neediness is a way to fulfill a need. Cynthia once worked with a fellow (Stan) who often presented "impossible" situations, complimented Cynthia by telling her how much he admired her ability to solve problems, and asked for advice. Of course, Cynthia was flattered to be asked and sometimes took the bait. When her advice failed to solve the problem, Cynthia was exasperated to find that Stan would blame the "bad advice," saying, "Well, I didn't know what to do, but Cynthia suggested this course of action so I did what she recommended. It was really her idea, not mine."

If you like to help others, it's easy for a manipulator's show of weakness to become a siren call. A manipulator will welcome your attempt to take over responsibility for her actions. Be careful. Don't get into the habit of rescuing people or making their decisions for them out of a feeling of guilt or the illusion that you can control their behavior. This sort of savior behavior is disrespectful when applied to a healthy individual. When applied to an unhealthy manipulator, your rescuing conduct can result in even greater damage to the manipulator and to yourself.

> *Don't get into the habit of rescuing people or making their decisions for them...*

A way to simultaneously protect yourself, extend respect, and help a manipulator come to a lasting solution that she makes for herself, is to employ open communication. This involves the practice of listening.

For example, if someone gushes about your skills and experience, looks at you with adoring eyes, and begs to sit at your feet to learn everything you know, resist the temptation to bask in her praise. Instead, check to see if she is working toward an alternate agenda. Ask clarifying questions like, "What are your goals?" "How will you achieve them?" Listen closely and respectfully, discount the smooth talk, and seek out (and attempt to reward) consistency and honesty in her answers.

When working with Stan, Cynthia learned to turn questions back to him. If Stan asked, "What would you do in this situation?" Cynthia would reply, "I've never dealt with a situation quite like this one. How do you think you should handle it?"

In addition to promoting honesty in your communication, you must be honest with yourself by listening to your gut. Lucy's original comments to her team about Randall—"I'm sure you can handle him; it's ten against one"—could be read as innocent humor, but humor often points to underlying tension. If Cynthia had followed this up with a qualifying question, she may have successfully clarified Lucy's true motives and warned her to play fair.

These principles and practices sometimes prove insufficient. In such cases, you'll need to pick your peer power strategy to transform the relationship.

Strategy: Collaborating

As long as you have adequate time and patience, and the manipulator's needs are not mutually exclusive from yours, we suggest employing the Collaborating strategy. Meet face to face with the manipulator and work to uncover the full story. As the dialogs show, the Collaborating strategy attempts to combat the manipulator's trickery through honesty, integrity, and communication.

The tools that Collaborating employs can bring you closer to becoming someone who can't be manipulated. And if you're clear enough, your manipulative coworker may come one step closer to becoming an open communicator.

A Collaborating strategy can be used to:

- Respond to withholding information and lying
- Handle flattery

Scenario: Responding to withholding information and lying

When you find that someone has told you a blatant lie or has withheld information in order to get you to do something, find a way to meet everyone's needs by asking questions. Begin by surfacing the missing and correct information. An exchange might sound like this:

MANIPULATOR: How are those graphics coming along? Time is of the essence if we're going to have that prototype done by the deadline.

YOU: They're coming along nicely. I'm curious about something though. When I was speaking with Gerard, he mentioned a different deadline than the one you gave me. I worked the last two Saturdays to meet my deadline. Gerard told me that the deadline you gave him was three weeks out. What gives?

MANIPULATOR: Well, you're right. We actually have until the end of next month to finish the segment you're working on. But your graphics need to be done before Gerard can do his piece.

YOU: (Though you may be tempted to point out that she withheld the real deadline, it's more constructive to listen well and focus on finding a solution that meets her need and your need.)
So, you're saying that you gave me an earlier deadline so that Gerard would have more time to complete his work. Is that right?

MANIPULATOR: That's right. Gerard told me that he can't do anything on the project until he gets your finished graphics. That's just the way it works. I'm sorry you had to work on the weekend but we all need to do what it takes to get this done. We're a team, right?

YOU: (Avoid labeling the manipulator as a "liar" but instead offer corrected information.)
I'm surprised that Gerard would tell you that. In the past, he has used a placeholder so that he only needs the dimensions of the diagrams and illustrations. The finished graphics are required from me three days before his deadline. That's been our working practice in the past. Is there any reason that might have changed? I really need accurate and complete information.

Dear Cynthia and Ray,

I'm a telecommunications major and was thrilled to get a position in our school's cable TV network as an investigative reporter. I've been befriended by two fellow reporters, both with more experience, who have helped me come up to speed with my new job.

Now I've been given my first major segment and get to recommend which producer I want to work with. I've selected Tom, a producer who is well respected by the desk editor. The problem is that my two friends have warned me away from him. Tom's success (they say) is due more to kissing up to the boss than performing his job well. They keep telling me stories that call Tom's integrity into question.

I have a feeling that my new friends are lying, but I don't have any proof. They want me to choose their buddy Rob as my producer. What should I do?

— Suspicious at the U

Dear Suspicious,

In this situation, we'd strongly advise you to apply your investigative skills to the task. Take time to see if your suspicions are well founded, even if it means delaying your decision. Study the buddy's work to see how effective it is. Discuss both producers' work with the desk editor and others who can provide insight about their job performance. If you find that your friends' advice is sound, it will feel good to know that they are watching out for you.

Of course, if you conclude that they are manipulating you because of a hidden agenda, ask them to clarify their intentions and then collaborate to explore any options that might work for you and them. Whether or not they acknowledge their intentions, recommend the person you think is best suited to do the assignment. To discourage them from manipulating you in the future, state clearly the objective reasons for your choice.

And one more thing: If you really can't delay this decision, trust your intuition. If you suspect your friends are lying, they probably are. Go with your instincts and make the best decision.

— Cynthia and Ray

MANIPULATOR: Well, even if that's true, there are lots of moving pieces that mean we have to stick to the date I gave you. Look, Gerard and I are on the same page here. I know that overtime is no fun, but everyone else is doing it and if one person fails, the team fails. Can I count on you to make this work?

YOU: (Don't react to her further attempt to manipulate. Instead, continue to collaborate. Don't agree to the manipulator's request unless you are totally comfortable with it. Anticipate some venting if you don't agree.)

You're saying that this is a complicated project and you need my commitment. You set deadlines that vary from the standard policy because you're worried about the results. I want to assure you that Gerard and I will work together to meet this deadline. We've always been a good team. Would you be willing to adjust my deadline to the standard of three days before Gerard's deadline? I'll ensure that I follow our standard practice of giving Gerard the dimensions of the diagrams and illustrations so he can get started now.

MANIPULATOR: Look, I just want to be sure that we get this done on time and with the highest quality. If I can't see what you've designed until three days before the deadline, I'm afraid we won't have time to fix it if I don't like it.

YOU: (Since the manipulator has finally disclosed the motivation behind her attempts to manipulate you, you can now suggest another alternative.)

I can tell you're worried about delivering a great result on time. It really helps me to get the full story from you. What if I were to share with you some of the graphics I've already developed?

MANIPULATOR: Do you have something I can look at right now?

YOU: Sure, we can take some time to look at these graphic concepts. If you're satisfied with the initial approach, would you let Gerard know that I'll get him the dimensions this week and then I'll take another week to finalize the graphics?

MANIPULATOR: That sounds like a plan. Let's see what you've got.

Scenario: Handling flattery

Manipulators will often appeal to your pride or vanity rather than clearly communicate what they want. Turn them away from buttering you up and toward collaboration by acknowledging their praise and moving to understanding their needs.

MANIPULATOR: I just wanted to tell you how much I enjoyed your presentation to the Help Desk team. I think we all really understand what's expected of us a lot better now. In fact, I'm going to go out on a limb here and tell you that may have been the best Help Desk presentation that's ever been delivered here. It was really, really effective. Have you considered applying for a job in the technical training department? You seem to have a natural talent for explaining information so that people really get it.

YOU: (With this much gushing, you may be feeling skeptical. Acknowledge the praise, but then move on to understand the manipulator's needs.)
Thanks. I enjoy communicating complex information clearly so people can understand and use it. It sounds like I succeeded.

MANIPULATOR: You certainly did. I was very impressed. In fact, that's why I wanted to speak with you.

YOU: Oh? What did you want to speak with me about?

MANIPULATOR: Communicating well is something I've always valued a lot. In fact, I really admire your way with words.

YOU: (Be neutral and interested at this point so the manipulator can tell you what she's thinking.)
Uh huh. Go on.

MANIPULATOR: I'm doing a lot of writing in the evenings. I think I have a knack for it. Writing well can be useful in our line of work, don't you think?

YOU: (Paraphrase and then probe to learn more about her real needs.)
So, you're developing your writing skills. It sounds like you feel

good about them. Is writing something you want to do more of here?

MANIPULATOR: Exactly. It seems like writing would be a really useful skill for the Help Desk support team. Do you agree?

YOU: A number of people on the Help Desk support team have good writing skills. That's true.

MANIPULATOR: I guess I was thinking mainly about the technical writers, the ones who document our processes and user guides. I know that there'll be an opening after Jane leaves.

YOU: Are you thinking of applying for Jane's position?

MANIPULATOR: I thought I might. Would you be willing to put in a good word for me? I think you have a lot of credibility with that team.

YOU: (The manipulator has finally gotten to the point. Now you can address her real need.)
I think you should apply, by all means. They usually look for someone with several years of technical writing experience. It sounds like you are developing your writing skills. Do you have technical writing experience?

MANIPULATOR: Not on-the-job experience. You're so skilled at writing; I was hoping I could show you some of my writing samples. If you like what you see, you can recommend me to the manager.

YOU: (If you don't want to be led to where the manipulator would like you to go, try to suggest some mutually satisfying alternatives.)
Without on-the-job technical writing experience, you might be at a disadvantage when compared with other candidates. I'm happy to take a look at your writing samples and make any suggestions that would help you continue to develop your skills. After you've made some changes, you might be able to include your samples when you apply for the job.

MANIPULATOR: That sounds great. And you'll write me a recommendation too, won't you? It would mean so much to me, coming from such a skilled writer as you. You really know your stuff.

YOU: (Don't agree just to please the manipulator.)
I can certainly tell the manager that I reviewed your writing samples. Since I've never worked with you as a technical writer, I can't really recommend you. But I can certainly give him my assessment of your writing samples.

MANIPULATOR: Thanks. I appreciate that.

Plan B (If Your Initial Strategy Fails)

The conversion of a manipulator into an open communicator through Collaborating is possible, but it's not easy and it often takes time. The feeling of powerlessness and victimization that led to her coping strategy won't be undone overnight. If Collaborating fails completely, you may be left feeling angry, guilty, and a little powerless yourself.

At this point, it may seem like you're on the horns of a dilemma, with only two choices: to strike back or give in. Resist them both. Be careful not to assert your power or authority, embarrass the individual in front of others, or try manipulation yourself. On the flip side, ignore any feelings of guilt you may have for not complying with the manipulator.

Instead, pick a middle ground. Your Plan B strategy is Compromising. The goal of Compromising is to come to agreement on a course of action that partially works for both you and the manipulator. It's an appropriate choice if the manipulator's behavior is not so destructive that you can still maintain a good relationship. For example, if the manipulator doesn't want to complete an assigned task, she may falsely claim she doesn't have time to do it and insist that it would take much less time for you to do it (due to your vast experience). Instead of completing the task for her, you might offer to provide suggestions before she begins, or review her first draft. By Compromising, you neither give in and complete the task for her nor abandon her to complete it on her own.

In extreme situations though, even Compromising won't stop a manipulator. In this case, focus on Caring-for-Self. Avoid the person who is attempting to mislead you or find allies within the team. If you make a decision based on limited information, develop contingency plans to deal with unintended consequences. As a last resort, you may have to move to another group.

Moving Forward

Your Plan B approach should encourage the manipulator to become an open communicator in the future. Support this process. Acknowledge any positive changes that occur, but continue to draw attention to negative behavior. If lying or withholding critical information continues, for example, work on a roadmap toward its resolution. This might take the form of saying, "What needs to happen for this to stop?" If the deceitful behavior continues, besides Caring-for-Self you will need to turn to Going Head-to-Head. Tell the manipulator you won't continue to work with her (unless you have no choice) and disengage from the conversation. Document the deception and invite the person to join you to discuss it with management.

The Rest of the Story

In the opening story, a manipulative manager created conflict for her colleague by whispering in the ears of her team. Once Cynthia realized that she had been manipulated by the outgoing manager who was settling a political score inside the organization, she began to collaborate willingly with her new boss. They developed a productive working relationship built on mutual trust that lasted for several years. In hindsight, she wishes she hadn't relied on gossip and innuendo to develop her opinion of her new boss.

Cheat Sheet for the Manipulator

Definition: The manipulator is a coworker who attempts to influence your attitude or behavior through deception or secrecy.

Clues

The manipulator:

- Offers unusual favors or gives you gifts

- Flatters you or is unusually sweet

- Appeals to your sense of guilt

- Deceives you, or you begin to feel deceived

- Presents only positive reasons for an action, with no balancing negatives

- Misrepresents or excludes data to support her position

- Whispers in your ear, sharing confidential information with you alone so that you feel privileged or flattered to be selected

- Asks a leading question that she already knows the answer to

- Asks for input when she has already made the decision

- Tells stories that are inconsistent

Helpful Assumptions

- Manipulators fear the consequences of telling the truth or being open.

- They have learned to exercise power indirectly behind the scenes to meet their needs.

- Manipulating is a coping strategy used when people feel powerless.

- You have probably manipulated others, too.

- You have a right to take care of yourself.

- Manipulators usually have many strengths.

Key Principles and Practices

Take Responsibility

- Be responsible for your own experience. Be aware of your own hooks and how you can be manipulated.
- Perform well. Do your homework.
- Respect your needs. Become someone who can't be manipulated.
- Communicate and set ground rules.

Extend Respect

- Avoid rescuing behavior.
- Use good listening and questioning skills to encourage openness.
- Be a good listener—pay attention to your gut/intuition.

Strategy: Collaborating

- Call her on a lie without calling her a liar. Offer the correct information.
- Don't do what she wants unless you really want to.
- Expect and allow her to vent when you refuse.
- Acknowledge her praise. Then move to understanding her needs.
- Probe to uncover her needs. Ask, "Is there something you need from me?"
- Use statements like, "I need more information," or "I need to hear the opposing view."
- Jointly come up with alternatives.

Plan B (If Your Initial Strategy Fails)

- Don't strike back or give in.
- Don't embarrass the manipulator in front of others.
- Don't resort to manipulating behavior yourself.
- Don't placate or feel guilty for not complying.
- If Collaborating fails, move to Compromising.
- Caring-for-Self: Avoid the person or leave the department; find allies within the team; develop contingency plans to deal with unintended consequences; move to another group.

Worksheet

1. What clues make you suspect you may be dealing with a manipulator?

2. Assuming you've determined the person is a manipulator, what might be her legitimate needs?

3. What are this manipulator's strengths?

4. How could you Extend Respect or Take Responsibility with the manipulator?

5. Write the opening statement you might use to begin working with the manipulator.

6. What response do you anticipate and how will you handle it?

7. What will you do if your strategy fails?

chapter 9

from the clueless colleague to the considerate teammate

Cynthia once worked with a fellow manager who had been in her human resources position for 20 years and was close to retirement. Every day at 10:30 a.m., she would drop by Cynthia's office, holding coffee cup, to chat. Li would stand just inside the door to Cynthia's office and chatter away, not noticing that Cynthia was busy and wasn't interested in Li's comments.

Li was what we call the clueless colleague, the coworker who is insensitive to her negative impact on the work environment. Clueless colleagues litter the environment with excessive conversations, dirty dishes, loud or unpleasant sounds, smelly food, inappropriate posters, jammed printers, messy spaces, etc. While these conditions often don't directly affect your work, they do make it unpleasant to come to work.

Cynthia tried everything: continuing to work on the computer, taking phone calls, breaking eye contact, and even filing papers while Li randomly explored her own ideas and opinions out loud. After about 15 minutes, Li would wander back to her own office. Cynthia began to dread the morning break.

Li had a long history with the organization and handled the employee issues that crossed her desk easily and quickly. She was often sought after by other managers for her good advice about the organization's policies and practices. Cynthia felt terrible that she found Li so annoying.

Clues to the Clueless Colleague

Our clueless coworkers are often well meaning and committed workers. They just have a limited awareness of their impact on everyone else. Social cues, such as people politely coughing to signal that a long monologue should come to an end or an employee's pointed look at the time on his cell phone, go unheeded. It may seem as if the clueless colleague doesn't care about the needs or feelings of others.

You may be experiencing the oblivious behavior of a clueless coworker if she:

- Places inappropriate posters on the wall
- Doesn't clean up her messes
- Talks too loudly in the hallway, at her desk, or on her cell phone
- Inadvertently broadcasts private or personal information
- Interrupts others frequently
- Borrows items or money and doesn't return them
- Jams the printer or photocopier (and doesn't fix it)
- Leaves dirty dishes in the sink
- Clips her fingernails (or toenails) at work
- Makes inappropriate sounds—whistles, burps, slurps, sniffs
- Plays loud music
- Sets the thermostat too high or low
- Has body odor
- Leaves dirty tissues all over her desk
- Makes long-winded pronouncements on topics or talks excessively
- Leaves long-winded voice mail messages
- Copies you on e-mails you don't need to see

- Causes people regularly to complain about her impact

- Causes you to feel annoyed or disrespected

These are just examples of clueless behavior and it's not likely that any single clueless individual would exhibit them all (thank goodness).

Cynthia recalls a tightly wired coworker who was always rushing to complete his next deadline. Laboring under constant self-imposed pressure, he found it very easy to interrupt any other conversation going on in the office to ask a question or get help. From his worldview, nothing was more important than the task at hand (his

It's helpful to realize that your colleague's preferences and sensitivities are different than your own.

hand). She and her coworkers often reacted with annoyance to his interruptions. In his mind, whatever they were discussing was far less important than his work. This self-focus marks a clueless colleague.

Helpful Assumptions

While Cynthia was annoyed at Li's insensitive behavior, she was also well aware that Li's contributions were valuable and contributed to the department's success. Clueless colleagues are a lovely bundle of strengths and weaknesses, just as you are.

In fact, many clueless colleagues are more focused on their own goals and getting the job done than they are at building relationships. Feeling this internal sense of pressure and stress, they may go about their work without realizing that others are irritated with their actions.

It's helpful to realize that your colleague's preferences and sensitivities are different from your own. Her behavior is not directed at you. If you can stand back and look at her behavior objectively, you may see that it is not personal. While we don't excuse leaving the dishes unwashed in the office kitchen for someone else to clean up, it's possible that in her household this is common behavior, while in your household this is a sign of chaos and disrespect.

The same applies to coworkers from different cultures. An important assumption to make is that things you find disconcerting— from the amount and scent of your colleague's perfume to the seeming invasion of personal space—do not necessarily signal insensitivity or boorish behavior, but are totally acceptable in their culture.

Take a good look in the mirror and ask yourself the last time you exhibited clueless behavior. Cynthia will admit that she is a talker and when she's upset about something she processes her feelings out loud. Recently she talked aloud for several minutes with a friend who responded kindly, "Perhaps you need to pay for a counseling session." In that moment, Cynthia realized that she had not been registering the nonverbal signals that told her that her friend was uncomfortable with the conversation.

Once you accept that you, too, have been clueless, you may find it easier to deal compassionately with someone else's lack of sensitivity. We want to stress that you have a right to care for yourself in these situations. You can speak up, set boundaries, or explain your own needs and preferences. If you give your clueless colleague the opportunity to change her behavior, she will usually become a considerate teammate.

Key Principles: Take Responsibility, Build Relationships, and Be Real

Like a bull in a china shop, your clueless colleague may be shattering teacups while attempting simply to cross the room. Oblivious to the organization's values, she may post a photo or motto that offends her teammates. Oblivious to your personal preferences, she may eat a cheeseburger at her desk, getting greasy fingerprints on your latest report. Ignoring technology protocol, she may leave long, rambling voice mail messages or copy e-mail recipients inappropriately.

Let's examine the principles and practices that will support your addressing these kinds of situations in a constructive manner.

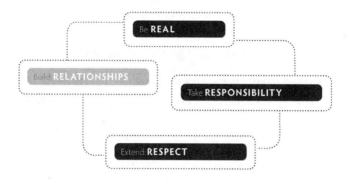

Take Responsibility

Crazy though it may seem, your behavior may actually be contributing to the very problems that you're experiencing. You may hate the greasy fingerprints that appear on your latest report; however, if you're the person who made the run to the fast food restaurant for the burgers, you're sending a mixed message. Part of the Take Responsibility principle is the practice of being responsible for your experience. If you hate interruptions yet you keep a candy bowl on your desk, notice the incongruence between what you say you want and what you are doing. A candy bowl is an open invitation to interrupt you any time someone wants a snack.

Demonstrate respect for your own needs by removing the extra chairs from your office that may invite people to plop down and start talking. Put up "I'm busy now" signs when you are working under tight deadlines. Stand up when your clueless colleague barges in and walk her back to the door. Get yourself a pair of ear plugs if the office conversations are too loud for you to concentrate.

One of the most powerful ways to influence behavior change and evolve a clueless colleague into a considerate teammate is to perform well. Model the behavior you want to see. Don't like to be interrupted? Stop interrupting others when you're under pressure. Expect others to wash their dishes? Don't leave your own unwashed dishes in the sink, even if it's only for a few minutes. Expect people to be on time for meetings? Start meetings on time. Tired of improper use of e-mail, voice mail, and teleconferencing? Model good use of technology. (Refer to Chapter 14 for technology tips.)

Take time to communicate your expectations and needs. Ask your clueless colleague to share her expectations and needs. Then come to agreement about the ground rules that will guide your work relationship. When we first began to collaborate on the writing of this book, Ray made it clear that he wanted to review Cynthia's feedback on chapter drafts before they met to discuss changes. Until he did, Cynthia would bring her feedback to the meeting for discussion, oblivious to Ray's need for reflection ahead of time. By taking responsibility for clear communication at the outset, you may very well eliminate the unskilled behavior demonstrated by a well-meaning colleague who didn't "get" you.

> *Though you may be tempted to simply avoid your clueless coworker, you'll get better results from improving your relationship with her.*

Build Relationships

Though you may be tempted to simply avoid your clueless coworker, you'll get better results by improving your relationship with her. If your stressed-out colleague is wreaking havoc, try to determine what you might do to help reduce that stress. Can you offer support on a project? Are there resources you might share?

Invite her to lunch and begin to get to know her. Find out what motivates her. Chat about her work challenges and interests. And share more about your work, your hobbies, your interests, and your life. The goal is to build a personal relationship so that your colleague will find it difficult, if not impossible, to remain in her clueless state. If she's more aware of your needs, the genie is out of the bottle and she may never be able to stuff it back.

As your relationship with her improves, demonstrate the Build Relationships practice of showing empathy for her challenges and stressors. Demonstrate that you care for her success and well-being. When she tells you about her frustrating morning driving through traffic behind a crazy guy texting at every red light, take a moment to commiserate. By empathizing, you will begin to strengthen your relationship so that you're able to address lingering concerns. (For that excessively chatty clueless colleague, your lingering concern might be when and where she chooses to bend your ear.)

Protect your clueless colleague's self-esteem even when you are dealing with annoying issues. Ray recalls working with a colleague (Roger) who started to have terrible body odor. After watching his teammates pinch their noses and fan the air behind Roger's back, Ray knew he needed to have a conversation. He took Roger aside privately. He was careful not to say, "Everyone here thinks you smell bad." Instead he told him that he had started to notice a strong body odor recently and asked him if he was okay. Roger told him that his spouse was very ill, and with all of the care he had to give at home, he had been unable to get his shirts to the dry cleaners. Ray empathized with his situation, and his colleague thanked him for bringing the problem to his attention. By protecting Roger's self-esteem, Ray made it possible for him to correct the problem without embarrassment.

Be Real

This principle means that you will not allow problems to fester. In the example above, Ray didn't join in the complaining behind Roger's back. Instead he shared his concerns candidly and privately. It can be especially difficult to Be Real with the clueless colleague, since the issues can be very sensitive. Nevertheless, it is essential if clueless colleagues are to learn to become more considerate.

Your ability to raise your legitimate concerns in these situations is made easier by taking responsibility for your own behavior and maintaining a good working relationship with the clueless colleague. These three principles—Take Responsibility, Build Relationships, and

Be Real—work in tandem. However, they sometimes aren't sufficient to turn your clueless colleague into a considerate teammate.

Strategy: Collaborating

The Collaborating strategy often is necessary to accomplish that transformation. Collaborating with your clueless colleague means that you will take the time required to engage your coworker in discussion. Because these conversations tend to be sensitive, arrange to meet or converse in private. It's likely that your coworker is unaware of her impact and she may feel hurt, surprised, embarrassed, or defensive when faced with your constructive feedback.

> *One of the most helpful stances you can adopt when applying the Collaborating strategy to the behavior of a clueless colleague is one of curiosity.*

Remember that there are no absolutes or "shoulds" in these conversations. Speak about your own needs and preferences for workplace behavior and ask your colleague to share her preferences. Be careful not to ascribe negative motives to your coworker and take time to acknowledge her good intentions. Also, acknowledge any improvements you notice after your conversation.

One of the most helpful stances you can adopt when applying the Collaborating strategy to the behavior of a clueless colleague is one of curiosity. Rather than leaping to the conclusion that she is insensitive or uncaring, approach her with interest. After all, if she understood the effect she had on others, you probably wouldn't be having this conversation.

Here's how to use your peer power to handle:

- The excessive talker
- A jammed printer
- Loud noises

Dear Cynthia and Ray,

My boss is a total slob. He acts like everyone who works here should clean up after him. Literally! It drives me wild to have to wash his dirty dishes at the end of the day. Oh, and worse than that, he leaves food containers in the refrigerator until they turn green. You seem to be telling me to collaborate with clueless people, but I don't see how to make that work with my inconsiderate boss. How would you handle that?

— No More Mothering

Dear No More,

Unless it violates a contract, your boss has the right to decide that you should wash the dishes at the end of the day. We agree, however, that you shouldn't have to touch your boss's "science experiments."

Collaborating with your boss can work. Speak up and communicate your needs to your boss. Acknowledge that he is very busy and suggest a weekly refrigerator clean-out. You might offer to remind him on Thursday to take his old food items home. Ask for his ideas as well.

If he consistently forgets, a compromise might be that you sack up his old food containers on Friday and leave them on his desk to take home.

— Cynthia and Ray

Scenario: Dealing with the excessive talker

CLUELESS COLLEAGUE: Hey, what are you up to? You look busy this morning. I just had this great conversation with my old boss. Remember I told you about my old boss and the mansion she made an offer on? They accepted her offer. Unbelievable! She got it. She's really excited. It's a gorgeous house.

YOU: (Bring up the issue with your clueless colleague.) Ummmm...yes, I am busy. Li, this brings up something that I'd like to talk about for a minute. I've noticed that you drop by my office many mornings to talk. And usually I'm in the middle of something that I want to finish. Can we talk about a better time to socialize?

CLUELESS COLLEAGUE: (Sounding hurt)

No problem. If you don't want to talk, just tell me.

YOU: (Make an assertive request.)

I like talking to you, Li. But I'd like to chat when I'm not focused on getting work done. It's hard for me to get refocused after I've been interrupted.

CLUELESS COLLEAGUE: (Still sounding hurt)

I didn't mean to be an interruption.

YOU: (Acknowledge her good intentions.)

I know you didn't intend to interrupt me, Li. One of the things I like about working with you is how much fun we have talking about our friends. I don't want to lose that connection and I know you don't either. Frankly, I'm having a hard time being much of a friend when I feel so swamped by my work.

CLUELESS COLLEAGUE: My job is so tedious sometimes. Right now I have to code these legal documents until my eyes start to cross. There are hundreds of them. I just need to hang out for a few minutes and connect with humans instead of codes. Then I can get back to it.

YOU: (Paraphrase.)

It sounds like you get bored and just need a break in the morning. Is that it?

CLUELESS COLLEAGUE: Yes. I'm going crazy.

YOU: (Explore options that might satisfy you both.)

I enjoy chatting with you during the day but it doesn't work for me to interrupt my work. Can we agree to schedule time to socialize? I wouldn't mind joining you for a break in the lounge around 10:30. Would you be okay going to the lounge instead of coming to my office? I can meet you there.

CLUELESS COLLEAGUE: You mean that you'll only talk to me at scheduled times?

YOU: Not exactly. Of course, I'll talk to you at other times. I just won't interrupt my work when I'm trying to stay focused. Can we agree to take a break at 10:30 this morning? I'd love to hear about your old boss's new house when I can really take in the details. You're a great storyteller.

CLUELESS COLLEAGUE: Well, okay. I guess we can try that. You could also post a sign that said "Please don't interrupt me right now." That way I'll know to go talk to someone else.

YOU: (Summarize your agreement.)
Sure, I can do that, too, if it helps you to know when I'm busy. So, we've agreed to meet for breaks at 10:30 in the lounge, right?

CLUELESS COLLEAGUE: Sure. Let's try that and see if it works. And you'll post a sign so that I can see that it isn't a good time to talk.

YOU: Right. Now, I need to get this project done. See you at 10:30 in the lounge. Save me some chocolate-covered peanuts, please.

Scenario: Dealing with jamming the printer

YOU: Li, thanks for spending a few minutes with me to talk about a situation that's been bothering me.

CLUELESS COLLEAGUE: No problem. What's up?

YOU: In the last few days, when I've gone into the copy room, I've found that the printer is jammed.

CLUELESS COLLEAGUE: Yeah, I hate that printer. It jams all the time, just when I'm in a rush to get a project copied for Tom. And it never jams in the same place twice!

YOU: I'm sure you don't know this but over the past few days, I'm the one who has unjammed the copier when it's been left jammed. It's been frustrating to me that I have to fix the printer before I can use it.

CLUELESS COLLEAGUE: Aw, gee. I'm sorry about that, leaving the printer for you to fix. If it's any consolation, I unjam the copier all the time. I've just been in a hurry this week trying to get this rush project done for Tom. You know, we really ought to buy a new printer so that we're not constantly fixing these jams.

YOU: (Rather than arguing with her, agreeing with her, or proving her wrong, acknowledge her need.)

It sounds like you've had a busy, stressful week working on an important project.

CLUELESS COLLEAGUE: Yes, and unfortunately Tom has had to make additional corrections to the report, so we'll have to do the whole printing project again.

YOU: (Empathize. Then gain her agreement to the underlying issue.) That's too bad. Sounds like you are going to be spending a lot of time in the copy room this week. Li, several of us have to share the printer. And when the printer jams, someone has to fix it. Would you agree with that?

CLUELESS COLLEAGUE: Well, yes, certainly. We all need to cooperate to keep the printer humming along.

YOU: (Paraphrase her point of view.) You're also saying that you are working on important projects and don't always have time to unjam the printer.

CLUELESS COLLEAGUE: Right. C'mon. You can't tell me that you don't look the other way sometimes when that printer locks up.

YOU: (Laughing) (Define the problem and brainstorm solutions.) Well, I will admit I'm tempted to walk away when it makes that high-pitched, squeaky noise. However, I think we need to come up with a solution to this pesky printer that works for everyone. What ideas do you have?

CLUELESS COLLEAGUE: You mean besides taking care of my own print jams?

YOU: (Avoid the temptation to blame her for this problem.) Certainly, one way to handle it is for everyone to agree to fix the printer when it jams on her job.

CLUELESS COLLEAGUE: That won't work when we're all in a rush.

YOU: (Ask for more ideas if she rejects yours.) What are some other options?

CLUELESS COLLEAGUE: Another idea is to buy a new printer that is a heckuva lot more reliable than this one.

YOU: (Don't discount her idea, even though you may think it is unworkable. Continue to brainstorm.)
Or we could assign the responsibility for fixing jams to one person each week. We could keep a schedule for printer duty.

CLUELESS COLLEAGUE: That's an interesting idea. I like the idea of knowing when it's my week to obsess about paper jams. I really think I need more training, though, on how to clear some of them. Have you seen that bright yellow light that flashes on the panel just before the printer conks out? I have no idea what I've done that makes it do that. It's really weird.

YOU: Why don't we schedule a 30-minute training session with Margot next week? She's the expert when it comes to these printers.

CLUELESS COLLEAGUE: Great. I can learn from the master.

YOU: (Be careful not to rescue Li by doing all of the work. Ask her to contribute to the solution.)
Would you be willing to discuss this with Margot and put together a proposed schedule for next month?

CLUELESS COLLEAGUE: Sure, I can do that by tomorrow.

YOU: Thanks, Li. I knew we could figure this out.

Scenario: Dealing with loud noises (e.g., music playing, loud conversations)

YOU: Li, would you mind turning down Pandora for a minute so we can chat?

CLUELESS COLLEAGUE: (She turns down her computer speakers.)
I love Pandora. It's so cool to be able to play my favorite music on my computer while I work.

YOU: Well, that's what I'd like to talk with you about.

CLUELESS COLLEAGUE: I can show you how to use it. You just go to this website and create an account. Do you want me to walk you through the steps?

YOU: No, thank you. Believe it or not, I actually can't concentrate when music is playing.

CLUELESS COLLEAGUE: No way. Really? My brain works way better when I've got my favorite tunes playing.

YOU: (Define the problem by summarizing your needs.)
It sounds like you concentrate better when Pandora is on. And I concentrate better when it's quiet.

CLUELESS COLLEAGUE: If you're about to tell me I can't play my music, I just want to remind you that company policy says that we can listen to music. I looked it up. Stand up and look over these cubicle walls. Bob is listening to something. Jennifer is practically dancing on her desk.

YOU: (Reduce the defensiveness as much as possible. Stress that your goal is to meet her needs as well.)
I admit that you and others enjoy listening to music. I just find it very distracting. I'd like to find a way that we can both get what we need. Last week, I had to write up the cost figures for the management team report. It took me forever. And I made a bunch of dumb mistakes that my boss caught, fortunately before the report went to senior management.

CLUELESS COLLEAGUE: And that's my problem, because...?

YOU: (Don't respond to her use of sarcasm. Explore options that you can both live with.)
Would you be willing to kick around some options that still give you the opportunity to listen to music but also give me the quiet that I need to concentrate?

CLUELESS COLLEAGUE: Well, okay, as long as you're not telling me I can't play music at all. I suppose I could turn it off completely a few hours a week.

YOU: (Encourage her contribution. Continue to explore options.)
Thanks for suggesting that. I like that idea. What about using a headset? That way you never have to turn Pandora off.

CLUELESS COLLEAGUE: I hate wearing a headset. I'd rather just turn the volume down and move the speaker closer to me. You know, you could wear a headset and listen to white noise, like ocean sounds, to cancel out the music playing in the office.

YOU: (Summarize your agreement.)

You're right. I could listen to ocean sounds. That might just work. So, it sounds like we have some good options here. First, I'll tell you some hours of the week that I really need you to turn off the music completely.

CLUELESS COLLEAGUE: Okay. I'll fix these speakers so they're not pointing in your direction, and I'll go into the audio settings and turn down the volume.

YOU: And I'll look for a recording of soothing ocean waves crashing on the beach. That may take me a few days.

CLUELESS COLLEAGUE: No, it won't. My daughter was a light sleeper when she was a baby. I actually have a CD of ocean waves that we used to play in her room to help her sleep at night. I'll bring it to work tomorrow.

YOU: Great. Thanks, Li, for being such a considerate teammate and helping to find a solution that works for both of us. Let's try it out for a couple of weeks and then see if we're both happy with the results.

Plan B (If Your Initial Strategy Fails)

If your clueless colleague won't collaborate or become a considerate teammate, the Plan B strategy is Compromising. When you compromise to negotiate a solution, you give a little to get a little. For example, you might agree to wear ear plugs so you don't have to listen to loud music if she agrees to turn the music off when she's not at her desk. Or you might agree to take responsibility for fixing the printer jams if your colleague agrees to take responsibility for emptying the trash at night.

If you aren't able to come to agreement even using the

Dear Cynthia and Ray,

I work with several people who love to eat fish for lunch every day. They heat up their lunch in the microwave in the kitchen and the smell wafts through the office the rest of the afternoon. I feel terrible because they're all from the same country and they eat a lot of fish. I hate that smell. I wonder if I'm being culturally clueless, but it's getting so bad that I'm thinking of quitting my job. How should I handle this?

— Culturally Clueless

Dear Culturally,

Microwaves do intensify odors whether that smell is of fish, hearty spices, or something else. This situation calls for the Collaborating strategy. We suggest you approach one person (not the whole group) and let her know of your concern. As with any sensitive issue, have this discussion privately so that your coworker can save face over the issue.

Acknowledge that everyone has likes and dislikes. You might say, "I know this isn't intentional and you're probably not aware of how this is affecting me." Or "I may be more sensitive to smells than other people." Ask for help in solving this problem so everyone feels good about the outcome. Then ask for her ideas and suggest a few options that might help (for example, liberal use of air freshener or turning on the ventilation fan). When you notice improvements in the office odor during the day, be sure to thank your coworker.

— Cynthia and Ray

Compromising strategy, you may have to shift to the Going Head-to-Head strategy and take the issue to your manager for resolution. If you choose to follow this course of action, invite your coworker to go with you rather than complaining about the situation behind her back. You might say, "Li, I've been trying to work with you to come to an agreement that we can both live with. However, we just don't seem to be able to work this out. I would like to take our issues to our boss because I think he needs to hear about this. He's free now for a conversation. Would you like to come with me to discuss what's happening?"

As a last resort, you may need to use the Caring-for-Self strategy to handle your clueless colleague's behavior. Wear a sweater if the office is too cold. Put on ear plugs if the office is too noisy. Post signs if you don't want to be interrupted. Use air freshener if you dislike the smells emanating from the kitchen. Move to another office or another job if you can.

Avoid turning these situations into control battles that mimic the squabbling between siblings.

- Don't escalate the conflict by getting into a childish battle of wills over your coworker's behavior.

- Don't retaliate by doing it back to her, only louder or messier.

- Don't rescue her by agreeing to do something that you resent (for example, washing all of the coffee mugs left in the sink).

Moving Forward

If there is an ongoing pattern of clueless behavior that is not eliminated by dealing with the immediate issue, then you need to address this pattern. Bring it up and ask what your coworker needs in order to be able to change the pattern. Be sure to acknowledge any improvements in her behavior so that she'll continue them. Consider using the Going Head-to-Head strategy as a last resort.

The Rest of the Story

Cynthia began to close her door to indicate when she was not available to talk. She and Li agreed to meet for coffee or lunch once a week and socialize at that time. Li continued to wander down the hall looking for someone to talk to during the day, but she stopped seeking Cynthia out for idle chit-chat. By setting clearer boundaries and communicating them to Li, as well as meeting Li's need to socialize, Cynthia was able to manage her relationship with her clueless colleague.

Cheat Sheet for the Clueless Colleague

Definition: A clueless colleague is a coworker who is insensitive to her negative impact on the work environment.

Clues

The coworker:

- Places inappropriate posters on the wall
- Doesn't clean up her messes
- Talks too loudly in the hallway, at her desk, or on her cell phone
- Inadvertently broadcasts private or personal information
- Interrupts others frequently
- Borrows items or money and doesn't return them
- Jams the printer or photocopier (and doesn't fix it)
- Leaves dirty dishes in the sink
- Clips her fingernails (or toenails) at work
- Makes inappropriate sounds—whistles, burps, slurps, sniffs
- Plays loud music
- Sets the thermostat too high or low
- Has body odor
- Leaves dirty tissues all over her desk
- Makes long-winded pronouncements on topics or talks excessively
- Leaves long-winded voice mail messages
- Copies you on e-mails you don't need to see
- Causes people regularly to complain about her impact
- Causes you to feel annoyed or disrespected

Helpful Assumptions

- Clueless colleagues often make valuable contributions.
- They are a mix of strengths and weaknesses (like you).
- They are often more focused on goals and tasks than on building relationships.
- They may not realize others are irritated by their actions.
- Their behavior is not personal.
- You may have differing values and preferences.
- You may be clueless at times.
- You have a right to take care of yourself.

Key Principles and Practices

Take Responsibility

- Consider your role and how you might have contributed.
- Respect your needs. Anticipate her needs and take preventive action.
- Perform well by modeling behavior you would like to see.
- Communicate your needs. Establish ground rules.

Build Relationships

- Reduce her stress.
- Network with and help her so she gets to know you.
- Show empathy for her challenges and stressors.
- Protect her self-esteem.

Be Real

- Bring up your concerns.

Strategy: Collaborating

- Take time to engage in a discussion.

- Arrange to talk privately.
- Adopt a stance of curiosity about your differences.
- Bring up your concerns.
- Acknowledge her needs and good intentions.
- Use lots of paraphrasing and listen well to her.
- Clarify each of your needs.
- Explore mutually satisfying options.
- Summarize agreements.
- Acknowledge improvements.

Plan B (If Your Initial Strategy Fails)

- Use Compromising to give a little and get a little.
- If Compromising fails, shift to Going Head-to-Head and take the issues to management (invite your coworker to join you).
- As a last resort, use Caring-for-Self: Do what is necessary to reduce the clueless colleague's impact.
- Don't escalate the conflict by getting into a childish battle of wills.
- Don't retaliate by doing it back to her, only louder or messier.
- Don't rescue her by agreeing to do something that you resent.

Worksheet

1. What clues make you suspect you may be dealing with a clueless colleague?

2. Assuming you've determined the person is a clueless colleague, what are her legitimate needs?

3. What are this clueless colleague's strengths?

4. How could you Take Responsibility, Build Relationships, or Be Real with the clueless colleague?

5. Focus on one clueless behavior. How can you use the Collaborating strategy to calmly address your issue? What might you say?

6. What response do you anticipate and how will you handle it?

7. What is your Plan B if you are not successful?

from the faux-smart boss to the knowledgeable leader

Some bosses are not open to any input. Everything must be done, as Frank Sinatra sang, "my way." They discourage suggestions by arguing with any they get, and they sometimes even say they don't want your ideas. They are very poor listeners. They micromanage and don't delegate. Their behavior can lead to damaging decisions and poor morale. We call them faux-smart bosses. They think they are smart but they are blind to their own flaws. What distinguishes them is their unrealistic confidence in their own ideas and skills, often accompanied by a lack of confidence in their employees.

While Ray has been blessed with many good managers, early in his career he reported to a faux-smart boss. Tom had been a production manager in an aerospace company for many years. Just prior to hiring Ray, he had become a manager in Human Resources. When he interviewed Ray, he said he was counting on him to help create a new performance system for the company.

Very quickly Ray discovered that Tom was not open to his input. Tom had a lot of expertise in performance systems and he already knew what he wanted. Tom disagreed with almost every suggestion Ray made. He told Ray that he was under a tight deadline and that there was no time for discussion. At one point he yelled at Ray, told him he was not a "team player," and put himself back in charge of the project. He began to micromanage Ray on his other assignments. Ray saw Tom behave the same way with his other employees. Consequently team morale and productivity were low.

Clues to the Faux-Smart Boss

A variety of clues indicate that you are dealing with a faux-smart boss. From his position of power and leadership, he:

- Argues when others give input

- Insists upon doing things his way

- Makes impulsive and unwise decisions

- Micromanages his employees

- Asks his employees to ignore company policies or procedures

- Refuses to delegate much

- Takes back tasks once delegated

- Rates his employees too critically

- Hires employees who tend to agree with him

- Shows favoritism to people who agree with him

- Pontificates at the drop of a hat

- Refuses to acknowledge mistakes

Let's look at the assumptions you might hold after accumulating clues that point to a faux-smart boss, and how you might shift them in order to survive and thrive under his knowledgeable leadership.

Helpful Assumptions

The faux-smart boss appears to be a commanding control freak. The loud and clear signal of "it's my way or the highway" seems to break every best practice in the book on how to manage effectively. Such a boss doesn't listen well, doesn't utilize his employees' unique talents, and doesn't value ways of learning and contributing other than his own.

If your style and mindset don't magically match your boss's, your choices seem obvious: hit the proffered highway or become a yes-person. Neither of these is an optimal solution for you or your company.

Organizations need differing opinions, not yes-men and yes-women. There are too many examples in business and political history where disasters occurred because a groupthink mentality ruled or those with contrary opinions were reluctant to express them. A famous one involved the tragic explosion of the space shuttle Challenger in 1986 due to defective O-rings. Long before the accident occurred, NASA engineers had expressed concerns about the reliability of the O-rings, and yet management at higher levels failed to address the issue for fear that project funding would be cut. Nobody had the courage to use peer power to express a view contrary to the desired one. We can look to the disastrous oil spill in the Gulf of Mexico to confirm that nearly 25 years later, we are still living through catastrophes caused by faux-smart bosses. The message is not (necessarily) to go above your boss's head, but to recognize your right, and perhaps your duty, to voice your views.

> *Organizations need differing opinions, not yes-men and yes-women.*

Before you run to a more accommodating supervisor, consider trying to see your boss in a different light. This might allow you to prompt changes in his style or at least find ways to work with him that benefit you, your coworkers, and your organization.

Softening your reaction to your boss begins by understanding that his difficult behavior is driven by hidden needs. He may desperately want to be right. He may value expertise highly. He may desire perfection. He may refuse to entertain other people's viewpoints because he can't imagine there is validity to any opinion other than his own. He may be adapting to a culture that punishes failure.

It's easy to make certain assumptions of the faux-smart boss's drives. You might imagine that he prefers his way because of egotism and arrogance; that he hires people like himself because of a sense of elitism. But before you continue painting him as evil, consider that deeper anxieties or fears may trigger his approach. Perhaps the faux-smart individual:

- Feels humiliated when he is exposed as unknowledgeable

- Is insecure about his job or himself

- Feels uncomfortable with change

- Bases his self-esteem on a display of expertise

- Feels pressured by a work culture that rewards the wrong priorities

Do any of these sound familiar? It's easier to be empathetic when we remember times that we chose a well-trodden path in times of uncertainty, feigned a false immodesty to hold off humiliation, or brazenly acted as a braggart when trying to impress.

You're probably familiar with the Peter Principle,[4] which suggests that employees tend to rise to their level of incompetence. The career path of the controlling, micromanaging boss typifies this principle. He's a productive employee because he independently applies smarts and skills to the problem at hand. But he's a poor player at the strategic level for exactly the same reasons. His independence relies on his own contributions and negates others'.

He probably does have considerable expertise with a good track record in his field. This was true in Ray's experience with Tom, whose expertise with performance systems was impressive. If you feel less negatively toward a person, it's easier to recognize his strengths and see ways that you can work with him effectively.

And consider that someone who seems like a know-it-all isn't

---

[4] Laurence J. Peter and Raymond Hull, *The Peter Principle: why things always go wrong.* (New York: William Morrow and Company, 1969).

necessarily stingy with what he knows. Instead of hoarding their knowledge, faux-smart bosses can be very active mentors because they want to share their understanding. This can be used to your and your organization's advantage.

Key Principles: Take Responsibility, Extend Respect, and Be Real

To all outward appearances, the faux-smart boss is arrogant, conceited, and egotistical. Within, he has fears and anxieties and defense mechanisms like the rest of us. Knowing that we share some of his anxieties makes it easier for us to work with him in a caring, respectful way.

But it's only helpful to a point. We still want to have our own vision and style and to feel like our contributions are respected. By employing the following principles and practices in your daily routine, you can work more effectively with your manager and help him evolve from a faux-smart boss to a knowledgeable leader.

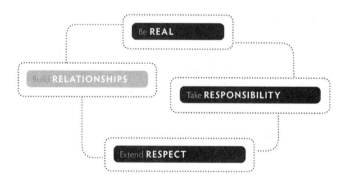

Take Responsibility

When you decide to be responsible for your own experience, you begin by examining the causes for your boss's behavior, then addressing how you can work with your boss and team to achieve your shared goals. Since his managing style is directed at your entire team, begin by resolving not to join your coworkers in a blame game, pity committee, or whining convention. Shift your focus from powerlessness to taking the reins of control over your experience (without, of course, becoming controlling yourself!). If others emulate your pragmatic approach, your team may survive intact and live to work together for better bosses in the future.

Communicate your progress and accomplishments frequently with your manager to build his confidence in you. E-mail is often the appropriate technology for status updates, since the updates are primarily informational in nature, and the boss can peruse them at his leisure. But when your boss is faux-smart, consider making it a point to update your status in face-to-face meetings. Once he feels he can rely on you for regular updates, his urge to seek you out will be reduced. Eventually it will be easier to expand the time between meetings and to deliver your reports electronically, if that works best for your boss. In these first few sessions, clarify his expectations and set ground rules that relate to his tendency to control, like establishing reasonable target dates or taking on additional responsibilities upon reaching milestones.

Though you've identified him as faux-smart, he's still your boss. Help him by supporting his efforts to reach his goals and the company's goals. It is not rescuing when you help your boss; it builds his respect for you and your opinions. Since he values expertise, help to educate him by feeding him information—articles, websites, contacts, workbooks, etc. If he becomes a more knowledgeable leader with your help, perhaps he'll lose some of the rigidity and intellectual pride that makes him "faux-smart."

You may not get many kudos from a boss who is used to receiving them himself. Respect your own needs by not letting his lack of praise hurt your ego. Reward yourself for incremental improvements in your relationship, even if they remain unacknowledged.

Of course, for all of these efforts to work you'll need to be on top of your game to earn your boss's respect. Follow the practice of performing well. Before you suggest a plan or solution that is new or that differs from your manager's, do your homework. Make sure you have prepared your talking points and considered his preferences. Reduce the risks by double-checking your work for accuracy. Performing well also applies to habits: don't make excuses; don't make promises you can't keep; don't slack (slackers don't last long in this environment).

Extend Respect

Your faux-smart supervisor may behave very differently from you, even if you share some of the same fears. For example, you can both be uncomfortable with change, but your boss may be more apt to stick to the tried and true than dive into a new direction. Or when battling self-esteem issues, you might prefer to let others have their way while your boss argues with anyone who questions that he has the correct answer.

Your frustration with these differences can lead to conflict and tension. You might say to yourself, "If only my supervisor were a better listener," or "I wish my supervisor would delegate more." These statements usually mean, "I wish my supervisor would become more like me." This wish is no more than a pipe dream. You may be able to influence your boss through information and education. However, it is extremely rare for any supervisor—or even non-supervisor—to change his style significantly.

An important practice in the Extend Respect principle is to honor differences. With a faux-smart boss, try to mirror his style while interacting with him. Keep your messages brief and focused on the task and demonstrate decisiveness. Use the forms of communication and technology he prefers. Also, keep in mind that just because your boss's opinions are different from yours, his views probably have some merit.

Ray had a boss who frequently asked for his advice. Ray usually presented several alternatives with their advantages and disadvantages. During one of these discussions she told him his approach was frustrating her. Her approach was action oriented—she wanted a recommendation, not alternatives. Afterwards Ray modified his approach to mirror her style. Not only did their relationship improve considerably, but when he gave his recommendation first she would frequently request additional alternatives.

Use the practice of listening well so that you *can* honor your faux-smart boss's opinions and acknowledge their merits. And who knows? By modeling good listening, you may get him to listen as well. Request your boss's opinions in situations where you truly welcome them, especially if they fall within his area of expertise. Say, "I know that you have some experience with this issue. Can you help me brainstorm some approaches to deal with it?"

> *Request your boss's opinions in situations where you truly welcome them, especially if they fall within his area of expertise.*

In writing this book together, Cynthia would occasionally take a passionate position, arguing her points vigorously. Ray, using his best listening skills, would often hear her out and then calmly state, "You are making some good points," followed by skillful paraphrasing of Cynthia's thoughts. His open listening made it possible for Cynthia to relax her position and listen to Ray's concerns. Good listening works just as well with faux-smart bosses who, finding their opinions respected, may even begin to rethink their own faulty conclusions and become knowledgeable leaders.

You'll find that listening to a faux-smart boss has additional advantages. Since you are dealing with someone who tends to micromanage, it's to your advantage to be totally clear on your assignments and perform them correctly. Your boss will respect you, pay more attention to your ideas, and perhaps trust you enough to micromanage less. Don't be afraid to use lots of paraphrasing and questioning in your interactions. The same listening skills can benefit you when it comes to dealing with criticism: ask for specifics, don't get defensive, thank him for being open, and acknowledge your mistakes. Following these guidelines for honoring differences and listening well does not guarantee that your faux-smart boss will have confidence in you and your opinions. There are no guarantees in life, except death, taxes, and work challenges. But using the guidelines can reduce your work challenges with your boss. (We're sorry that it won't help with the other two items.)

Respect the organizational hierarchy and culture. Our conversations with management over the years have helped us identify some employee behaviors that they find particularly unproductive:

- Bad-mouthing the boss or organization
- Making unreasonable requests
- Breaking confidences
- Ignoring the boss's time pressures
- Bringing problems without suggesting any possible solutions

If you want to gain your boss's support, try to avoid these behaviors.

Be loyal. When your boss is ready to make an impulsive decision without the input of his team, communicate your concerns in private, tactfully, and at a time when he is receptive. After their initial clashes, Ray had some success

> *Once a decision has been finalized by your management, stop arguing or criticizing it.*

with Tom using this tactic. When approached with respect one on one, Tom seemed more open to hearing other ideas than when in a group setting.

Once a decision has been finalized, stop arguing or criticizing it. You can privately point out disappointing results as long as you are trying to improve things rather than trying to prove that you were right.

Be Real

It should come as no surprise that a key practice when dealing with a faux-smart individual is to express what's on your mind. Unless you share your thoughts, you can't respect your own needs or act toward your boss responsibly and with integrity. Remember the Challenger O-rings. Rather than think critical thoughts about his decisions in silence, openly and authentically express your observations and questions.

The faux-smart boss has a tendency to steamroll employees into his way of working. Don't let that happen. To build your courage, skill, and tact in voicing your concerns, begin with relatively easy situations and agreements. Anticipate his objections and plan your responses. Practice what you'll say before you meet. And reward yourself after a tough conversation, no matter how it turns out.

Strategy: Coaching or Collaborating

The suggested principles and practices stress the importance of communication, acting professionally and with integrity, and showing expertise. They are aimed at understanding your boss and adapting your behavior accordingly, so that you can continue to contribute effectively to your team and your organization. When they don't transform your faux-smart boss to a knowledgeable leader, turn to either the Coaching or the Collaborating strategy.

In some situations your boss's blind spot, pride, or micromanagement results in behavior or decisions that affect the organization more than you. In these cases, such as when your boss is implementing a new performance strategy that will not work, try the Coaching strategy. Though a faux-smart boss may not be receptive to this strategy, you owe it to the organization to give peer power a try. When his behavior primarily affects you personally—such as when your boss micromanages you, delegates little to you, or is convinced your performance is worse than it is—

> *Though a faux-smart boss may not be receptive to this strategy, you owe it to the organization to give peer power a try.*

Dear Cynthia and Ray,

It seems like you are suggesting we "kiss up" to an incompetent boss. I don't want to be seen as a "kiss up" by my coworkers. Can't this partnership with my boss go too far?

— Opposed to Kisses

Dear Opposed,

Our view is that it is not "kissing up," unless this phrase means to try to work well with someone in order for both of you to be successful. Yes, without becoming buddies, you will do nice things for your supervisor, but you will do them openly, sincerely, and with no ulterior or selfish motive. You will do them because it is in the best interest of your supervisor as well as yourself and, most importantly, of your organization. And at times you will even disagree with your supervisor.

While working well with your boss is likely to be a key to your productivity and job satisfaction, there are some risks. One is that your peers might be jealous of this relationship and resent you for being the "teacher's pet." To reduce the chances of this, show them the same respect you show your boss, do not build your relationship with your boss at your peers' expense, and do not gloat about your relationship with your boss.

— Cynthia and Ray

choose the Collaborating strategy. Whichever you choose, meet face to face or by teleconferencing when you both have adequate time to work through the issues.

We'll look at a sample case that involves Coaching. Remember that Coaching usually involves asking good questions that help the person figure out what is happening ("What results are you now getting?" "What will be the effects of implementing that policy?"); what he wants to happen ("What is your goal?"); and some possible solutions ("What are your suggestions?" "Where can you get more information?").

The Coaching strategy can be used to advantage when the faux-smart boss:

- Makes an organizational mistake

Later we'll see how a Collaborating strategy is employed with:

- Micromanaging
- Unfair performance feedback

Scenario: Dealing with making an organizational mistake

When you strongly feel that your boss is making a mistake that has company-wide consequences, you owe it to the organization to state your case. A faux-smart boss will be reluctant to listen to direct counterarguments for fear of humiliation. Ask questions that let him think through the decisions he is making. Give him a way to save face.

FAUX-SMART BOSS: Thanks for writing up the conclusions for the performance management recommendation. I appreciate your reviewing the report and ensuring that it is 100 percent accurate. I know we have plenty of time before the presentation, but we don't want to look sloppy in front of the executive team.

YOU: (Show sincerity in acknowledging his expertise.)
Tom, I see a lot of value in this approach. However, I notice that you decided to stay with having a single incentive plan for all the non-sales departments. As you'll recall, I had suggested that it might make sense to use a different approach for the sales support team.

FAUX-SMART BOSS: I remember. It was not a bad idea, mind you. I know you once worked in that group. But in the end, I felt it unnecessarily complicated things.

YOU: (When a request or suggestion is rejected by your faux-smart boss, don't debate the decision. If you feel his decision will harm the organization, acknowledge your concerns and ask for permission to provide information or coaching without using the word "coaching.")

I still have some reservations. My goal, like yours, is to see that the plan enhances productivity. Would you be open to exploring this further?

FAUX-SMART BOSS: Sure, I'd be happy to help you understand the grand strategy. It's pretty fascinating how incentives affect behavior. Once you learn to control incentives, you can control behavior.

YOU: (Sincerely demonstrate curiosity about his position.)
Perhaps I'm wrong, but I've always been under the impression that incentive plans should be tied to revenue or profit goals. What is your thought about this?

FAUX-SMART BOSS: Well, I know from experience that it doesn't pay to be too transparent. By not being explicit, we have more flexibility. For example, we can just state that the bonus will be based on a combination of revenues and profits. We can determine the exact formula and therefore the exact impact on our bottom line when our financial picture is clearer at the end of the year.

YOU: (Paraphrase to check your understanding.)
You're saying that if we are less explicit about the relationship between finances and bonuses, we can adjust the formulas so that we can better control how much money is spent in bonuses at the end of the year.

FAUX-SMART BOSS: That's right. I couldn't have said it better myself. This company has never given bonuses, you know. The rank and file are not going to sweat the details.

YOU: (Acknowledge where he's right.)
I understand how that approach allows us to better control our expenses. That seems like it would be accepted just fine with the general employee. They probably won't question the details that much, as you say.

FAUX-SMART BOSS: And the sales team of course has a separate incentive plan. We decided not to touch that. Sales are unique in that they are closer to the numbers; their actions directly affect revenue. We don't want to mess with their motivation.

YOU: (If you still think your boss is making a mistake, you owe it to the organization to continue to ask coaching questions. Don't argue with him, however, and stop coaching if he becomes defensive.)

From your experience, how will the new plan be accepted by the sales support team? They are unique in that, like sales, a portion of their salary is closely tied to the financial results within their territory. I see some risks here.

FAUX-SMART BOSS: Well, that's a good question, Ray. Their salary will still be tied to their territory, but it will use the same formula as we use for everyone else. Yes, they won't know until we make our final decisions what that formula will be, but their paycheck won't vary too much from previous years. So there should be no reason for concern.

YOU: (Paraphrase. It will help the faux-smart boss to hear something stated back to him.)

I hear you saying that because the sales support team will end up being paid approximately the same as before, they won't be concerned that the incentives aren't explicitly stated until the end of the year.

FAUX-SMART BOSS: Well... I guess there may be some uncertainty. They are closer to the action; they'll be watching the numbers. But they needn't worry.

YOU: You mentioned that incentives affect behavior. How do you think the new incentive plan might affect the behavior of sales support?

FAUX-SMART BOSS: Hmm. It's hard to say. Uncertainty tends to make behavior unpredictable. You've worked with that group. What do you think?

YOU: (While coaching, it's okay to provide training, information, or options when asked or given permission.)

I agree that there will be uncertainty. The sales support group is like the sales team. They keep a very close eye on the revenue numbers, and their individual effort more directly affects revenue than other teams. That's probably why they are rewarded in a way that is similar to sales. Because of the uncertainty, I wouldn't be surprised if they ease up somewhat on their efforts.

FAUX-SMART BOSS: Those are good points. I'll have to think about this.

YOU: (Make it clear that while you are giving feedback, the decision is your boss's to make. It's also important to let the faux-smart boss save face if he realizes he has made a mistake.)
Of course, this is just my opinion. I understand that the incentive plan is your responsibility.

FAUX-SMART BOSS: Yes, that's right. I pride myself in gathering all the data that will affect behavior. My former company didn't have this hybrid style of reward structure, you know.

YOU: Tom, if you'd like, I can send you information on how sales support is currently compensated.

FAUX-SMART BOSS: Thanks, Ray. I would appreciate that. I believe we should modify the plan somewhat to accommodate sales support. That information will be useful.

Coaching in front of others is trickier. You still need to ask if the person is open to other input. If you get approval but don't quickly work things out, then drop the attempt. You don't want the boss to go through a possibly lengthy coaching session while others are watching. Afterwards you can ask the boss if he would like to continue the discussion in private.

Now let's look at how the Collaborating strategy works when the boss's mistakes affect you personally.

Scenario: Dealing with micromanaging

Coaching is not an appropriate strategy when your boss's behavior affects you personally, as in the case of micromanagement. In this situation, choose the Collaborating strategy. The goal of this strategy is to meet the needs of you both. You want freedom from control so you

Dear Cynthia and Ray,

I am dealing with a faux-smart person who is a coworker rather than my boss. He is a complete know-it-all. He disagrees with almost everything I say and won't listen to any of my ideas. It is particularly frustrating when he does this in our team meetings. He seems to monitor my tasks constantly and tells me how to do my job. Should I use Coaching with him even though he is not my boss?

— Too Many Bosses

Dear Too Many,

Coaching would not be appropriate since your coworker's behavior mostly affects you, not the organization. Decide how harmful it is, and if you can't ignore his actions, then try Collaborating. Meet with him privately and let him know how you would like his behavior to change. Try to discover the reasons for his behavior and what needs he is trying to meet. See if you can come to an agreement that will satisfy both of you. If you can't work it out, you may need to use the Going Head-to-Head strategy, a strategy you would avoid using if he were your boss.

— Cynthia and Ray

can work at a highly productive level. Your boss needs to have confidence that you are doing your job the way he wants it done. Let's look at a scenario involving your boss, Judy.

YOU: (It is very important when making your assertive request to allow the faux-smart boss to save face by sincerely acknowledging her good intentions. Stress your desire to meet her needs, too.) Judy, when I make a decision to go forward with implementation that is then countermanded by you, I find my need for autonomy challenged. I am the kind of employee who really appreciates autonomy and tends to be most productive when I have that. Also, I can lose my team's respect, which affects their productivity and mine. I really want to be productive for you and our department. I realize that you care a lot about what we do and our success and you want to make sure what we are doing is effective. I am hoping it will work for you to let me make these decisions in the future. What do you think?

FAUX-SMART BOSS: Hmm.... I am glad you brought this up. I just have some real concerns about the decisions that are being made. I worry that our customers won't like them.

YOU: (It is important to demonstrate that you are listening and that you care about her concerns.)
Well, it seems you are saying that you do this because of your desire to please our customers. I, too, am eager to do that. I feel that what I am asking of you will please them.

FAUX-SMART BOSS: I just can't agree to letting you make these decisions on your own.

YOU: (Pose alternatives that would work for you.)
Well, another alternative would be for me to find out from you ahead of time what you want me to keep in mind when I make the decision. Then I could make the decision on my own with your concerns in mind. Would that work for you?

FAUX-SMART BOSS: I think so, at least most of the time. I just want you to consider my concerns when you make decisions. Let's give this a try.

YOU: That works for me. I will check with you before making these decisions. Thanks so much for being flexible.

Afterwards acknowledge any improvements that occur and offer coaching if she needs help implementing the plan.

Scenario: Your performance feedback is unfair

The faux-smart boss tends to rate his employees more critically than other bosses. His expectations are often higher, and he is not hesitant to take back tasks that were once delegated. It's as though he judges performance through a lens that compares his employees to perfection instead of to reasonable standards.

This may result in unfair performance feedback. In this scenario, the employee uses the Collaborating strategy so that she can meet her need for a fair appraisal and her boss's need for strong workplace performance.

FAUX-SMART BOSS: I'm afraid I have to give you a less than stellar appraisal of your mid-year performance. (He hands you the review.) I know you have worked long hours and have the respect of your project team. But I have heard grumblings from your client, and your schedule has slipped. Not only has it slipped, but I did not realize there was a change in the milestone dates until I heard it from the rest of the management team at the status meeting. You requested more autonomy at the start of this period, and I granted it to you. But I still expected to be made aware of important changes in a timely manner.

YOU: (After listening very carefully to make sure you have understood the criticism, paraphrase it to determine if you understand properly.)
I hear you saying that my performance rating is negatively impacted because the project schedule has slipped and the client is unhappy, though the project team appears content. You are also unhappy because you felt blindsided about the new milestone dates. Is that correct?

FAUX-SMART BOSS: Yes, that's correct. Right now I feel that our experiment in giving you more freedom is in danger of failing.

YOU: (Do not get defensive or try to convince the boss he is wrong. Instead, attempt to collaborate to meet your needs [a positive appraisal] as well as your boss's [good performance from you.])
I appreciate your telling me your concerns. Would it be okay if I provided additional information that you may not have that shows that the project is performing well?

FAUX-SMART BOSS: Well, I am willing to listen, but I have already thought about this sufficiently.

YOU: (If the boss agrees, provide the information in a non-argumentative way. Tactfully point out why and how the appraisal should be changed and check to see if the changes work for the boss.)

Our agreement as I understood it at the start of the project was that I would give you a weekly status update of the project, but at a high level. You'll remember that I provided separate status indicators for schedule, budget, and resources, and that I documented red-flag issues. I feel I have followed through with that promise. Do you agree with this?

FAUX-SMART BOSS: That doesn't explain the low client satisfaction or the schedule change. With the old status reporting system, I would have known in detail what was going on so that I could nip problems in the bud.

YOU: (Do some more paraphrasing rather than getting into an argument.)
It seems you are saying that I did give you the reports, but that you needed more detail in them. Is that right?

FAUX-SMART BOSS: Yes, that is what I was expecting.

YOU: I did not realize that is what you wanted. Could I give you some more information about the clients grumbling?

FAUX-SMART BOSS: Okay.

YOU: All I can tell you is that my business liaison is extremely happy with our progress. Things are moving very well with no major hiccups. The schedule slippage is at the Marketing team's request. They have members of the project team who are working on both this project and their regular jobs—maybe that's where the grumbling is coming from. They will be even more overwhelmed near the end of the year. My Marketing liaison asked if we could push one of the milestones back. I've juggled the schedule to make sure this will not impact the end date.

FAUX-SMART BOSS: But there is still the issue of me finding out about the slippage in a meeting with other managers. I felt a little humiliated, to tell you the truth.

YOU: I am sorry about that. I am sure I gave the schedule a yellow status, meaning there were issues but not important ones. I only enter details with red flags, not for yellow ones. I am now clearer on what you are looking for. With my explanations for the slippage and the client satisfaction, would it be possible to update your comments and change the grading of my review?

FAUX-SMART BOSS: Well, you've been a good employee. I accept your explanation of the client satisfaction issue and the health of the project. I'll remove those negative comments from the review and give you a few more points on your rating. But we still need to make improvements to the status reporting.

YOU: (In this scenario, the boss has agreed halfway. If there are open issues, you should clarify what the boss needs in the future and agree to it or pose other alternatives that hopefully will work for both of you.)
I appreciate that. Would it work for you if I changed the status reporting guidelines to include a detailed explanation of any yellow-flag issues, in addition to red ones?

FAUX-SMART BOSS: Yes, that works for me. But set up a meeting to discuss if we need to add more information to those reports.

If the negative feedback on the performance appraisal is not resolved using Collaborating, it may be necessary for you to move to Plan B.

Plan B (If Your Initial Strategy Fails)

It's natural to feel discouraged if your attempts at Coaching or Collaborating fail. You've attempted to handle a characteristically stubborn individual with care and respect, and think his decision was an obvious mistake. However, it would be a mistake to undermine that decision or criticize it to others. Your reaction would model how to abdicate responsibility for your own experience.

And don't bother revisiting the issue with your boss. If he didn't budge after your first attempt, he's less likely to budge after the second. Ray realized the hard way with Tom that any decision made in the face of an opposing view against it was now cast in cement. This is not unusual for a faux-smart boss, as he is very unlikely to admit that he made a mistake.

When the Collaborating strategy fails, try the Compromising strategy. If your boss won't agree to give you more freedom in decision making, for example, you might offer to write up the various options, listing your recommendation along with advantages and disadvantages. That way he can get a sense of your reasoning and judgment. When his judgment differs, perhaps he might agree to give his reasons. This appeals to his desire to mentor. In time he may feel comfortable enough with your decisions (or overwhelmed enough with micromanaging the rest of your team) to offer you the independence that you're seeking.

Remember, the Caring-for-Self strategy is always there when all else fails. All three previous strategies have attempted to meet your boss's needs at least partially. It may be time to focus solely on yourself. If your negative performance appraisal isn't changed by the boss, you might tactfully note your disagreement in the comments section of the appraisal form. If you are losing time due to micromanagement (which is usually a time sink for both the manager and employee), be as time efficient as possible but refuse to work overtime perpetually. If your boss is making poor decisions that affect the attitude or emotional health of your team, do whatever is possible to salvage the situation to benefit you and your coworkers.

After all your efforts, if you think your manager still has you under his thumb with no relief in sight, consider taking him up on the message "it's my way or the highway." Do it with integrity (don't round up your friends to follow you; they need to make their own decisions). Of course, it is fine to answer questions truthfully and professionally during your exit interview. Don't leave your position rashly—research where you want to go and what form of management works best for you. While you're researching, continue to use the strategies and apply the principles and practices.

> ## Moving Forward
>
> If your boss continues to micromanage you on multiple projects or to habitually ignore your suggestions, it will not be effective to Collaborate with or Coach him on every issue. Select a few situations that are the most important to you. For other issues beyond your abilities, leave it to the boss's boss to address his managerial approach.

The Rest of the Story

The performance system that Ray worked on with Tom was implemented moderately successfully. A few of Ray's suggestions were later adopted. However, several of Tom's employees, including his most productive one, left the company within a few months. Ray found employment elsewhere in a little more than a year. Ray later heard that Tom was "retired" from the company shortly afterwards.

Cheat Sheet for the Faux-Smart Boss

Definition: The faux-smart boss has unrealistic confidence in his own ideas and skills, often accompanied by a lack of confidence in his employees.

Clues

The faux-smart boss:

- Argues when others give input
- Insists upon doing things his way
- Makes impulsive or unwise decisions
- Micromanages his employees
- Asks his employees to ignore company policies or procedures
- Refuses to delegate much
- Takes back tasks once delegated
- Rates his employees too critically
- Hires employees who tend to agree with him
- Shows favoritism to people who agree with him
- Pontificates at the drop of a hat
- Refuses to acknowledge mistakes

Helpful Assumptions

- The faux-smart boss:
  - May have a high need to be right
  - Values expertise
  - Wants perfection
  - Refuses to entertain other viewpoints
  - Feels humiliated when exposed as unknowledgeable
  - Can be very insecure about job or self

- - Can be uncomfortable with change
  - Feels pressured by a work culture that rewards the wrong priorities
  - Likes to mentor others and share what he knows
  - Usually has good intentions
  - Often has considerable expertise and a successful track record
- We all have been faux-smart at times.
- You have a right to express your opinion.

Key Principles and Practices

Take Responsibility

- Focus on what **you** can do. Don't become a whiner.
- Communicate frequently with your boss. Ask his opinions.
- Help your boss succeed.
- Respect your needs. Honor your own accomplishments.
- Perform well (so your boss will have confidence in you).
- Prepare thoroughly when presenting your ideas.

Extend Respect

- Honor differences. Adapt to your boss's style.
- Listen to clarify your boss's expectations.
- Be loyal. Correct misinformation but don't undermine.
- Respect the organization's culture.

Be Real

- Express what is on your mind.

Strategy: Coaching or Collaborating

Coaching (when the issue mostly affects the organization)

- Approach the issue using sincerity and tact.
- Ask for permission to provide information and coaching.
- Be curious. Listen well; paraphrase without arguing.
- Allow for face saving.
- Empathize with his situation; acknowledge his expertise.
- Ask questions that help your faux-smart boss assess the situation, determine goals, and come up with solutions.
- Do not dominate the conversation. Get his ideas first.
- Give options rather than a single solution.
- Allow the boss to save face when altering a position.
- Do not embarrass the boss in front of others.
- Let your boss come to his own conclusions and decisions.

Collaborating (when the issue mostly affects you personally)

- Schedule face-to-face discussions to resolve issues.
- Make assertive, clear requests that meet your boss's needs. Acknowledge good intentions.
- Do not get defensive or convince the boss he is wrong.
- Paraphrase frequently to demonstrate you are listening.
- Explore alternatives. Create joint solutions.
- If your boss evaluates you unfairly, ask to provide more information.
- Agree on the steps to implement joint solutions.
- Acknowledge any improvements afterwards.

Plan B (If Your Initial Strategy Fails)

- Avoid undermining your boss's decision or criticizing it to others.

- Avoid revisiting the issue with your boss.
- When Collaborating fails, move to Compromising.
- Caring-for-Self: Write a professional response to an unfair appraisal; manage your time well but refuse to work overtime perpetually; salvage situations caused by poor decisions; look for another job.

Worksheet

1. What clues make you suspect you may be dealing with a faux-smart boss?

2. Assuming you've determined the person is a faux-smart boss, what are his legitimate needs?

3. What are this faux-smart boss's strengths?

4. What principles and practices are particularly relevant for dealing with your faux-smart boss?

5. Write the opening statement you might use to begin Collaborating with the faux-smart boss or write the questions you would use if you used the Coaching strategy.

6. What response do you anticipate and how will you handle it?

7. What will you do if your discussion is not successful?

from the slacker to the contributor

Do you have a coworker or project team member whose poor performance or lack of support makes you crazy? His poor performance is probably harming your performance. At times you may even be frustrated with the performance of an entire team or department. We call these individuals or teams who hurt your performance slackers.

Ray once had the misfortune of working with a peer who was a slacker. Both Jared and Ray were managers in the Organizational Development Department in a manufacturing firm, reporting to the same Director. Ray provided services at Jared's assigned site and sometimes needed to call on Jared's employees to contribute their time and skills. Jared cared a lot about his employees and sometimes refused to make them available to help.

Ray's employees also frequently contributed services to Jared's assigned site. In order to evaluate his employees' work, Ray needed performance feedback from Jared, who often failed to provide useful feedback. If Ray followed up to get his input, Jared became evasive and defensive, insisting his input was unnecessary and that he was too busy to provide it. In the face of Ray's pleading, Jared would promise to respond, but usually broke these promises. If he did respond, his feedback was cryptic and not very useful. Ray resorted to drafting comments about his employees that Jared could simply read and approve. His resentment continued to build.

Clues to the Slacker

When you are working with a slacker, notice that he:

- Annoys you with his performance
- Ignores policies that affect your performance
- Breaks commitments or doesn't perform tasks you need
- Delivers projects late or of poor quality
- Fails to communicate with you or provide information you need
- Doesn't respond to your messages
- Repeatedly asks for your help
- Doesn't consult you on tasks, procedures, or decisions that affect you
- Causes your project to fall behind because of poor performance

Sometimes you can overreact to a coworker's failure to follow through. But if you consistently experience these frustrations with the same person or group and your performance is suffering, odds are good you have slackers in your life. (It sounds like an infestation, doesn't it?)

Helpful Assumptions

Your ability to turn your slacker coworker into a contributor will depend upon the assumptions you hold about his behavior. In Ray's example, Ray could not understand why Jared was so uncooperative. Ray assumed that Jared disliked him and only cared about his own success. Eventually Ray realized that Jared cared a lot about his employees' happiness and workload, and that Jared had a hard time juggling multiple priorities. In hindsight, Ray's perspective contributed to his difficulties with Jared.

You may need to work hard to give slackers the benefit of the doubt. Keep in mind that the slacker has many positive traits and probably is doing what he feels is best. Try to imagine that the slacker's behavior is the result of his legitimate needs, even if it conflicts with your and the organization's needs.

For example, if the slacker does not respond to your e-mails, you might choose to assume that the slacker is extremely busy, rather than jumping to the conclusion that he doesn't care about you. Making this assumption even when you are skeptical of it prevents you from overreacting and getting stressed. And it might even turn out to be true.

Keep in mind that everyone has both shortcomings and strengths. Certainly Jared did not cope well with multiple priorities, but he was very concerned about his people. How about you? Have you ever, like Jared,

> *You may need to work hard to give slackers the benefit of the doubt.*

had difficulty coping with multiple priorities? Acknowledging your own shortcomings should increase your patience with your slackers. Expecting perfection is unrealistic. You may still need to confront them, but you can do so calmly.

Peer power gives you the right to meet your needs. Having patience does not mean you are a pushover. The slacker does not have a right to hurt your performance or morale. Action is often called for and it can turn things around. The slacker can become a contributor if you take some appropriate steps.

Key Principles: Take Responsibility and Build Relationships

Applying some of the principles and practices described in Chapter 2 will help you eliminate or deal with slackers. The key principles to use are Take Responsibility and Build Relationships.

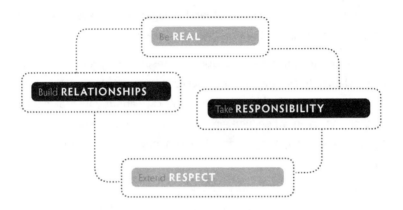

Take Responsibility

First, look in the mirror and acknowledge if you are contributing to your difficulties. Is it possible the slacker sees *you* as a slacker? Perhaps he is trying to get even for your failure to follow through on an issue critical to his success. It's possible that you need to change your own behavior in order to get the slacker to change his.

> *Is it possible you are encouraging the slacker?*

Be responsible for your experience. Ask yourself if you are being reasonable. Are you distorting what is happening? Are your biases getting in the way of seeing things clearly? Are you making a mountain out of a molehill? You may be calling him a slacker because he is failing to live up to your own perfectionist expectations.

Is it possible you are encouraging the slacker? Ray realized that he was reinforcing Jared's poor performance by drafting comments for Jared to approve. When Ray stopped doing his work for him, Jared's performance improved. There are times we need to help someone who is struggling, but not when the person takes advantage of our support.

Consider how you might need to change the way you make your

requests of the slacker. Do you ask courteously? Do you consider the slacker's needs and style? Do you stress the importance of the task to both him and the organization? Is it possible you don't receive what you want from him because you give him insufficient or unclear information? After making a request, you can check this out by saying, "I might not have been very clear. To see if I was clear or if I left something out, please give me your understanding of what I am requesting." Notice how you take full responsibility for the communication and don't imply he wasn't listening.

Are you making it easy for him to express his reservations about your requests? If not, you might say, "You may have some concerns about what I have requested. I would be very open to hearing them." If he has any reservations, it is best to find out about them up front. If you don't, he might not follow through. If you discover any objections, you can address them or prepare a contingency plan.

People you perceive as slackers may actually be focused on other priorities that you don't share. They may have agreed to support you, realize now that they are overwhelmed, and are focusing on their own goals instead of supporting you with your goals. Cynthia serves on a board for a non-profit organization that relies on the work of volunteers. Over many years, she has watched slacking behavior when it comes to the organization's priorities—situations in which volunteers say "yes" to work that they don't complete. From these experiences, she has learned not to pressure folks to take on tasks they may not want and to encourage people to say "no" if they are too busy to help.

Are you relying too much on e-mail? We've learned from much experience that using e-mail to make requests of slackers should be avoided if possible, unless the request is clear-cut. The written word is subject to multiple interpretations. You can't easily uncover the recipient's understanding or reservations and encourage questions. Talk to him face to face or voice to voice. Then use e-mail to document any agreements made in your conversation. (See Chapter 14 for guidelines on using technology.)

Look at how you follow up on your requests. Do you check to see how it's going, pick up items when you say you need them, and give credit to your coworker for his contribution? If not, you need to focus on what *you* can do to eliminate your problems.

Take Responsibility by communicating with the slacker. Create or reestablish ground rules with him. Include your boss in this process if necessary. The goal is to mutually agree to the rules that will guide future performance, not to lay blame for the problems of the past.

When Ray worked at a bank, he was very dependent upon the Print Shop. After a few occasions when Ray was disappointed with its service, he sat down with the Print Shop Manager. Ray agreed to give her the original documents five days in advance and to recognize her department in the training materials. She agreed to complete jobs in less than five days in rare emergencies and to review the Print Shop's performance with him monthly. As a result of these ground rules, he regularly received outstanding service. On the rare occasions when he didn't, he referred to the ground rules to turn things around.

> *Communicating is very important when you lead a project team.*

Communicating is very important when you lead a project team. A slacker who is assigned to your team can undermine the project by failing to carry out his responsibilities. Communicate extensively with each team member's boss. Meet with them before they assign their employees to the project. Ask that they stress the project's importance and evaluate their employees based on their contribution to the project. And keep them informed of their employees' performance throughout the project's duration.

Once the team is formed, agree on team ground rules, including how to handle failure to deliver an assignment on time. Create a chart that clearly communicates everyone's responsibilities, due dates, and dependencies on others. Post this chart in a visible location and use it to track project progress. Hold regular meetings with each individual and the entire team, and provide regular feedback.

Build Relationships

When was the last time you helped your biggest adversary at work? Do you tend to cooperate with people you know and like? You're not alone, and your slacker is not likely to be different. Use peer power to build a relationship with your peers, even the slacker who frustrates you. Spend time together and get to know him, his challenges, and his needs. Do sincere favors for him. Seek to achieve joint successes. In fact, it's not a bad idea to do all of this with others, too. The more allies you have, the more likely people will want to be on your good side.

We hope you won't do these things solely to gain some advantage. We want you to be honest about your intentions. For example, if you decide to do someone a favor because you hope for reciprocation, tell him so: "Hey, I want to help you because I want you to be successful and because I hope you will help me when I need it someday." Your openness will create trust.

When Ray began work at a bank, his manager asked him to attend an out-of-town conference with Sarah, one of Ray's coworkers. Ray spent a lot of time with her at meals, discussing the conference sessions as well as personal interests, experiences, and backgrounds. After they returned, even though they did not work much together, they continued networking with each other and occasionally involved their spouses in social activities. Over time Ray discovered that others sometimes perceived Sarah as unreliable. Nevertheless, on the infrequent occasions when Ray needed Sarah's assistance, she always came through, probably because of her relationship with Ray.

The way you make requests can influence whether or not a person behaves like a slacker. To reduce the likelihood of slacker behavior, solicit a person's input. If a coworker supports your work or your team's work, ask for his ideas on how you can get your needs met. You are not obligated to accept his idea, of course, but there's a chance that he may come up with options that work as well as or better than the existing situation. And by involving him in the brainstorming process, he will accept solutions with more enthusiasm.

Getting input will also enable you to seek solutions that benefit both you and the slacker. The goodwill that this produces may lead to the slacker's cooperation in the future.

A common objection to these practices is that they are time consuming, but ask yourself how much time you lose due to slackers at work.

These practices don't always work to prevent slackers or turn them into contributors. Sometimes you also need to employ one of our strategies.

Strategy: Collaborating

The best strategy to use with the slacker is Collaborating, especially when the relationship is very important (as when you need a slacker's help to succeed) and you have time to communicate, negotiate, document, and review progress.

Collaborating relies on a personal approach—using e-mail as your method of communication is not effective. Sit down with the slacker and present your concerns in order to come up with a solution that works for both of you. Do this in private, preferably in a neutral location, and at a time that is mutually convenient.

Make an assertive request. Tell the slacker your purpose, the exact, observable behavior that is troubling you, the impact of his behavior on both of you, and your proposal for meeting both his and your needs. Your statement should be brief and specific. It should address just one of your concerns and not include any exaggerations. Avoid commenting on his personality, attitude, or motives. Acknowledge your contribution, if any, to the problem. Allow for face saving and finish up by asking if he can agree to your request.

Some people are uneasy being assertive and are tempted to reduce their discomfort by including compliments in these statements.

Don't make this mistake. If you do, you will confuse the slacker and he will anticipate a criticism every time you compliment him.

Here is how Ray might approach Collaborating with Jared (with a serious expression and a calm, but firm, tone):

Jared, my goal here is to see that we are both happy with our working relationship. There are times when I need input on my employees for their performance appraisals and I am not getting it. This makes it difficult for me to give my employees a fair appraisal in a timely way. It prevents them from getting the raises they deserve and causes our boss to be unhappy with you and me. I don't think that is your intention. I would like to receive brief input from you at least a week before the appraisals are due. Would this work for you?

Since the slacker has already failed to provide what you need, he probably will not agree to your request. There are other possible responses which we will cover when we discuss common obstacles to successful Collaborating in Chapter 13. Since rejecting your request is the most common response, in this chapter we will show how to handle that. The approach is similar to times when someone rejects an idea of yours.

In Collaborating, the first step is to identify each of your needs. This enables you to explore options that will meet those needs. You may be able to come up with a solution that satisfies you both.

In order to identify the needs of the slacker, you must listen very carefully to his reasons for rejecting your request. His reasons will suggest his needs. You may need to draw him out by paraphrasing his reasons for objecting so he will expound on them. As you listen, don't argue. Ask questions if you are unclear, but do so honestly and without aggression. When he makes a good point, acknowledge it and try to incorporate it into future solutions.

Sometimes it's difficult to determine his reasons and to extrapolate his needs from his reasons. Hidden psychological needs such as avoiding risks, getting even for perceived past injustices, and achieving the respect of others underlie the rejection of many

Dear Cynthia and Ray,

This is all well and good, but I work with a slacker whose poor performance really doesn't affect me. He comes in late, wastes a lot of time, violates some policies, and doesn't perform very well. Granted, it doesn't affect me in my job, but I just don't think it's fair, and his customers aren't getting good service. What should I do when a slacker doesn't affect me personally?

— Perturbed

Dear Perturbed,

Though your coworker's behavior may not affect you personally, it certainly makes the organization look bad to its customers.

Since it doesn't affect you personally, try Coaching rather than Collaborating. Discuss your concerns directly with your coworker. Point out that you are worried about the organization's customers. He might respond by telling you it is none of your business, but it is also possible he will improve now that he is aware that he's been "caught." Ask him if he is aware of the company policies and offer to coach him on them if he would like.

If his performance does not improve and he reports to the same boss you do, you can let him know you will encourage the boss to address performance problems on the team (without naming him, of course). Avoid ratting out your coworker to the boss. Such tattling can create a parent/child relationship between the boss and your coworker (with you playing the part of the tattletale sibling). (Of course, if your coworker is doing something illegal or unethical, you may need to report that behavior.)

You may want to encourage the team to develop ground rules, including clear standards for individual performance and guidelines for how to address the poor performance of a peer.

— Cynthia and Ray

reasonable requests. You will need to plumb deep in order to identify these hidden factors without offending the slacker.

The following scenarios will show how to Collaborate when the slacker rejects your request because:

- He thinks he is too busy to do what you want.

- He thinks your request is unimportant or not his responsibility.

- He is angry at you about another matter.

Each scenario is modeled on the opening case between Ray and Jared. Imagine that you have made an assertive request of Jared.

Scenario: Dealing with the slacker who thinks he is too busy

SLACKER: I'm sorry; I just don't see how this proposal will work.

YOU: (Draw him out to clarify the reasons for his objection.) Perhaps we can tweak it. Tell me what aspects of it you are unsure of.

SLACKER: My schedule is hard to predict. I won't always have time the week before the appraisals are due.

YOU: (Paraphrase his concern.) It sounds like you believe you might be too busy during the week these are due.

SLACKER: That's right.

YOU: (Acknowledge good points that are made. Try to show how your proposal addresses his concerns.) That's a valid point. I know it could be difficult to predict how busy you'll be from week to week. I, too, am concerned about this not taking much of your time. That is why I am requesting just brief input. This will get me what I need without taking much of your time. Won't that work for you?

SLACKER: I don't think so.

YOU: (If the slacker still does not agree to your request, seek to define the problem by identifying your individual needs. Your needs should be the purpose of your request rather than the request itself.)

Well, what I think you need in this situation is to get your other activities done. What I need is to give my employees a fair appraisal and to see that they provide you with good service. Do you agree that these are our needs?

SLACKER: Well, that sounds about right.

YOU: (Keep working to clarify the needs.)

Is there anything else you think you need?

SLACKER: No, I can't think of anything. I think you have covered it.

YOU: (Once the needs are agreed to, ask the slacker if he has ideas to meet both sets of needs. It is better to get his ideas rather than rely on yours.)

Well, let's see if we can come up with something that meets both your needs and my needs. Do you have any suggestions?

SLACKER: Another option would be that you give me a brief form to fill out right after your employees provide me with service, rather than at the time the appraisals are due. This would mean that I could fill it out at my convenience with plenty of lead time.

YOU: (If his proposal doesn't work for you or he has no suggestions, continue to explore options. If you reach agreement, discuss next steps.)

Wow, that's a great idea. Let's give it a try. I will draft a form and run it by you to see if it works for you.

SLACKER: Sounds good. Please keep it brief.

YOU: (Express appreciation and confidence.)

I will. Thanks for helping me with this. I am confident we have a good plan.

Scenario: Dealing with the slacker who thinks your request is unimportant or not his responsibility

SLACKER: I am not going to do this.

YOU: (Draw him out to clarify the reasons for his objection.)

What's the problem with it?

SLACKER: This is not my job. It is your responsibility to evaluate your employees. You really don't need my input. What they do for me is very limited.

YOU: (Paraphrase his concern.)
It is my understanding that you feel that what I am requesting is not your job and that I don't really need it. Is that correct?

SLACKER: That's right.

YOU: (Courteously express disagreement and emphasize the benefits of your request.)
I agree that they don't work a lot for you and that doing their appraisals is my responsibility. However, I don't feel I can be fair to them and make sure they give you good service unless I have your feedback on what they do for you. Would you agree?

SLACKER: No. I don't feel you need my input or that it is my job to do this.

YOU: (If the slacker still does not agree to your request, seek to identify both of your needs. Your needs should be the purpose of your request rather than the request itself.)
What I need is to give my employees a fair appraisal and to see that they provide you with good service. What I think you need is to feel that your input to the appraisal is really necessary and that it truly is your responsibility. Do you agree that these are our needs?

SLACKER: Well, that sounds about right.

YOU: (Keep working to clarify the needs.)
Is there anything else you feel you need?

SLACKER: No, I can't think of anything. I think you have covered it.

YOU: (Once the needs are agreed to, ask the slacker if he has ideas to meet both of your needs. It is better to get his ideas rather than rely on yours.)
Well, let's see if we can come up with something that meets both of our needs. Do you have any suggestions?

SLACKER: I don't. This is not my job.

YOU: (Try again to get him to suggest something. It is best if he comes up with the solution.)
Can't you think of anything that will work for both of us?

SLACKER: I already said I can't.

YOU: (Offer some options if he seems stuck.)
One option might be for you to ask my employees if they want you to do this. That could show you how important your input is and that it is something you need to do. It will work for me if they say they feel they can have a fair appraisal without your input and you are not concerned about improving the service they give you. Another option would be for us to discuss it with our boss, Joan. We could find out whether she wants you to do this. If she doesn't, then we can agree that it isn't your responsibility.

SLACKER: Well, I am open to discussing it with your employees, but not Joan. I don't want to involve her.

YOU: (If you reach agreement, discuss next steps and express confidence.)
If they indicate that they want you to do this, will you?

SLACKER: I will.

YOU: (Give him another chance to bring up any reservations. It is better to discuss them now than to discover them later.)
Do you have any reservations about this?

SLACKER: No. I am fine with it.

YOU: Okay. I will ask my employees to contact you in the next week. Then I will check with you about what they said. Thanks for helping me with this. I feel good about our plan.

Scenario: Dealing with the slacker who is angry at you about another matter

SLACKER: No way.

YOU: (Draw him out to clarify the reasons for his objection.)
What is your objection to my request?

SLACKER: Oh, it just seems like a lot of busy work.

YOU: (If his objection is vague, try to get clarity.)
Tell me a little more. I am not sure I understand your concern.

SLACKER: I'm just saying I don't want to do this.

YOU: (Plumb for psychological reasons without criticizing.)
It would really help both of us if I knew more about that. Is there something on your mind that I need to know? I am open to whatever it is.

SLACKER: There is nothing.

YOU: Are you sure? Are you upset with me about our past interactions? If you are, I would be happy to discuss it.

SLACKER: Well, to tell you the truth, I am still pretty upset about your not supporting me when I proposed a modification to our department plan. I was really counting on you.

YOU: (Express appreciation for the honesty.)
You seem to be saying that you are mad that I did not back you on the plan. Hey, I really appreciate your telling me that. I knew you were upset then, but I did not realize you were still upset about that.

SLACKER: Yes, I guess I am.

YOU: (Clarify the reasons for his not accepting your request.)
So is that why you don't want to provide me with the appraisal input?

SLACKER: I guess so.

YOU: (Seek to identify both of your needs. Your needs should be the purpose of your request rather than the request itself.)
Well, what I think you need in this situation is to feel that I will support you and treat you with respect. What I need is to give my employees a fair appraisal and to see that they provide you with good service. Do you agree that these are our needs?

SLACKER: Well, that sounds about right.

YOU: (Keep working to clarify the needs.)

Is there anything else you feel you need?

SLACKER: No, I can't think of anything.

YOU: (Once the needs are agreed to, ask the slacker if he has ideas to meet your individual needs.)
Well, I would like to satisfy both of our needs. Do you have any suggestions?

SLACKER: If you would agree to support me in the future, I will agree to provide you with the input.

YOU: (If his proposal doesn't work for you or he has no suggestions, continue to explore options.)
Well, I really can't commit to supporting you every time. Sometimes I might not agree with you. What I could agree to is to support you when we agree and to give you a heads-up if I can't support you. At least I won't catch you by surprise. I am sorry I did that last time. I want to respect you. Would that do it for you? Would you be comfortable giving me the input if I commit to that?

SLACKER: Yes, I would. That would make me feel a lot better.

YOU: (Express appreciation and confidence.)
Thanks for helping me with this. I am confident we have a good plan. I am really glad we discussed this.

Keep the commitments you make during these discussions. If the slacker becomes a contributor, it is very important to acknowledge the improvement. Do this even if he has not agreed that he needs to change. Often people make requested changes but hear nothing about their improvement. They conclude that it wasn't very important since their change has not been acknowledged. As a result, their behavior often reverts back to its old form.

Plan B (If Your Initial Strategy Fails)

If Collaborating is not successful, avoid the temptation to retaliate by withholding your support of the slacker. This might seem justified because of his lack of cooperation. However, your reputation will only

Dear Cynthia and Ray,

My slacker (Jon) works in another department. He provides me with monthly statistical reports that help me conduct my analyses. I need these reports by the end of every month and without any errors. Sadly, often I don't get them on time and I frequently discover errors in them.

I don't know what to do to improve the situation. Since he is not in my department, I don't know whether I should talk to him about this. I am afraid his manager might be upset with me if I do. On the other hand, I am afraid to discuss it with his manager because I don't want to get Jon in trouble with his boss.

I feel helpless. What should I do?

— Nowhere to Go

Dear Nowhere,

Because this situation involves another department, discuss it first with your boss. Try to get permission to communicate directly with Jon. If your boss disagrees, follow your boss's directions to address this situation. He may prefer to take it up with Jon's boss, rather than including you in the discussion.

— Cynthia and Ray

suffer and the slacker will now be justified in continuing to escalate the conflict. Do not vent by copying the world on your angry e-mails. Humiliating a coworker will keep him and others from wanting to work with you. Attacking and bullying, while tempting at this stage, won't improve things.

This does not mean you should cave in and accept the status quo, even though that, too, might be tempting. You have the right to expect the cooperation of your coworkers. Avoid becoming the slacker's informal trainer or boss. It is not your responsibility to show the slacker how to do his tasks. A long-term commitment to train the slacker will stifle both your productivity and his accountability. Only accept this role if your boss assigns it to you.

First, try the Compromising strategy. Attempt to solve the issue directly with the slacker. A possible compromise with Jared would be to get his feedback every other year rather than annually.

If that fails, try Going Head-to-Head. Tell the slacker you want to take the issue to his boss. This strategy may be all it takes to change the slacker's behavior. Invite the slacker to join you in this conversation. The boss should hear the slacker's side of the story, and the slacker should hear what you say to his boss. The boss could make the decision to assign the task to someone else on the team or require the slacker to change his approach. If the slacker refuses to talk with the boss, you might decide to go alone.

Use Caring-for-Self as a last resort. Try to reduce your dependence on the slacker. The less you need him, the less he can hurt you. When Jared refused to assign his employees to provide Ray's services, Ray streamlined his services. Streamlining increased Ray's efficiency and productivity and decreased his need for Jared's employees.

You might be thinking that there is no way you can alter your dependence on slackers. But sometimes you can find others who will meet your needs. Or you can find ways to reduce your needs, or meet them yourself. As your dependence on the slacker goes down, your accountability and productivity will go up.

Moving Forward

The slacker might have a pattern of slacking off with you. He might fail to provide what you need on many occasions and on many items. Bring this up with him and try to collaborate on the pattern rather than on a single specific issue. Your odds, however, of succeeding are lower when there is a pervasive pattern. You most likely will need to turn to Going Head-to-Head or Caring-for-Self.

The Rest of the Story

If your frustrations become unbearable, you may decide to look for another job, though that can be difficult. Ray discontinued drafting material for Jared, who became somewhat more responsive. While Ray's relationship with Jared improved, Ray ultimately left the organization for greener pastures. This move was the best choice for Ray because the slacker seriously affected his job satisfaction.

Cheat Sheet for the Slacker

Definition: The slacker is a coworker whose poor performance damages your performance.

Clues

The slacker:

- Annoys you with his performance
- Ignores policies that affect your performance
- Breaks commitments or doesn't perform tasks you need
- Delivers projects late or of poor quality
- Fails to communicate with you or provide information you need
- Doesn't respond to your messages
- Repeatedly asks for your help
- Doesn't consult you on tasks, procedures, or decisions that affect you
- Causes your project to fall behind because of poor performance

Helpful Assumptions

- The slacker's behavior is the result of his needs.
- Everyone has both shortcomings and strengths.
- You probably have been a slacker at times.
- You have a right to meet your needs.

Key Principles and Practices

Take Responsibility

- Don't be a slacker yourself.
- Ask if you are being reasonable.

- Make requests of others effectively.
- Establish ground rules with your coworkers.
- As a project manager, communicate extensively with your team members and their bosses.

Build Relationships

- Network with others.
- Get input.
- Seek solutions that benefit all.

Strategy: Collaborating

- Tell the slacker your purpose, what is troubling you, the impacts of his behavior, and your request for meeting both your needs and his needs.
- Paraphrase his responses frequently and draw him out if necessary.
- Use his response to determine and identify his needs.
- Link your request to his needs and how it benefits him.
- If your request is rejected, identify mutual needs.
- Get him to generate options to meet both your needs and his needs.
- Suggest options if he is truly stuck.
- If there is a deadlock, explore psychological needs such as resentments towards you.
- Make sure he has no reservations about any agreement.
- Express confidence and acknowledge any improvements.

Plan B (If Your Initial Strategy Fails)

- Avoid retaliating.
- Do not vent to others.
- Try not to attack or bully.

- Do not accept the status quo.

- Avoid becoming his informal trainer or boss.

- If Collaborating fails, move to Compromising or Going Head-to-Head.

- Going Head-to-Head: Invite the slacker to join you in a meeting with his boss.

- Caring-for-Self: Find others who will meet your needs; reduce your dependence; look for another job.

Worksheet

1. What clues make you suspect you may be dealing with a slacker?

2. Assuming you've determined the person is a slacker, what might be his legitimate needs?

3. What are this slacker's strengths?

4. What principles and practices are most relevant?

5. Write the statement you will use to begin Collaborating with the slacker:

6. What response do you anticipate and how will you handle it?

7. What will you do if your Collaborating is not successful?

8. How could you reduce your dependence on the slacker?

from the bully to the assertive leader

We'd like to introduce you to Darcy, a sales representative who used anger, impatience, and threats to force others to give her what she wanted. Cynthia watched Darcy steamroll any employee who dared to question her demands.

Darcy would often pressure the support teams to meet customer requests at the last minute and respond with threats if she was told that there were higher customer priorities. She refused to use the company's planning processes, yet expected immediate compliance with her demands. Once Cynthia saw Darcy reduce a well-meaning employee to tears by threatening to have her fired, long after the employee had corrected the problem and apologized for the inconvenience. We call people who use unreasonable demands and inappropriate threats to get their way bullies.

Darcy was a smart and focused high achiever who often hit her sales targets. While alienating most of the team, Darcy developed a strong relationship with the sales manager who valued her sales results. But her interpersonal skills were her greatest weakness. When the phone rang and Darcy's number appeared on caller ID, the entire staff gritted their teeth and sighed. Cynthia recognized that this situation couldn't continue without losing strong employees.

Clues to the Bully

It's not hard to recognize bullying tactics at work. Bullies respect power and wield it to force people to obey them. Because bullies are most concerned with accomplishing results, they often have little regard for other people's needs. Their motto might be "Just do it!" and they wear this slogan like a badge of honor.

Clues that tell you you're dealing with a bully include:

- Making demands that you ignore procedures to meet her needs
- Insisting that you do things her way without the authority to require that
- Threatening to take a problem to your boss rather than trying to resolve it with you first
- Threatening to criticize you to others
- Threatening to block your promotion unless you cooperate
- Delaying a decision until you comply with a demand
- Withholding support for a project unless you give her what she wants
- Refusing to listen to your objections to complying

The workplace is full of bullies and, unfortunately, many have used their aggressive tactics to move into higher-level technical and managerial positions.

Helpful Assumptions

When you are the target of bullying behavior, it can be helpful to notice what seems to be motivating the bully's actions. Beneath her abrupt or gruff demeanor lurk her hidden motivations. It's possible that the bully craves success and achievement. It's also possible that the bully fears failure. The bully believes that the people around her will disappoint her, cause her humiliation, or make her fail. In the bully's worldview, she sets high standards and expects others to meet them. The bully believes that her standards are the only thing preventing the company from crumbling. Darcy was convinced that both her success and the organization's success depended upon her achieving her sales targets.

Behind bullying often hides a control freak who is afraid that the spinning plates are about to crash to the ground. Bullies have developed an aggressive coping strategy to ensure that they succeed—no matter how incompetent or unsupportive the people around them. This strategy is particularly prevalent when they are under stress. Keep in mind that the bully's behavior is rarely about you.

If you recognize that fear of failure or humiliation and a commitment to high standards drive the bully to threaten consequences or demand compliance, you may be less hostile and more effective in responding to her threats and demands. This does not mean you necessarily comply. It means you

> *Notice that bullying is a common human failing.*

focus on your mutual goals, rather than become obsessed with how badly the bully behaves. In doing so, you may better appreciate the strengths she brings to your organization—her personal power in achieving objectives, her commitment to do what's right by her customers, and the care she displays in a job well done.

Ask yourself if you have ever bullied another person with subtle (or blatant) threats or outright demands. Notice that bullying is a common human failing. Then stop judging and complaining about the bully and focus on getting the work done. Whoever crafted the old expression, "What doesn't kill you makes you stronger," probably worked with a bully.

Key Principles: Take Responsibility and Extend Respect

It's not a pleasant experience to work with a bullying coworker or boss. But instead of feeling victimized, rely on two principles that will help you work with her more effectively and transform her into an assertive leader: Take Responsibility and Extend Respect.

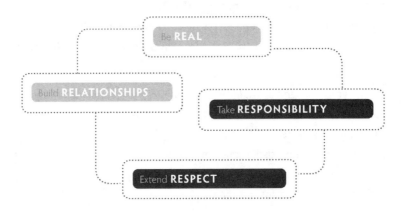

Take Responsibility

As you work with the bully, there are steps you can initiate to develop a constructive working relationship. Let's start with some basic communication practices that may prevent or nip her bullying in the bud. The first of these is to establish clear expectations and ground rules.

Because bullies essentially mistrust their colleagues, gaining clarity about what they expect of you and what you expect of them eliminates some uncertainty (and reduces their frustration level). You might say, "Darcy, as your new Sales Support Representative, I want to be sure that I understand your expectations. What part of pre-sales activities do you like your SSR to assist you with?"

Ground rules are the working agreements that you make to guide your work together. If you document three to five ground rules at the outset, they serve as an objective reminder of agreed-upon behavior.

With a bully, you might suggest ground rules such as: hear the other person out without interrupting; focus on the problem when giving feedback; give me the opportunity to correct a problem first. If you ask her for ground rules, you might hear, "Do what you say you're going to do. Don't take things personally."

Try to gain agreement with the bully regarding the formal systems, policies, and practices that have been established in your department and organization. Without this agreement, many bullies will work around the system to get what they want, creating havoc and ill will as a result. Think of this step as orienting the bully to the way it works so she can get what she wants with less hassle.

Frequent, focused updates on tasks you are doing for the bully will reduce her anxiety. Regularly communicate your status on these tasks and advise her of any difficulties you are having.

Another important Take Responsibility practice is to perform well. Bullies are often high achievers, like Darcy, and hold others to high standards. Try to anticipate their needs (as long as they are reasonable) by offering suggestions that will help them succeed. When making proposals, make sure you've thought them through—be prepared to answer questions or counterarguments. Demonstrate by your good example how to make proposals without bullying. Gain the bully's respect by becoming someone she can count on for high-quality work.

But if the worst happens and you screw up a task or request, take the initiative to present the mistake and apologize. Never hide your mistakes and hope the bully won't discover them. Take a deep breath and explain clearly what went wrong. Be responsible for the problem. Say, "I'm sorry and I'll fix it."

Most bullies admire strength even as they vent their frustrations toward the people who disappoint them. You may listen to the bully's rants without defending or explaining your actions further. When the bully has run out of steam, say, "Again, I'm sorry, and I need to hang up now so I can correct this error."

By performing well and acknowledging errors, you are using your peer power to model how to achieve competency and success in a non-bullying way. It's possible that the bully may come to realize that there are less confrontational ways of reaching her goals. In time she may use her passion and skills to become less of a bully and more of an assertive leader.

Until you reach a less taxing relationship with the bully, be sure to respect your own needs. You may be tempted to go overboard in performance by working too many hours or refusing to say "no" to a request that pushes past the envelope of your abilities. Don't do what a bully wants unless it meets your needs, too.

If you find yourself the recipient of a tirade from a bully, remember to maintain steady breathing. If you rise to the bully's bait and react defensively or emotionally, consider some positive reinforcement instead of being too hard on yourself. Tell yourself, "I am getting better and better at developing a positive working relationship with a colleague who has a strong personality."

Extend Respect

Honoring style differences is part of the Extend Respect principle. In the case of the bully, you might honor her focused, results-oriented nature. You can practice respect by aligning your style to these positive characteristics. After all, the bully's assertive emphasis on answers and action is often applauded by an organization's management. So applaud it yourself, for the positive benefit it brings to the company.

> *Another key practice within the Extend Respect principle is that of listening well.*

When communicating with the bully, accommodate the method of delivery that she prefers. But be aware of the drawbacks of e-mail, voice mail, and instant messaging. Read through "Technology: A Blessing and a Curse" (Chapter 14) for tips on the benefits and pitfalls of each of these modes of communication.

Another key practice within the Extend Respect principle is that of listening well. When the bully vents, make eye contact and just listen. Don't interrupt, don't defend, and resist using logic to rebut her arguments. Assume that, after you remove the emotion from her words, her complaints may be reasonable. Say, "Darcy, I hear what you are saying. You have a very good point." You don't want reasonable complaints to escalate into bullying.

When giving bad news, expect the bully to voice her frustrations. Instead of wincing through this one-sided exchange, stay calm and allow her to express her dissatisfaction. Act the same as you would toward a non-bullying friend. To show you have listened well, you might nod your head while she speaks. If she is only venting, there is no need to repeat the emotional content. If she has expressed genuine points, show you have listened well by paraphrasing her words. If the bully has expressed threats and demands, acknowledge her needs.

When the bully makes reasonable requests, ask questions to get more information, clarify your understanding, or confirm details. Because bullies present their needs so assertively, you may be tempted to submit or agree quickly. Later, you may realize that you're not clear on the bully's request. So pause to clarify any areas of potential confusion or uncertainty. Try phrasing it this way: "Darcy, I want to make sure I complete your request accurately. Did you mean that you want me to prepare the customer's quote for you, and that you will then route it through the proper channels?" Take notes as you clarify her needs rather than relying on your memory. If appropriate, follow up with an e-mail documenting your understanding.

Another way to Extend Respect to the bully is to resist the temptation to rescue her. Don't comply with her demands when you don't want to. And because the bully wants to remain in control, give up your own desire to control how she does her job. Instead, focus on giving the bully choices, like this: "I can fill in the quote for this customer and have you review it, or give you the details so you can create the quote yourself. Which option do you prefer?"

Acknowledge that the bully is in charge. Say, "Darcy, this is your customer and I want you to be satisfied with the solution." Let her know that her role or job is important by saying, "Darcy, I want to ensure your success because your role as a sales rep is important to the organization's success."

In addition to respecting the bully and her role, respect the organization. You should not circumvent established policies and procedures because a bully is pressuring you to do so. Another way to respect your organization is to respect the roles and hierarchy. If the bully is your boss, she has a right to "demand" performance from you and to discipline you when necessary. If you are in a support role relative to a bully, respect the unwritten rules as well as the formally established ones. This might mean deferring to her judgment in situations where she has more seniority and experience, even if the reasons for her decision are unclear.

Strategy: Compromising

These principles and practices will go a long way toward alleviating the bully's concerns and reducing her perception that she needs to sweep in and set things straight. However, there are times when they won't be sufficient and you will need to pick a strategy.

> *However, the bully often has little interest in your needs and not much patience with the process of Collaborating.*

Workplace conflicts can usually be handled with the Collaborating strategy, in which both people focus on meeting their respective needs. However, the bully often has little interest in your needs and not much patience with the process of Collaborating. You can certainly try to collaborate by first attempting to find out what she needs and then clearly expressing your need for no bullying in the future. You can also attempt to come up with a mutually satisfying solution for the current situation. But it is not likely you will be successful.

Peer power requires flexibility. Rather than Collaborating, we suggest that you adopt the Compromising strategy to deal with unreasonable demands and inappropriate threats. With this strategy, you offer the bully some of what she wants in exchange for some of what you want. This is a classic negotiating stance in which you basically give up a little to get a little. It works when each party has something the other party wants. It takes less time than Collaborating, and most bullies prefer it.

Compromising is most effective if done face to face. However, you should not agree to a compromise that produces significant negative consequences such as antagonizing your boss, other coworkers, or customers.

Let's see how the Compromising strategy works when you need to handle the following situations:

- Demands to make an exception to a procedure
- Threats to go over your head

Scenario: Dealing with an unreasonable demand to make an exception to a procedure

It's not pleasant to stand firm against a bully's belligerence. But being an accomplice to breaking the rules can have even more unpleasant consequences. Not only does it disrespect your organization's policies, it reinforces the bully's behavior. To keep the bully from making unreasonable demands in the future, seek a Compromising solution.

YOU: (Don't agree to a bully's request unless you are totally comfortable with it.)
Darcy, I'm afraid I cannot place the Newton Pharmaceuticals order into the system. You are offering them an extra year's maintenance at the regular price. According to the policy, that requires approval of upper management.

BULLY: You know there's no way in hell I can route this through the process in three hours—not on the last day of the quarter. I promised Newton two years of maintenance in order to get this sale, and I will get this sale today. And if you don't want my boss talking to your boss about this, you'll help me out.

YOU: (Show that you've listened to the bully by paraphrasing her demand, without the hostility or threats.)
I understand that this sale is very important to you to get booked today, and you made a promise that you want to deliver on.

BULLY: Damn right, it's important. Newton needs our product, and this contract is a winner for them and for us. And it means I'll make top sales rep of the quarter. I know very well you can override the computer without management because this is a judgment call, not a hard and fast rule. I've seen it done before. All it takes is a little guts.

YOU: (Acknowledge the bully's good intentions to serve the customer, but don't surrender when it comes to her unreasonable demands. Explain the rationale of the policy.)
I'm sorry, Darcy. This is a clear exception to policy, and any exception requires approval. I appreciate that you worked hard to come up with terms that will satisfy the customer. This policy is in place for a very good reason. It promotes a fair price for both the company and our customers.

BULLY: You can't sit there and tell me that other salespeople don't push through exceptions without approval. They're not playing by the rules. Why should I?

YOU: (Paraphrase the bully's point to demonstrate you've heard it.)
It sounds like you think that other salespeople are allowed exceptions all the time without getting the required approval. If they don't play by the rules, you don't want to play by the rules.

BULLY: I know they don't play by the rules.

YOU: (Ask the bully how others might feel if the policy were ignored, explaining how the policy works for the bully as well.)
I can only tell you that I do play by the rules. The exception process only works if everyone follows it, Darcy. It promotes a level playing field. The rule protects you from others who might want to be unfair. How do you think others will feel if I make an

exception for you?

BULLY: (Allow the bully to vent when you say no.)
I'll tell you how I feel right now. You're taking money out of my pocket. I don't appreciate that, and I can assure you I won't forget it. If Jonathan were not out sick today, I'd be having this conversation with him, not with you, because I know he would push it through.

YOU: (After listening to the bully vent, don't refute what she said or focus on logic. Try to seek a compromise.)
Darcy, I'm well versed in the policies and practices of the sales department. I can help you get your order in today without the need for an exception and without going outside the system. It would require you to make a quick call to the customer to gain their agreement to a longer term on their contract.

BULLY: That sounds interesting.

Scenario: Handling threats to go over your head

The bully's threats to take a problem to your boss are attempts to intimidate you into resolving an issue quickly and doing it her way. One option when you hear a threat, of course, is to say, "I don't think that will help, but go right ahead, Darcy." Before saying that, try the Compromising strategy.

BULLY: Look. You're in Tech Support. Your job is to provide technical answers to our customers. I'm not sure what part of that you don't understand.

YOU: (Don't take the bully's words personally. Stay professional and remember to breathe.)
Is there a problem, Darcy?

BULLY: Yes, there is. My contact at Newton said that you refused to help them with an issue. That's unacceptable customer service, in my opinion.

YOU: (Acknowledge the bully's concern for good results.)
Darcy, I know that you are loyal to your customer and want to do what's best for them. Do you realize that Newton doesn't have a

maintenance support contract with us?

BULLY: Yes, I realize that. But they are a growing company with a good relationship with us. A little less rigidity on your part might mean that they purchase more licenses next year. We both know that it's acceptable practice to allow a customer a quick question, even if they don't have a support contract. If we are nice to them, perhaps they'll buy a support contract next year.

YOU: (Paraphrase the bully's words, so she knows you have listened.) It sounds like you think that answering a quick technical question might help the company win more license sales next year.

BULLY: Yes.

YOU: I can't do that.

BULLY: I am going to discuss this with your manager. He knows how the game is played.

YOU: (Don't overreact to the threat.)
You are certainly welcome to call my manager if you think that's necessary, Darcy. But I think we can resolve your concerns right now. May I propose a compromise?

BULLY: Go ahead. But it better be good.

YOU: I propose that we answer one question for Newton, as long as it takes less than 15 minutes. We will provide that service to your other non-contract customers as well. We will notify you when they call, in case you want to talk to them about getting a maintenance contract. In return, you let them know that we cannot answer any more calls for them until they have a contract.

BULLY: No, that's way too strict. Sometimes there are emergencies and we have to get their software up and running, contract or no contract.

YOU: (If the bully rejects your proposal, offer another compromise.)
In that case, we will take a call from them only if you give the okay, and only if it truly is an emergency.

BULLY: I can live with that.

YOU: (Clarify next steps.)

Good. Let's try this for two months to see if it works. I will let my manager know about this new process with your customers. I will keep both of you informed of the results.

In this scenario, you have given up a little of your time by agreeing to take these extra calls, and she has given up some of her time as well. This is an effective compromise.

Notice that you never take the bait put out by the bully in these scenarios. You remain professional and clear in your communication. And notice, too, that bullies don't melt under this positive attention. They're often still impatient and abrupt. The difference is that you're not hooked by their behavior.

In neither scenario did you request a halt to the bullying. In a sense, you're tolerating the bully's obnoxious behavior in the interest of completing a task or fulfilling a request. However, your hope is that the bully will learn that you don't cave when she bullies. Realizing this, the bully might stop the bullying when expressing her needs. You have contributed to her becoming an assertive leader.

Plan B (If Your Initial Strategy Fails)

There are times when Compromising is not possible or is not successful. And sometimes when it is successful, it encourages rather than discourages further bullying because the bully feels rewarded for her behavior. In these cases, turn to the Going Head-to-Head and Caring-for-Self strategies (in that order).

When using the Going Head-to-Head strategy, hold firm and disengage from the discussion without offending the bully ("I really can't help under these circumstances"). You might call her bluff by asking her to put the threat in writing or suggesting she go ahead with it. If the threat is serious or continues over time, you can take it to your manager or the bully's manager. Unless her demand is illegal, invite the bully to join you. Management is responsible for preventing and dealing with an intimidating work environment.

Dear Cynthia and Ray,

I work with a bully who presents demands and threatens me, and the bully is my boss. I'll call him Mr. Bull's Eye. The assignments he gives me are unreasonable. I have been his executive assistant for six months now, ever since he replaced my former boss (whom I never had any issues with!). Mr. Bull's Eye has gone so far as to threaten me with going on performance probation! Should I treat this bully differently because he is my boss?

— Shoot the Bull

Dear Shoot,

We encourage you to closely examine Mr. Bull's Eye's actions to see if they are true bullying or represent a style difference. Your new boss may simply have more demanding expectations and present them in a more forceful way than your previous boss. He has a right to give you "unreasonable" assignments or point out negative consequences, such as discipline, if you do not do assignments he gives you.

If you believe your boss's requests are really unreasonable or come with an inappropriate threat, respectfully let him know that you understand why he wants them done, but they can't be done well, and that as a result his needs won't be met. Try to compromise. Ask him if he would be willing to reconsider. Then give him some alternatives that would make the task more reasonable. Of course, if your boss does anything illegal or asks you to, you should go to Human Resources or his management, depending upon your organization's policies.

If your boss continues bullying, do your very best, and if it is intolerable, invite him to discuss it with higher management or HR. You can also look into finding another job. But before taking those final steps, try to work it out with your boss. Bullies and demanding people exist in any organization at all levels, so you are likely to come into contact with them again.

— Cynthia & Ray

Do not retaliate or refuse to work with the bully. Your reputation will suffer and the bullying will just escalate.

Oddly enough, some bullies respond well to direct confrontation. They see you as an equal who is capable of playing the game within their rules. If you can stand the constant battles, you might be able to meet the bully on this jousting field and forge a workable relationship. The bully may realize that she can't push you around and soften her approach.

Adopting the Caring-for-Self strategy means that you choose to take care of your own needs. If you make an exception and agree to a bully's request, then make sure you can fulfill it without undue stress to yourself. In working with Darcy, you may need to get help from a coworker to prepare that sales document. If you're frustrated with Darcy's communication style, you may need to talk with a coworker about how best to communicate with her. Or possibly you and a coworker could decide to rotate the responsibility of working with Darcy. When you care for yourself, you accept that Darcy is not interested in meeting your needs, and you try to find creative ways to make sure your needs are met without her participation.

If nothing else works, you may decide to leave the organization, rather than be bullied any longer. This Caring-for-Self strategy is always a last resort because, unfortunately, there are bullies waiting to bedevil you in most workplaces. Learning to work with them is a career-enhancing move.

Moving Forward

Some bullies make frequent unreasonable demands or inappropriate threats. If you handle one of these situations well, they might discontinue using this approach with you. However, often the pattern continues on a variety of issues. In such cases, point out the pattern and ask them to break it. Acknowledge any improvements that occur.

The Rest of the Story

Darcy continued to make unreasonable demands, loudly venting at the sales support representatives on the team. However, one particular SSR seemed to enjoy the challenge of keeping her happy. Because he maintained his equilibrium and objectivity while refusing to go over the policy line on her demands, Darcy overreacted less often. She trusted him to give her good service and requested that he provide the primary support for her sales region. Of course, the team was delighted to turn Darcy over to their colleague whenever she called, and in time the team stopped wincing when she negotiated a sales order, picked up the phone, and demanded immediate attention.

Cheat Sheet for the Bully

Definition: The bully is a colleague who uses unreasonable demands or inappropriate threats to get her way.

Clues

The Bully:

- Makes demands that you ignore procedures to meet her needs
- Insists that you do things her way without the authority to require that
- Threatens to take a problem to your boss rather than trying to resolve it with you first
- Threatens to criticize you to others
- Threatens to block your promotion unless you cooperate
- Delays a decision until you comply with a demand
- Withholds support for a project unless you give her what she wants
- Refuses to listen to your objections to complying

Helpful Assumptions

- The bully craves success and may fear failure.
- She believes that the people around her will disappoint her, cause her humiliation, or make her fail.
- The bully sets high standards and expects others to meet them.
- Her coping strategy is meant to ensure her success.
- Don't take her behavior personally. It is more about her than about you.
- Bullies have many strengths.
- You have probably bullied others, too.

- Don't be judgmental, but don't cave either.

Key Principles and Practices

Take Responsibility

- Establish ground rules and clear expectations.
- Provide frequent updates on tasks you are doing for her.
- Perform well to gain the bully's respect.
- Acknowledge any mistakes you make.
- Respect your own needs by not succumbing to pressure.
- Congratulate yourself for successful encounters with her.

Extend Respect

- Notice and honor style differences. Adjust your behavior to reflect the bully's emphasis on results.
- Listen well to her concerns and requests.
- Don't rescue the bully by caving to her pressure.
- Respect the organization's policies and hierarchy.

Strategy: Compromising

- Take a deep breath and don't take things personally.
- Paraphrase what the bully says, including her emotions, but without the hostile component.
- Acknowledge the bully for her concern for good results.
- State your unwillingness to comply with unreasonable demands.
- Don't react to threats.
- Allow for some venting. Don't rebut what is said or focus on logic.
- Show how policies sometimes work for her.
- Seek a compromise solution. Propose alternatives.

Plan B (If Your Initial Strategy Fails)

- When Compromising fails, switch to Going Head-to-Head.

- Disengage from the discussion without offending her.

- Call her bluff if she threatens you.

- Invite her to join you to discuss the situation with management.

- Do not retaliate.

- Do not refuse to work with the bully.

- Stand up to the bully and she may respond positively.

- Caring-for-Self: Manage your stress; get help from coworkers; meet your needs without the bully's participation; reward yourself when you handle situations well; as a last resort, look for another job.

Worksheet

1. What clues make you suspect you may be dealing with a bully?

2. Assuming you've determined the person is a bully, what might be her legitimate needs?

3. What are this bully's strengths?

4. What Take Responsibility and Extend Respect practices are most relevant for your situation?

5. What compromise could you suggest to the bully?

6. What response do you anticipate and how will you handle it?

7. What Plan B steps will you take if your discussion is not successful?

from challenges to collaboration

As we have seen in the case chapters, many issues with uncooperative coworkers can be resolved by incorporating the principles and practices of Chapter 2 into your everyday activities. When that isn't enough to resolve conflicts or keep them from occurring, we have suggested applying specific strategies introduced in Chapter 3.

As you develop peer power, you may realize that the most appropriate strategy is usually Collaborating. Because of its emphasis on providing a joint resolution to conflict, successful Collaborating efforts not only resolve problems but set the stage for an improved working relationship.

However, special obstacles often occur on the way to a mutual agreement. By understanding these challenges, it's often possible to overcome them without having to resort to Plan B (one of the other strategies). This chapter illustrates five obstacles in the order that they generally occur and offers tips on how to deal with them. We will illustrate these tips with scenarios involving the slacker, but the tips apply to the other challenging coworkers as well.

Recall that a slacker is a coworker (or an entire department) who not only performs poorly, but whose performance harms your own performance. The slacker provides poor service or a poor work product, breaks commitments, ignores policies, or fails to communicate or provide information. In the case study in Chapter 11, Ray's team provided services for Jared's employees, and Ray occasionally required feedback so he could complete performance appraisals. By failing to provide useful feedback, Jared, a slacker, made it impossible for Ray to evaluate the work that was done by his team.

> *The obstacles to collaborating typically surface after you assertively request that your challenging coworker change his behavior so that it works for both of you.*

Note that our approach to outlining the strategies and their usage is based upon Western/ American values and culture. You may need to adapt this approach when dealing with people from other cultures. For example, when dealing with Asians it is often important to allow the person to save face (by discussing things in private, acknowledging his good intentions and factors beyond his control, sharing responsibility for problems, not pushing him to agree verbally to an error, etc.). Of course, not all people will fit a cultural generalization—it's important to treat everyone as an individual.

The obstacles to Collaborating typically surface after you assertively request that your challenging coworker change his behavior so that it works for both of you. Here is Ray's assertive request of Jared:

> *Jared, my goal here is to see that we are both happy with our working relationship. There are times when I need input on my employees for their performance appraisals and I am not getting it. This makes it difficult for me to give my employees a fair appraisal in a timely way. It prevents them from getting the raises they deserve and causes our boss to be unhappy with you and me. I don't think that is your intention. I would like to receive brief input from you at least a week before the appraisals are due. Would this work for you?*

Let's look at how to handle each of the five obstacles that might occur with Jared.

Obstacle 1: The other person refuses to discuss the issue because trust has eroded

When you initiate Collaborating, a colleague may refuse to discuss an issue with you. Perhaps he feels uncomfortable because he expects conflict or does not trust your motives. You often employ Collaborating when you need the slacker's assistance to deliver a service or conclude a successful project. But sometimes slackers will not respond to your request to meet and talk things out. Let's look at how you might respond when a slacker (or any challenging coworker) refuses to collaborate.

The first step is to build your relationship with your coworker. If you follow the Build Relationship principle and practices, you will have gone a long way toward this step already. The practices involve developing relationships, respecting the impact of your actions on others by talking things over with them first, being attentive to others' self-esteem, and showing compassion and empathy.

Try to stress the benefits of Collaborating to your coworker. More than any other strategy, it offers the best opportunity to fully meet both of your needs. While communicating with him, act as non-threatening as possible. Your goal is to gain his agreement to a solution, not to win an argument.

If your coworker is still reluctant to discuss matters with you, try to dig deeper to determine the reason. If you think that he distrusts your intentions, consider suggesting a mediator. Address the issue by saying, "Let's look at our relationship and what can be done so that this discussion works well for you."

Imagine that you are responding to Jared's refusal to discuss the issue.

Scenario: The slacker refuses to discuss the issue with you

SLACKER: I don't want to discuss this. Performance appraisals of your team are your job, not mine. I've said all I'm going to say on the matter.

YOU: (Laying the groundwork for a discussion on how Collaborating can benefit both parties)

Jared, because my team provides services to your employees, we can only be successful if you are successful. It seems that the successes of our teams are intertwined. Would you say that this a fair statement?

SLACKER: I'm not convinced of that. It may be true that your success depends on ours, but I don't think the reverse is true. Your services are not necessarily a key to my team's success. Having to provide performance appraisals is time consuming, and it is not a good use of my time. That's why I'm hesitant to do it.

YOU: (Paraphrase what is said to make sure you have heard correctly, to show that you are listening, and to defuse any tension.)

It sounds to me like you are not sure that my team's services are critical to your success, and because of this your time is not well spent in helping my team to appraise its performance. Is that true?

SLACKER: I've really said all I want to say on this. I don't know how else to tell you that.

YOU: (Don't get defensive. Continue to try to make the situation as non-stressful as possible.)

Look, Jared. This is really important to both of us. We really need to discuss this. Perhaps I can approach this from a different perspective. The more my team provides quality services, the more our customers benefit. If we are not providing a level of quality that will benefit your team, the onus is on us to improve. Would you agree with that?

SLACKER: Perhaps.

YOU: By getting your help with performance appraisals, perhaps we can determine where my team has room for improvement. I'm happy to explore other options with you.

SLACKER: I don't agree. I think it's up to you to improve your services on your own. Again, I don't want to discuss this.

YOU: (If you still can't get the other person to see the benefit of Collaborating, offer to use a mediator.)

Without performance data that you and your team can provide, I feel that we will be working in the dark. I wish we could come to some agreement on this that will help us both. Would you be willing to discuss this if we get a third party, say Jerry, to help you and me talk the matter over?

SLACKER: I don't feel comfortable bringing other people into this.

YOU: (Try to find out the reasons for his refusing to Collaborate with you.)

Jared, let's look at our relationship and how we can improve it so that things work well for you. I think the issue goes beyond the appraisal input. I would be very receptive to hearing what's on your mind about me.

SLACKER: Well, there are several things I am unhappy about. I am willing to tell you about them tomorrow.

YOU: Thank you for agreeing to work with me on this.

If the slacker continues to refuse to talk, then it's time for Plan B.

Obstacle 2: The other person becomes defensive when you bring up your concerns

People who become easily defensive are often those who doubt their capabilities. They may sense blame or disapproval when you bring up a concern, even if that is not your intention. Because defensiveness is a barrier to Collaborating, do what you can to reduce a defensive reaction in your coworker; if that fails, try to reduce or manage his defensive posture.

To keep your coworker from becoming defensive, work at providing feedback constructively and skillfully. When discussing your concerns, make the situation as safe as possible. Try to keep blame and disapproval out of your voice and, of course, don't get defensive yourself. Stress that your goal is to meet his needs as well as yours. That is what Collaborating is all about, after all.

Identify when your coworker is being defensive. Typical reactions might include making excuses or changing the subject. Other clues range from inappropriate emotional reactions such as anger or attacks to a seeming loss of emotion, as when someone clams up or denies that there is a problem. Try to bring the defensive behavior into the open by acknowledging there is something wrong. Say, "I didn't mean to put you on the defensive," or "What's happening now? This doesn't seem to be working."

Of course, acknowledging defensiveness can be a tricky strategy. No matter how sincere you sound, it is possible that a challenging coworker will react to your honesty with more defensiveness. If your dialogue appears to deteriorate, consider taking a break and regrouping.

Let's return to your discussion with Jared the slacker to illustrate the different defensive reactions and attempts to overcome them. Trying to reduce a defensive posture in Jared, you should keep from assigning blame and stress that your goal is to meet Jared's needs, as well as your own.

Scenario: The slacker attacks you

SLACKER: You are so unreasonable and compulsive. You think you are the only one who needs my help. And who are you to talk anyway? You don't help me when I need your help.

YOU: (Paraphrase what he says to make sure you have heard him correctly, and to demonstrate that you are listening to him. Good listening will help you understand his side of the discussion.) You seem to be saying that I am expecting too much of you and that I'm also not cooperative. Is that right?

SLACKER: Yeah, that's for sure. Pretending that you want a solution that benefits me. I can see right through you. You're only in this for yourself.

YOU: (If the slacker continues to attack you after you paraphrase, try to get back to the issue.)

I am happy to discuss how you perceive my motives later. I would like to focus now on my request. Can you agree to my request?

SLACKER: Well, I have some problems with it.

Continue by exploring his reasons for objecting to your request and Collaborating to come up with a solid solution. (For more on this approach, return to Chapter 4 to see how to handle an attacker.)

Scenario: The slacker uses excuses for his behavior

SLACKER: Look. I could not do this because my laptop has been crashing, and the only time I have to work on things like appraisals is at night. I haven't been able to use my laptop at home to do that, and I just don't have time during the day.

YOU: (Ignore inappropriate bids for sympathy. Paraphrase and try to capture any indication that the slacker agrees with you that it would be best if you could solve the problem.)
It seems you are saying you are unable to give it to me because your laptop isn't working properly. It does seem that you are agreeing that it would be best if I could get the input in a timely way.

SLACKER: Yes. I can't use my laptop so I can only work on the appraisals during the day at work, and I really am too busy to do that.

YOU: (The best way to handle reasons or excuses after paraphrasing is to accept the excuses rather than to argue about them, and to ask what he can do about the situation. Avoid the temptation to offer suggestions unless the slacker becomes genuinely stuck. You don't want to take responsibility for his problems. If your suggestions don't work, you will be blamed, and he will expect you to come up with other suggestions.)
Well, do you have any ideas about what you can do about this situation?

SLACKER: There's really nothing I can do. I can't get a new laptop and this one is shot.

YOU: (Don't point out that the excuse is phony. Keep collaborating.)

What can you do to get it fixed?

SLACKER: Well, I'm so busy that it's been difficult to get my laptop in for service. But I suppose I could make a call to the IT Department. Maybe they would lend me one.

YOU: I would appreciate that. Does this mean you would get me the input?

SLACKER: I believe so.

Scenario: The slacker denies that he is doing what you claim

SLACKER: Well, I think I am giving you the input when you need it.

YOU: (Paraphrase what you have heard.)
Hmm. If I am hearing you correctly, you seem to feel that my concern is not accurate. Is this right?

SLACKER: Yes, that is correct.

YOU: (The best way to respond to denial after paraphrasing is with specific examples or evidence. This requires careful preparation before meeting with the slacker.)
Well, let me try to show you why I feel it is accurate. I have some copies of our e-mails around this issue. I requested the input by the 1st, and the response I got was not until the 10th, after another request. The second and third requests show similar situations. Wouldn't you agree that this is happening?

Scenario: The slacker says his behavior doesn't matter

SLACKER: I think you are making a mountain out of a molehill. You don't really need my input. You are still able to get the appraisals done. Just do them without my input.

YOU: You seem to be saying that the late input doesn't make much difference. Is that right?

SLACKER: Yep.

YOU: (The best way to handle the "so what?" response after

paraphrasing is to emphasize the negative consequences of the individual's behavior, especially any negative impacts on him, and to ask if it is better if they did not occur. This requires knowing what matters to him.)

I believe your input on the appraisals is important. I am concerned that your refusal to participate will be perceived negatively by our boss. Also, without the input I won't know if we need to improve what we do for you. Do you agree?

(In this example, you and the slacker have the same boss.)

Obstacle 3: The other person proposes a solution or makes a request that you don't like

Collaborating involves negotiating in good faith. If the person on the other side of the discussion appears manipulative or unreasonable, there is a risk that your efforts at finding a mutually satisfying solution might break down. One way to prevent this from happening is to clearly communicate your expectations from the beginning. Your coworker is less likely to present an idea that disregards your stated terms or needs.

If you consider a proposed solution to be off the mark, consider it a starting point for a better solution instead of rejecting it outright. Your colleague is more likely to work with you if you acknowledge whatever importance and value the proposed solution offers. Seek to understand the elements of the proposal that are most necessary to his needs, as well as his priorities.

When you are both more definite about what is important to you, it will be easier to identify and eliminate obstacles to agreement. Don't be dishonest or shy. Cite your reasons for not agreeing to your teammate's idea. If possible, explain how your refusal is in his best interest.

Your coworker may have placed a lot of importance on the proposed solution. Be prepared for accusations of being overly adamant or stubborn. Don't react to his venting. While it is necessary to stand firm against a solution that will not work for you, signal that you are not inflexible. Express to him that you are interested in exploring other possible solutions that will satisfy you both.

Let's return to your conversation with Jared.

Scenario: The slacker proposes a solution that you don't like

SLACKER: I'd like to propose that you draft comments about your employees that I can read and approve. That way you get the feedback you need in order to write your performance appraisals.

YOU: (You consider the request to be unreasonable. Instead of an immediate negative reaction, acknowledge any value that the proposal has, and clarify the slacker's needs and priorities.)
I appreciate that this offers a way to get your feedback in a timely way. What elements of this solution work best for you?

SLACKER: Well, it's quick and painless. As you know, I'm a very busy man.

YOU: (Use paraphrasing.)
It sounds like saving time is one of your biggest concerns.

SLACKER: Yes, that's the most important thing to me.

YOU: (Identify obstacles you have to agreeing. Cite your reasons for not agreeing without being adamant.)
Jared, any solution we come up with would have to provide accurate information for my appraisal while not placing an unfair burden on either of us. I feel that this solution, while saving you time, would redirect the entire lion's share of the work to me. Let's keep talking this through.

SLACKER: (Allow for some venting.)
Look, you wanted me to suggest a solution, and this one works for me. You say that this is an unfair burden on you, yet you are asking me to do the work. I thought you were a team player.

YOU: (Don't get hooked by the attack and guilt trip. Paraphrase again.)

It sounds like you feel I am being unfair, making you do more than your share.

SLACKER: Exactly.

YOU: (Indicate how your refusal is in his best interest. Express a desire to come to an agreement. Try to offer an alternative to what the slacker is proposing.)
Remember, there is benefit to you in sharing your knowledge of my team's efforts. These appraisals will help increase the quality of service we provide you. I'm sure that if we keep exploring, we can come to a solution that works to benefit both of us. An option would be for you to ask your employees to draft your comments for you. I believe they were aware of what my employees did.

Obstacle 4: You reach a deadlock or the person procrastinates making a decision

Following all your attempts at Collaborating, there are occasions when a mutually satisfactory result will still elude you. Don't be too hasty to admit defeat. There are other options that may allow you to salvage the situation.

One such option is to concentrate on solutions that, while incomplete, offer some progress. For example, you might agree to a tentative solution or to an initial step. Or you can break your issue into different components and focus on satisfying one or two of them. Sometimes progress made in this way will be enough to generate momentum towards a better working relationship that allows for a more complete solution.

Another approach is to take a break. Agree to continue the discussion later if you have the luxury of time. Set a date in the future to continue your efforts. Or identify research that can be performed to provide more focus on the issues or generate more alternatives.

After implementing a partial solution or taking a break, try to maintain the dialogue. You might ask, "What do you think is getting in the way of our solving this?" or "What are the advantages of my solution?" If you sense that the advantages of your proposed solution are still unclear, point them out. Stress that you will work hard to make your solution work and that you have confidence in its success.

If a deadlock threatens to terminate your discussions, it might be time for some more dramatic responses. Consider seeking a mediator that you both trust to be impartial and effective. Ask difficult questions, such as "What will the consequences be if we don't come to an agreement?"

If neither of these alternatives works, consider an informal moratorium. Your colleague may change his stance, given time. This might occur if he adopts a new point of view or if his reason for not accepting an immediate solution had to do with saving face. If he signals a change of heart, acknowledge any improvements.

Again, let's see how you do this with Jared.

Scenario: You and the slacker reach a deadlock; you work to keep the discussions alive

SLACKER: It seems like we're beating a dead horse. Maybe we should just agree to disagree on this.

YOU: (Suggest a first step as a means to keep the discussion alive, or try to deal with only part of the issue.)
Though we haven't been able to agree on a complete solution, I think we have made some headway. We both agree that you should be given enough advance notice to be able to provide feedback. Why don't we set that as a stake in the ground and work out the form that the appraisals will take later.

SLACKER: I don't know. It looks like we're at an impasse and we're just prolonging the agony.

YOU: (Try to break an impasse by proposing a break.)
I still think we can come to a solution that benefits us both. It might take a little research. Would you agree to pick this discussion up after the holidays? In the meantime, I can delve into this further.

SLACKER: Okay. Call me in four weeks.

Scenario: You and the slacker continue discussions after a break

YOU: Hi, Jared. How were your holidays?

SLACKER: Wonderful. I needed the rest.

YOU: That's great. I did a little research during our break. Here is a hybrid approach that other companies are using to gather information for performance reviews. It combines a narrative with survey questions.

SLACKER: Hmmm. A survey, you say?

YOU: Yes. Do you think there might be some advantages to that?

SLACKER: I'm not sure.

YOU: (Clarify the advantages of your solution. Emphasize how they benefit him.)
It will take you less time to give us the information that we need.

SLACKER: Hmmm. It still takes time to fill out.

YOU: (Show confidence in the solution. Stress you will work hard to make it work.)
But not too much time. It offers an alternative that will give us what we need to improve our services to your team. We're committed to making this work to everyone's advantage. I will make it really short.

SLACKER: I'm sorry, but I still don't think I can work with this.

YOU: Jared, we've discussed a number of approaches to a solution. In your opinion, what do you think is getting in the way of our solving this issue?

SLACKER: I don't know. I don't really have any good ideas on this, I guess.

YOU: (If you're at a deadlock that threatens failure, consider using a mediator, asking difficult questions that highlight the consequences of failure, or suggesting a moratorium.)
Well, I think the matter is important enough to continue looking for common ground. What would you say to having a mediator

facilitate these discussions?

SLACKER: I'll think about it. Not crazy about the idea. Can't really think of anyone I'd trust getting involved with this.

YOU: (It may be time to emphasize the negative consequences [especially to the slacker] of his lack of commitment. This requires knowing what matters to him.)
The appraisals are due in two months. In all honesty, I don't feel that I can give them to my team without your input. I am concerned that withholding appraisals will reflect negatively on both of us—and the boss will certainly not like it. I don't want that to happen and assume that you don't either. Do you agree?

Hopefully, presenting negative consequences can startle the slacker out of his slumber. Be prepared to follow through.

Obstacle 5: The other person agrees to a solution but does not keep his commitment

It wasn't easy, but your efforts to reach an understanding with your recalcitrant coworker have paid off. But agreement to a solution doesn't ensure that the solution will be carried out. Some coworkers are like Lucy in the "Peanuts" comic strip who continually breaks her promise to hold the football for Charlie Brown to kick. Obstacle 5 addresses the scenario of a person who doesn't keep his commitment.

The first step to prevent this from happening is to discourage your coworker from agreeing to something reluctantly. You don't want him to offer his consent just because he is weary of the process. Ask "What concerns do you have about this solution we are agreeing to?" Or touch base the following day to see if there are any lingering questions about your mutual decision.

Document your agreement so there are no surprises later. Plan to have a follow-up discussion after your solution has been initiated in order to monitor its success.

Even after taking these precautions, your coworker may still fail to follow through on his action items. Without attacking, point out this failure and ask for the reasons behind it. Verify that the original solution is still acceptable and offer to explore other solutions if it is not. If he needs help implementing the solution, assist him. Do what you can to make sure that the absence of follow-through doesn't occur a second time. Propose a deadline for action.

The following scenario continues where the previous one left off.

Scenario: The slacker agrees to a solution; you ensure that the agreement is genuine

SLACKER: I think I can work with this.

YOU: (Discourage the person from agreeing to something reluctantly.)
Are you sure, Jared? Do you have any lingering concerns about the solution we are agreeing to?

SLACKER: Nope.

YOU: (Document your agreement and plan a follow-up discussion after the plan is implemented.)
Okay, I'll write up what we discussed and send you a copy. The first performance appraisal will be due in three months. I'll put a meeting on our calendars to follow up after the first appraisal to see if there are any questions with the new form.

SLACKER: Sounds good to me. I'd better get going now. Things to do, you know.

Scenario: The slacker does not keep his commitment to the agreement

YOU: (Without attacking, point out the failure to follow through and ask for reasons.)
Jared, thanks for making the deadline for the performance appraisal using the new form that we agreed to three months ago. However, it was incomplete. Can we discuss the reasons for this?

SLACKER: What do you mean? I filled out the survey.

YOU: Yes, you did. But there was also a narrative section. We had agreed that this section should contain at least two paragraphs of text. Instead, you entered an average of a single sentence. Some appraisals had no entry at all.

SLACKER: I can't always remember what happened three months in the past.

YOU: (Paraphrase his concerns.)
I hear you saying that the form is difficult to fill out correctly because too much time has passed since the individual has performed his activities.

SLACKER: That's correct.

YOU: (Offer to explore other solutions if the original one isn't acceptable.)
Jared, we should be able to correct this easily enough. What would help you to fill in the form correctly?

SLACKER: I guess I just need to be given the forms at the start of the quarter. Maybe with an additional section in it that I could use to take notes as I go along.

YOU: (As you did when the solution was first agreed upon, discourage the person from agreeing to something reluctantly.)
Okay, that should be easy enough. Are you certain that this is your only issue and that your proposed fix will keep this issue from occurring again?

SLACKER: Right. You give me the forms at the start of the quarter, and I'll use them to take notes.

YOU: (Propose a deadline for implementing the solution.)
Great. I propose that we make the corrections in the form immediately and that I get them to you in the next two weeks. Do you agree that that would be enough time for you to use the form for the next appraisals that are due in three months?

SLACKER: Yes. Thank you for being persistent with this. I think this solution will work.

Final Thoughts

The best resolution of interpersonal conflict in the workplace is one that fully satisfies both parties. The best way to reach this mutually satisfying solution is through the Collaborating strategy. That's easy to see.

But dealing with challenging coworkers and bosses is, well, challenging. Their behavior doesn't easily lend itself to working in good faith to reach mutual goals. When encountering such resistance, it's perfectly natural to want to employ a strategy that attacks an individual, manipulates him, or gives him a taste of his own medicine. But these approaches won't produce the transformative results that you seek.

We hope you've learned from this chapter that Collaborating, like any strategy, involves technique and practice. It's not guaranteed to work, but by helping you identify and then address the obstacles that your challenging colleague puts in your path, we hope that you can see the potential for success with Collaborating.

If you're still uncertain about your ability to overcome obstacles, practice these tips in front of the mirror, role-play them with associates, and apply them with rational associates who are attempting to resolve conflicts in good faith. And then test them with the more uncooperative and frustrating among the people you meet in the workplace. The potential benefits of using peer power make it well worth the effort.

technology: a blessing and a curse

When we first began our working careers, we dealt with lack of information, confusion, disagreements, and conflict by walking down the hall and talking things out with the other party. But the world has changed significantly in the past decades. E-mail has become the most common communication tool in the workplace. Many organizations rely on instant messaging (IM) for quick updates, troubleshooting, and fast answers. Web conference meetings bring people from remote locations together virtually via the Internet. Cell phones and pagers make it possible to be connected 24/7. Social networking websites create opportunities to connect with friends and strangers alike. You can now tweet a thought the minute it occurs to you.

Despite the many positive changes brought about by these new technologies, there are dangers in their use. When misunderstandings occur or disagreements arise, the ability to communicate instantly (via e-mail or IM) can encourage poorly thought-out messages that lead to increasing conflict.

That puts employees in remote locations who never meet face to face at a significant disadvantage when problems crop up. Without the benefit of rapport and solid relationships built through personal contact, it may be difficult to address interpersonal obstacles. If employees relate to each other primarily through online chat messages, opportunities for miscommunication are often magnified. Criticisms and observations that are shared unfiltered on Twitter can easily have unintended consequences.

We want to share a few examples of communication snafus that have been created by the inappropriate use of technology:

- The company that laid off hundreds of employees via e-mail (what were they thinking?)

- A young man who wrote a frustrated, angry e-mail at the end of a challenging work day, resigning his position without giving notice (and, too late, regretted hitting the "Send" button)

- The voice mail message informing an employee that she was fired from her job (she didn't get the news until the next morning when she arrived for work and was stopped by security)

- A colorful complaint about a coworker posted on a public discussion board (a violation of the company's policies that led to the complainer's immediate termination)

- The spat between two coworkers that was carried on over IM (one of them copied the entire dialogue and sent it to Human Resources)

- The person who meant to reply privately to an e-mail but pressed "Reply All" by mistake and in so doing sent criticisms of one person to everyone on the thread

- The use of Facebook to complain about an organization's management team and build support among employees for a public meeting to vent their grievances

- The young employee who sent a short e-mail with text message abbreviations to a company's major client, who had to spend several minutes trying to translate it into English

Peer Power has focused on helping you gain the support of others and manage their difficult behaviors when they create problems. In an ideal world, our conversations with people would always occur face to face to minimize the potential for misunderstandings and maximize the potential for collaboration.

We don't live in that ideal world, however, and we didn't want to end this book without taking a deeper look at both the benefits and disadvantages of some of the most common technological tools available for workplace communication. We have a few suggestions for making them work for you, rather than against you, in on-the-job communication as you develop your peer power.

Voice Mail: Dangers and Guidelines

The obvious benefit of voice mail is that you have the ability to leave a detailed message giving information or requesting action. You move the task off your plate and into the hands of the other party. It is certainly a more personal form of communication than e-mail or IM. And it has the benefit of allowing the listener to hear your tone of voice, along with the verbal message.

Delivering bad news via voice mail is truly the way of the coward, as it gives no opportunity for your listener to react, ask questions, or engage in discussion.

But voice mail's greatest disadvantage is the phenomenon of voice mail tag, in which both parties leave repeated messages for each other. If you pick up the phone to discuss a problem with a colleague and get voice mail, it can be tempting to leave a lengthy message, full of irritation, for example, which may trigger a reaction on the part of your receiver. Delivering bad news via voice mail is truly the way of the coward, as it gives no opportunity for your listener to react, ask questions, or engage in discussion.

If you want to make voice mail work for you, consider these steps:

- Use voice mail for specific requests or to provide quick answers.

- Avoid delivering difficult or unwelcome news through voice mail (instead, leave a call back number and good time to reach you in person).

- Keep voice mail messages short and to the point, and indicate the subject and urgency at the beginning.

- Organize your thoughts on paper before dialing so that you don't ramble.

- If you request information, leave enough detail that the other party might be able to record a voice mail for you with the answers.

Voice-to-Voice: Dangers and Guidelines

By far the second best option (after face-to-face) when communicating about difficult issues, speaking voice to voice (either on the telephone or using a computer-based voice application such as Skype) allows two parties in conflict to hear and respond to both words and tone. (If your organization has video capability, that is even better.) In a phone call there are opportunities to exchange information, ask questions, clarify issues, and probe for details. Many organizations function quite well with voice-to-voice meetings, calls, and conferences.

Without body language, tone of voice becomes even more important to reach mutual understanding.

The downside, obviously, is that you lose visual cues about the other person's reactions, which can often create confusion. Without body language, tone of voice becomes even more important to reach mutual understanding. Also without face-to-face contact, it is hard to avoid interruptions and the temptation to express strong emotions.

To make voice-to-voice conversations work for you:

- Plan in advance how you will raise difficult issues diplomatically.

- Jot down key words and phrases using neutral (non-inflammatory) language.

- At the beginning of the call, clarify how much time each of you has for the call.

- State your objectives and allow the other person to state hers.

- Check assumptions regularly: put your assumptions into words and ask if you are both in agreement.

- Document issues, problems, solutions, and plans as you talk.

- Make certain the other person has finished before speaking.

- Paraphrase frequently.

- Let the other person know if you need a quiet break to think about something.

- Avoid multitasking.

- End the call at the agreed-upon time (or agree to continue).

- Follow up phone calls with an e-mail summary of the major issues discussed.

- Thank the other party for the willingness to collaborate.

Teleconferencing: Dangers and Guidelines

Telephone conference calls bridging communicators in multiple locations can be a godsend when a dispersed team needs to collaborate. The ability to speak to one another in real time reduces the potential for confusion or misunderstanding. Problems can be surfaced, discussed, and resolved quickly. Teleconferences add a nonverbal dimension (tone of voice) that can build rapport and strengthen relationships.

The biggest downside of teleconferencing occurs when employees are located in multiple time zones. It can also be difficult for busy employees to focus their attention in a rambling phone call. Because you can't see others and they can't see you, conversations via teleconference lack helpful visual cues. Multitasking often takes place and results in poor listening and comprehension.

You can make teleconferencing work by following these suggestions:

- Plan an agenda for your teleconference meeting and share it at the beginning of your call.

- Ask people to identify themselves before speaking.

- Call on quieter people by name to get their input in discussions.

- If you anticipate conflict, ask people to agree to basic ground rules for civil discussion.

- Frequently solicit others' questions or concerns.

- If there isn't too much background noise, ask people to keep their phone lines unmuted for immediate responses.

- Don't single an individual out by delivering constructive feedback in front of the teleconference group. (Remember the old adage: praise in public; correct in private.)

- If participants will need to discuss the contents of a document or review visual elements such as charts or diagrams, make sure these are e-mailed well ahead of time to all participants.

E-mail: Dangers and Guidelines

Lacking tone of voice, body language, or other non-verbal behavior, our receivers will often fill in the blanks with assumptions and misperceptions.

We love e-mail. (That's how you know we're baby boomers.) Those long e-mail strings leave a great trail of documentation that is easy to refer back to. It's a simple practice to summarize meeting notes and action items, sending them out to project teams. It's possible to reach multiple people with the same message at the same time.

However, the biggest weakness of e-mail is the lack of nonverbal signals. Was that short, pithy sentence a sign of anger? Were you just in a hurry? Or are you more task focused than people focused? Lacking tone of voice, body language, or other nonverbal behavior, our receivers will often fill in the blanks with assumptions and misperceptions. And unintended conflict may be the result. Poor communicators often hide behind e-mail because it allows them to make a point without considering the other party's point of view. Flaming e-mails blister work relationships!

Here is some basic e-mail etiquette to help you stay out of trouble:

- Avoid copying everyone on an e-mail reporting an embarrassing error or a customer complaint.

- Avoid copying the recipient's boss when you are expressing frustration with the recipient.

- If you are concerned about the meaning of an e-mail you received, ask a question to check out the concern, rather than making assumptions.

- Use good faith statements such as "I don't think you intended..." or "I'm confident we can work this out...."

- Pose questions that allow your reader to explain or give more information.

- When disagreements occur during e-mail exchanges, pick up the phone and call to resolve them.

- Whenever possible, don't deliver constructive feedback using e-mail.

- If you wouldn't say it to someone's face, don't use e-mail to vent frustrations or complaints.

- Before sending the e-mail, reread what you wrote with a mindful ear toward your tone. It's very easy to sound more negative than you meant to, so take the time to express everything in the most positive terms you can.

- When you write a difficult e-mail, save it as a draft and let it sit for a day before hitting the "Send" button. Give yourself a chance to cool down, read it again later, and perhaps choose to delete it. It's impossible to call back that e-mail once it has been sent (although Google Gmail gives you 30 seconds to change your mind after you hit "Send").

- Don't put anything in an e-mail you would not want your mother, friends, or an attorney to read.

- E-mail etiquette requires a style more similar to a business letter than a text message. Avoid abbreviations and acronyms that may confuse your reader.

Instant Messaging (IM): Dangers and Guidelines

We confess—we don't much like instant messaging for resolving challenging situations. Though we realize it is used successfully in fast-paced organizations, it's an invitation to be interrupted whenever someone else needs something from you. IM does have one key benefit. If a project team is working on an issue that requires a rapid response, IM facilitates quick communication at the moment of need.

> *...unless the issue is pretty darn simple or straightforward, IM is not usually the best communication tool.*

But unless the issue is pretty darn simple or straightforward, IM is not usually the best communication tool. Because IM lends itself to short, focused questions and responses, there is often a string of back-and-forth messages that ensues between two people. By its very nature, messages need to be short for IM to be effective. We don't think IM is very useful when you need to include other people and you want to flesh out a complex issue. By the way, being blasted by a blistering IM is no more pleasant than being blasted by a blistering e-mail.

Herewith, some suggestions for using IM constructively:

- Use it for quick check-in conversations about deadlines or deliverables.

- Send an IM when you need a fast answer to a simple question.

- IM someone to check availability for an unscheduled conversation.

- Don't use IM to complain or criticize anyone.

- Don't attempt to resolve differences or negotiate agreements via IM.

- (Do we have to say this?) Never use IM to deliver bad news.

- Turn off IM when giving a presentation projected from your laptop.

Social Networking and Microblogging: Dangers and Guidelines

The proliferation of social networking sites has made it possible for people to connect, commiserate, and bond over similar work challenges and industry issues. The ability to post a question or comment and review others' experiences and suggestions allows for learning and insight at the moment of need.

The greatest disadvantage of any public social networking site is the lack of privacy when posting questions or issues about your organization or your coworkers. Your observations, images, gripes, and complaints will never disappear once they have been posted in cyberspace (and they can be forwarded to anyone once posted).

A few suggestions for successful social networking and microblogging:

- Avoid career-limiting posts made in a moment of impulse.

- Before you post, ask yourself, "Would I want my mother (aunt, grandfather, boss, etc.) to read this post?"

- Avoid finger-pointing and blaming.

- Don't hang your dirty laundry (personal or organizational) on public discussion boards.

- Keep it positive (no whining).

- If your team is using an internal microblogging application, take complex or complicated discussions into a medium better suited to a group discussion.

Web Conferencing: Dangers and Guidelines

Like teleconferencing, web or video conferencing allows people in multiple locations to meet and collaborate. However, web conferences also include the visual component—being able to view documents, slides, or other files over the Internet. Teams that meet in real time to discuss issues or challenges are using web conferences more frequently. Many web conference platforms include the ability to display streaming video over webcams, which helps to personalize the interactions with others.

Web conferencing and teleconferencing have similar disadvantages: capturing and holding people's attention, scheduling across time zones, and the tendency for participants to multitask, listening with one ear tuned to the proceedings. In addition, web conferences frequently have unexpected (and annoying) technological glitches that can prevent smooth communication.

Adopt these suggestions to get the most from web conference meetings:

- Send out an agenda prior to the meeting.

- Pose questions, issues, or challenges to participants in advance.

- If you anticipate intense discussion, set ground rules at the outset.

- Avoid "monologuing." Instead, give people frequent opportunities to share their perspectives.

- Learn how to use the interaction tools in your web

conference platform (for example, polling allows you to easily gauge agreement or disagreement on an issue).

- Learn how to schedule web meetings on the fly (quickly e-mail a meeting invitation and open a web meeting).

- Consider using a neutral facilitator to help the team discuss difficult issues.

- Don't single an individual out by delivering constructive feedback in front of the web conference group.

Summary: When Face-to-face is Not Possible

You know our bias—communicating face to face is our preferred method of clearing up confusion, resolving disagreements, and working through conflict. You gain the benefit of verbal and nonverbal communication, developing a complete picture of the situation at hand. You are able to probe and problem solve in the moment. And you may leave a conversation with greater trust and a stronger relationship.

We also know that face-to-face communication can be time consuming. It requires a more advanced set of skills and practices. It may feel challenging, even threatening, to the novice communicator.

In our case studies and examples, we have given you dozens of suggestions for making face-to-face communication work for you during conflict. But we also recognize that you may not always have the luxury of sitting down for a face-to-face dialogue.

In cases where face-to-face connection is just not possible, here is a summary of our previous suggestions:

- Strive to speak with the other party over the telephone, voice to voice.

- Organize your thoughts before calling.

- If you must leave a voice mail message, avoid going into detail about the problem (wait until you can connect).

- If voice-to-voice communication is not possible, write a

clearly worded e-mail.

- File your e-mail as a draft; let it sit for 24 hours; read it again to be certain your language is neutral and not inflammatory.

- Add good faith statements to your e-mail, such as "You are probably on top of this..." or "I know you didn't intend to do this..." or "I'm certain we can work this out together."

- Ask questions in your e-mail to encourage the other party to share his point of view.

- Never carry on an IM conversation during a disagreement with an individual.

- For team meetings in which you expect conflict, consider using a neutral facilitator to guide the conversation (this works in teleconference and web conference meetings as well).

- Avoid airing dirty work laundry on discussion boards or social networking sites.

- Don't copy e-mails to others when you are confronting someone or air your grievances so others can hear them.

- Agree on ground rules when you expect difficulties.

When used with sensitivity, technology can lead to rapid results and enhanced peer power. Any time you need to deal with a difficult person or situation, choose the communication method that is likely to produce the best outcome (and is most feasible considering your geographic location)—for you, for the other party, and for the situation.

moving forward: from passive reader to active communicator

When we began to collaborate to write *Peer Power*, we had no idea a hearty meal in a noisy Italian restaurant would launch a five-year labor of love. On this writing journey, we have used all of the techniques we describe here with each other.

Cynthia has come to appreciate Ray's analytical, thorough, and logical approach to the content, and Ray has come to value Cynthia's creative storytelling and conversational writing style. We set ground rules early on to reconcile our differing communication styles and work practices. We addressed interpersonal frustrations quickly rather than letting issues fester.

What might some of those issues be? Just to give two examples: Ray, with his focus on logical details, can analyze the content and structure of a chapter way beyond Cynthia's tolerance level. And Cynthia, focused on running a training company, often juggles too many balls, frustrating Ray by missing deadlines for chapter drafts and edits. In any collaboration, issues like these can derail a project. We're grateful that we worked through our stumbling blocks and are certain that we have become more skillful communicators as a result of applying all of these principles, practices, and strategies to our own partnership.

Next Steps

Thank you for having the courage and commitment to change your communication practices. We want you to experience the freedom that comes from building your peer power and watching the positive changes that occur in your work relationships when you do.

If you have made it to this final chapter, we trust that you are beginning to incorporate new practices in your work with others. Remember to Be Real, Take Responsibility, Build Relationships, and Extend Respect at work. If you need to address difficult behavior, draw upon the five strategies: Collaborating, Compromising, Going Head-to-Head, Caring-for-Self, and Coaching. By consciously choosing the right strategy at the right time, you'll be able to transform difficult situations in the workplace. And don't forget Plan B (what to do if your strategy of choice fails to achieve the result you seek).

So what's next on your journey?

Practice, Practice, Practice

Remember the old joke? How do you get to Carnegie Hall? Practice!

Becoming a skillful communicator is a lifelong process. To take this journey, we suggest a few simple steps.

1. Monitor your current behavior non-judgmentally.

As you begin to notice the gap between what you are currently doing and what might get you better results, don't be too hard on yourself. Cynthia found herself looking again at the way she manages stress while working on the chapters about bullying and attacking. Ray got to revisit his approach to people who are slacking. There will always be opportunities for improvement.

2. Set a realistic goal for yourself.

You might decide to focus on improving one work relationship at a time. Begin by setting an achievable goal such as: "When working with Bob, I will focus on listening and paraphrasing before responding to his criticisms of my work." Once you've nailed that behavior change, you can set the next goal.

3. List the benefits of changing your behavior.

We were highly motivated to resolve our differences because we both wanted to get *Peer Power* written and published. If you identify the benefits of changing your behavior, you will be more motivated to persevere despite challenges.

4.   Write out a plan and share it with a confidant or coach.

We've provided Cheat Sheets and Worksheets for each case chapter to encourage careful planning. They will help you organize your thoughts and give you solid plans to share with a coach or trusted advisor.

5.   Post reminders.

Use sticky notes at your computer or inspirational quotes to remind you of your commitments. One of Cynthia's favorite quotes is posted on the wall next to her computer: "Keep your fears to yourself but share your courage with others" (Robert Louis Stevenson). It reminds her to focus on the positive rather than succumb to the urge to whine about life's challenges.

6.   Record and reward progress.

Acknowledge yourself for your own improvement. Notice the positive changes and the favorable outcomes. Keep a notebook or journal to record daily observations. And while you are recording your own positive changes, track the positive changes that your colleagues are making as a result. Say "thank you" to others for keeping their commitments. With this attention to results, it becomes easier to maintain new habits.

7.   Reflect on lessons learned.

We can't guarantee that every communication practice will work exactly as we've indicated. After all, we're talking about humans dealing with unpredictable humans. But continued reflection about your experience and lessons learned can guide you in making better choices in the future.

Visit our Website

To support your continued development, please visit our website: www.netspeedlearning.com/peerpower. There you can view videos, listen to podcasts, post questions, complete assessments, post testimonials, and communicate with Ray, Cynthia, and a skilled team of master trainers. We're interested in your success stories and your challenges.

Both the "About You" and "About Them" assessments are online at NetSpeed Learning Solutions. Please feel free to share the links with others on your team. These assessments are available at no charge.

Courses and Web Workshops

If you would like to join other people to explore these concepts further, consider registering for a public web workshop. You'll find the schedule at www.netspeedlearning.com/peerpower.

If you would like to bring *Peer Power* courses to your organization, contact us. We have a network of certified trainers who are skilled at delivery either in the face-to-face classroom or through online web workshops. We also license companies and organizations to deliver our programs, and we certify internal trainers. Call us at 877-517-5271 for more information.

Best of luck as you continue to develop your personal peer power. It's a commitment that will yield enormous dividends in your career. And please stay in touch!

Appendix 1: Interpreting Your Responses to the "About You" Questionnaire

In the Introduction you responded to the "About You" questionnaire, which contains statements about your interpersonal strengths, weaknesses, and beliefs. Here are Ray and Cynthia's comments on what your responses tell about you.

1. I can improve my communication skills.	Yes	No

If you answered "yes" to this statement, your head is in the right place. Everyone can improve his or her communication skills; it's within your control, and we'll offer many tips for achieving this goal.

2. What happens to me at work is usually not related to my own behavior.	Yes	No

If you agree with this statement, you may often feel victimized by others' actions. We invite you to consider the many ways your behavior may be helping or hindering the situation.

3. I prefer to take responsibility for my own actions.	Yes	No

This is a powerful statement. If you said "yes," you are indicating your readiness to act in new ways that will benefit your difficult relationships.

4. Even if I change my behavior, the situation usually doesn't change.	Yes	No

If you answered "yes" to this statement, you may want to try out some new behaviors, including respecting your own needs when necessary.

5. I am willing to make the first move to improve a challenging situation.	Yes	No

Answering "yes" to this statement puts you in the driver's seat. If you're at an impasse with a colleague, someone must make the first move. We're glad it will be you.

6. When someone is behaving badly, it's hard for me to feel compassionate.	Yes	No

If you find it difficult to feel compassion when someone's behavior is a problem, you're not alone. However, by the end of this book you may be able to answer "no" to this statement.

7. It's easy for me to put myself in the shoes of other people to imagine their point of view.	Yes	No

If you responded with a "yes," this is a great gift. Being able to view the world through another's eyes will allow you to respond with less defensiveness in difficult conversations.

8. I try to be open about my thoughts and feelings.	Yes	No

We encourage openness in most work relationships. If you answered "yes" to this statement, there are probably no hidden agendas in your relationships with others.

9. I find gossip to be a great stress reliever.	Yes	No

Let's face it—most people would answer "yes" to this statement. However, we'd like to suggest that when gossip is used in this way, the price you pay (in mistrust and conflict) is too steep.

10. I discourage complaining.	Yes	No

"Yes" is a great answer. Since complaining often seems like a national past time, learning to discourage it can take time. We guarantee that you will be happier, if not more productive, when you give it up.

11. I wish that the top leaders in my organization would just fix the messes at work and leave me out of it.	Yes	No

We bet the top leaders wish they had the power to fix the messes at work, too! If you answered "yes" to this statement, look for opportunities to reclaim some personal power.

12. I strive to listen before I speak.	Yes	No

This is a critical practice that takes discipline. If you answered "no" to this practice, you may wish to experiment by letting others speak while you listen with all ears.

13. If I have an opinion, I always put it on the table first.	Yes	No

While this statement sounds reasonable on the surface, if you answered "yes," you may be dominating others in work situations. Let others speak first and see what happens.

14. I often feel impatient with others.	Yes	No

When you have a to-do list a mile long, having to slow down to deal with others may seem like a trial. If you answered "yes" to this statement, your brusqueness may be blocking your success.

15. I try to leave my emotions at the door when I arrive at work.	Yes	No

If this were possible and we could teach everyone how to do it, we'd be rich. If you said "no," you know you're human—your emotions are part of the package. Don't try to check them at the door.

16. I expect others to apologize when they offend me.	Yes	No

Many a relationship has ended because that apology never came. If you answered "yes" to this question, you may find that you must move on in search of new people who will never offend you.

17. I offer an apology even though I may not be 100 percent at fault.	Yes	No

Answering "yes" to this question demonstrates a willingness to accept partial responsibility for problems that arise in relationships. You've probably learned it "takes two to tango."

18. I make sure I know who's at fault when things go wrong.	Yes	No

The impulse to assign blame is a strong one. If you answered "yes" to this question, you have the opportunity to consider just how damaging this impulse can be.

19. When it gets confrontational, I shut down.	Yes	No

For many of us, shutting down is the way to maintain peace of mind. If you answered "yes" to this statement, you may be missing opportunities to influence others.

| 20. I reach out to someone I may have offended. | Yes | No |

We hope that you were able to say "yes" to this statement. Reaching out, even when it may not have been your intention to offend, demonstrates your concern for the other person.

| 21. If I'm not sure what someone is thinking or feeling, I ask for his or her thoughts. | Yes | No |

Yes! Checking in to see what is happening for someone is the only way to know for sure what he or she is experiencing. We recommend it.

| 22. I take people at face value. | Yes | No |

While this sounds positive, if you said "yes," it may mean that you are relying more on the words people say and less on the unspoken messages sent by body language and tone of voice.

| 23. I'm good at reading others, so I rarely need to ask their opinions. | Yes | No |

If you answered "yes" to this statement, your confidence in your intuition may lead you astray. Unless you're a mind reader, you must ask others' opinions.

| 24. I thank others often. | Yes | No |

Yes, yes, yes! This simple practice makes a big difference at work. We can't remember the last time we met someone who thanked people too much.

25. My communication skills are as good as my technical skills.	Yes	No

If you implement the techniques and practices we recommend, you'll be able to answer this question with a resounding "yes!"

Appendix 2: Principles and Strategies Used in the Case Chapters

This table shows the principles and the recommended initial and Plan B strategies that are used in the case chapters.

		Attacker	Whiner	Scene Stealer	Drive-By Boss	Manipulator	Clueless Colleague	Faux-Smart Boss	Slacker	Bully
Plan B Strategy	Collaborating									
	Coaching									
	Caring-for-Self	✓	✓	✓	✓	✓	✓	✓	✓	✓
	Compromising	✓			✓	✓	✓	✓	✓	
	Going Head-to-Head		✓	✓			✓		✓	✓
Initial Strategy	Collaborating	✓		✓	✓	✓	✓	✓	✓	
	Coaching		✓			✓		✓		
	Caring-for-Self									
	Compromising									✓
	Going Head-to-Head			✓						
Key Principles	Build Relationships	✓		✓			✓		✓	
	Extend Respect		✓		✓	✓		✓		✓
	Take Responsibility	✓	✓	✓	✓	✓	✓	✓	✓	✓
	Be Real			✓	✓		✓	✓		

Appendix 3: References

Avery, C., Walker, M., and O'Toole, E. Teamwork Is an Individual Skill: Getting Your Work Done When Sharing Responsibility. San Francisco: Berrett-Koehler, 2001.

Bellman, G. Getting Things Done When You Are Not in Charge. (Revised ed.) San Francisco: Berrett-Koehler, 2001.

Block, P. The Empowered Manager: Positive Political Skills at Work. San Francisco: Jossey-Bass, 1987.

Brinkman, R. and Kirschner, R. Dealing with People You Can't Stand: How to Bring Out the Best in People at Their Worst. (Revised ed.) New York: McGraw-Hill, 2002.

Covey, S. The 7 Habits of Highly Effective People: Powerful Lessons in Personal Change. (Revised ed.) New York: Free Press, 2004.

Covey, S.M.R. The SPEED of Trust: The One Thing That Changes Everything. New York: Free Press, 2006.

Fisher, R. and Sharp, A. Getting It Done: How to Lead When You're Not in Charge. New York: HarperBusiness, 1998.

Fisher, R., Ury, L., and Patton, B. Getting to Yes: Negotiating Agreement Without Giving In. (Revised ed.) New York: Penguin Books, 1991.

George, B. and Sims, P. True North: Discover Your Authentic Leadership. San Francisco: Jossey-Bass, 2007.

Goldsmith, M., What Got You Here Won't Get You There. New York: Hyperion, 2007.

Hirsh, S. K. and Kise, J. Work It Out: Clues for Solving People Problems at Work. Palo Alto: Davies-Black Publishing, 1996.

Patterson, K., Grenny, J., McMillan, R., and Switzler, A. Crucial Confrontations: Tools for Resolving Broken Promises, Violated Expectations and Bad Behavior. New York: McGraw-Hill, 2005.

Patterson, K., Grenny, J., McMillan, R., and Switzler, A. Crucial Conversations: Tools for Talking When Stakes Are High. New York: McGraw-Hill, 2002.

Silberman, M. and Hansburg, F. People Smart: Developing your Interpersonal Intelligence. San Francisco: Berrett-Koehler Publishers, Inc., 2000.

Stone, D., Patton, B., and Heen, S. Difficult Conversations: How to Discuss What Matters Most. New York: Penguin Books, 2000.

Ury, W. Getting Past No: Negotiating Your Way from Confrontation to Cooperation. New York: Bantam Books, 1993.

Zenger, J. H. and Folkman, J. The Extraordinary Leader: Turning Good Managers into Great Leaders. New York: McGraw Hill, 2002.

Index

About the Authors

Cynthia Clay

Cynthia Clay's career has centered on helping managers, teams and individuals work together more effectively. She brings over 25 years in training and organizational development to her current role as founder and president of NetSpeed Learning Solutions. Her company provides learning and training programs that blend the best of instructor-led training (in person or on the web) with web-based performance support and measurement tools. In this capacity she has:

- Grown the company from a sole proprietorship to a global training company

- Developed 24 NetSpeed Leadership management and professional skills training programs (face-to-face and webinar delivery)

- Developed Blazing Service for customer service skill development (face-to-face and webinar delivery)

- Developed NetSpeed Fast Tracks, a social media platform for social learning

- Worked with clients as diverse as BP, Monsanto, Government Accountability Office, Microsoft, Pennsylvania National Gaming, and Nielsen

Prior to founding NetSpeed Learning Solutions in 1992, Cynthia managed the training and development department at a major hospital and held key positions in management development, human resources, and training at a national bank.

Cynthia is a popular presenter at the American Society for Training and Development (ASTD) International Conference and speaks frequently at ASTD regional chapter meetings around the country. She has also been recognized as an expert on effective web conference delivery of training by CLO magazine (August 2008), and is a featured webinar presenter for Adobe, CLO magazine and HR Industry.com. In 2010 she received the Contributor of the Year award from ISA (the association of learning providers).

Cynthia earned her Masters of Fine Arts (MFA) in Theater Directing from the University of Washington. She believes that directing theater productions requires the same interpersonal skills required for working successfully with peers and colleagues.

Ray Olitt

Ray Olitt has over 25 years of experience in the training and organizational development field. He currently consults with and coaches leaders in a variety of for-profit and non-profit organizations. He retired as Manager of Organizational Development for a health insurance company in 2003. Prior to that, he served as Manager of Management and Professional Development for a bank and as a Management and Organizational Development Specialist for two aerospace companies.

In these roles, some of his accomplishments included:

- Designing and conducting hundreds of classes for managers, employees and self-directed teams, averaging 9.2 on a ten-point course evaluation scale. Topics included "Dealing with Difficult People and Conflict," "Giving and Receiving Feedback," "Influencing Others and Selling Ideas," "Interpersonal Skills and Effective Listening," and "Working Well with People Over Whom You Have No Authority."

- Planning and leading over 100 strategic planning, team building, and group problem solving sessions, averaging 9.3 on a ten-point participant evaluation scale

- Gaining management support to implement and lead a new Employee Diversity Program and a new employee opinion survey process

- Receiving five merit bonus awards and two Human Resources Program of the Year awards

- Being selected as company Employee of the Year from over 2,000 employees

Ray's skills at engaging audiences with practical content have resulted in dozens of invitations to present workshops at home and abroad.

Ray designed and frequently taught the very popular workshop "Working Well with People Over Whom You Have No Authority" for a human resources organization serving all of Washington state. This workshop has attracted more attendees than any comparable program in the organization's history.

Ray earned an Ed.D. from the University of California, Los Angeles (UCLA) with a specialization in Adult Curriculum Development.

Bring Peer Power to your Organization!

Order via the Web

Purchase individual copies for $34.95 each plus
tax and shipping:
http://www.netspeedlearning.com/peerpower/

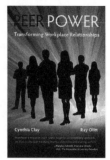

Order Copies for Your Organization

For larger orders, call us at 1-206-517-5271
(Toll-Free in US / Canada): 1-877-517-5271

2-10 copies $22.75 each
11-100 copies $21.00 each
Over 100   Please call us for pricing.

Customize This Book

We can tailor this book for your organization, including featuring
your logo and/or branding on the cover.

For more information, please call us.

Workshops and Webinars

Bring Peer Power to your organization. We deliver Peer Power
training programs in multiple formats:

- One-day Workshops (Classroom)

- Two-day Workshops (Classroom)

- Online Workshops (Virtual Delivery)

We also offer a train-the-trainer program and the ability to license
the program content for your internal use.

Please call or email for more information:
1-877-517-5271 or peerpower@netspeedlearning.com.